Canada's Pitching Sensation & Wartime Hero

with BRIAN KENDALL

VIKING

VIKING
Published by the Penguin Group
Penguin Books Canada Ltd, 10 Alcorn Avenue, Toronto, Ontario,
Canada M4V 3B2
Penguin Books Ltd, 27 Wrights Lane, London W8 5TZ, England
Viking Penguin, a division of Penguin Books USA Inc., 375 Hudson
Street, New York, New York 10014, U.S.A.
Penguin Books Australia Ltd, Ringwood, Victoria, Australia
Penguin Books (NZ) Ltd, 182-190 Wairau Road, Auckland 10,
New Zealand

Penguin Books Ltd, Registered Offices: Harmondsworth, Middlesex,
England

First published 1993

10 9 8 7 6 5 4 3 2 1

Printed and bound in Canada on acid free paper ∞

Canadian Cataloguing in Publication Data
Kendall, Brian

Ace: Phil Marchildon, Canada's pitching sensation and wartime hero

ISBN 0-670-85118-3

1. Marchildon, Phil. 2. World War, 1939-1945 - Aerial operations,
Canadian. 3. Baseball players - Canada - Biography. 4. Fighter pilots
- Canada - Biography. I. Title.

GV865.M37K46 1993   796.357'092   C93-093940-9

CHAPTER 1

PHIL MARCHILDON NIGHT

When I look back on that night now it seems almost like a dream. At the time I wasn't in the proper state of mind to really appreciate what was happening.

The date was Wednesday, August 29, 1945—Phil Marchildon Night at Philadelphia's Shibe Park and the official start of my comeback after almost three seasons away at war. Connie Mack, the legendary owner-manager of the Athletics, had decided to celebrate my return. There were 19,267 fans in the stands for the twi-night doubleheader against the Washington Senators—one of the biggest crowds that season, which saw the A's lose ninety-eight games and finish a bad last in the American League.

Before the start of the second game, the players of both teams lined up along the baselines for the official ceremony.

Byrum Saam, the Athletics' radio announcer, took the micro-phone and recounted the highlights of my short baseball career as well as my wartime experiences. How I'd made the jump from playing amateur ball in Northern Ontario to the major leagues in less than two seasons; how I'd won ten games in my rookie year and then become the ace of the staff as a sopho-more, heralded as one of the game's newest pitching stars for winning seventeen games with a last-place ball club.

The crowd applauded warmly as Saam recalled my enlist-ment in the Royal Canadian Air Force at the end of the 1942 season, and then my posting overseas as a tail gunner on a Halifax bomber. On my twenty-sixth mission our plane was shot down into the sea off Denmark. I spent the rest of the war in Stalag Luft III, the German prison camp that was the scene of the Great Escape, and on the infamous Death March, when the Germans herded thousands of cold and hungry POWs through the ruins of the Reich to prevent our liberation by Allied armies.

Now, less than four months after finally being set free by British troops, I was standing at home plate, waiting for the cheers of the crowd to subside so that I could step forward and say my thanks.

I was still weak from all I'd been through and knew I wasn't ready to pitch. But Mack, smelling a big payday at the gate, had insisted on holding the comeback day. Then in his eighty-second year, the Old Man, as his players called him, not only was the most famous owner in baseball, but also claimed to be the poorest.

My nerves were so raw I felt almost sick with apprehension. I'd been on edge since my return. Sometimes I felt like picking up a brick and heaving it through a window.

My problems had been building ever since I'd joined the RCAF. It started with the strain of all those missions spent fly-ing over enemy territory through radar-controlled searchlights and anti-aircraft flak, the endless hours of searching the dark-ness from my gunner's turret for the shadows of German night fighters. And then there were the awful memories of the night we went down. I kept seeing the faces of my five crew-mates who didn't survive the crash.

The applause of the crowd faded and I said a few words of thanks into the microphone. I appreciated the support of the Philadelphia fans. They had made me one of their favourites from almost my first big-league game and now, a little more than two weeks after the end of the war, I was more popular than ever, a returning hero.

With a wave, I walked to the mound and got on with my comeback.

I don't think it's giving too much of the story away to say that I was able to come back from my wartime experiences to regain my standing as one of the best pitchers in the American League. But there's no question that the war damaged my physical and mental health and cut short my career.

Looking back, I take great pride in the fact that I was one of the few Canadians to beat the odds and make it to the majors. In my day, professional clubs did almost no scouting in Canada, especially in the rural districts where I played amateur ball. Being hidden away in Canada probably cost me at least two or three seasons in the big leagues.

But I made it, and I became a winner in a decade now considered by many as the greatest in baseball history. I was a rookie during the fabled 1941 season, when Joe DiMaggio batted safely in fifty-six straight games and Ted Williams hit .406. I pitched against such other future Hall-of-Famers as Hank Greenberg, Bill Dickey and Jimmie Foxx, and duelled with Bob Feller and Hal Newhouser. I was also there for the racial integration of major-league baseball with the arrival of Jackie Robinson in 1947, the most important single change in the history of the game.

Sometimes I wonder how my life and career might have turned out if instead of the Philadelphia Athletics I'd played for the mighty New York Yankees, who tried to trade for me several times. Or if I'd been born forty years later and arrived in the majors in the age of free agency and multi-million-dollar contracts.

It would be pleasant to be a rich man. But I'm not certain I'd be willing to give up all my memories, not even for a few million bucks.

CHAPTER
2

PENETANG BABE

People are always amazed when I tell them I didn't begin to play baseball until I was in high school. Most American youngsters who grew up to be big-leaguers were given a bat and ball as soon as they could walk and were attracting the attention of talent scouts by the time they were in their early teens. Unfortunately, I never had those advantages. I was a small-town Canadian boy who, when I look back on it now, was probably an even bigger hick than most. It wasn't until I went south in 1939 to turn professional with the Toronto Maple Leafs of the International League that I even learned of the existence of the major leagues; I had thought the Leafs were it.

I was born on October 25, 1913, the fourth of seven children—four girls and three boys—in Penetanguishene, a town of about 3,500 set on an inlet of southern Georgian Bay, 90 miles or so north of Toronto by road. Penetanguishene is an Ojibway word that means "place of the white rolling sands."

There's nowhere I would rather have grown up than Penetang, as the name is almost always shortened by the locals. In many ways, it's the ideal Canadian town—a place where French and English have lived side by side for generations in harmony.

My father Oliver and my mother Elizabeth were French Canadians of pioneer stock. Along with hundreds of other farm settlers from Quebec, the Marchildons arrived in the area after Penetang was established as a naval base in 1817. The French farmers were joined by fur traders and commuted military pensioners from England. My mother's family, the Lavereaus, moved to the town from Fenelon Falls when she was a young girl.

While growing up I was always proud of the part my family had played in the building of Penetang. My grandfather, Hector T. Marchildon, was the contractor who cut many of the downtown streets through the virgin forest, and he supplied the lumber used in the construction of the railroad line from Toronto to Orillia. The present site of the nearby town of Port McNicoll was once known as Marchildon's Point because of his lumbering activities there. My grandfather was also a member of the first village council in 1878, served as the town's chief of police for seventeen years and was on the public school board for fifty-five years.

I remember him as a sweet-natured, hardy old man who single-handedly reshingled the roof of his barn when he was eighty-seven and was still chopping his own cords of firewood almost until the day he died at the age of ninety-two. One of my earliest memories is the sound of his cheerful whistling as he came up the sidewalk to our house every evening after walking in from his farm on the outskirts of town with a bucket of fresh cow's milk for my family.

I was called "Babe" as a boy, or "Bé" in French—although none of us kids ever learned French and it was only rarely used in the house by my parents. No one is certain how I got the nickname, but it caught on with my family and friends and stayed with me until I reached the major leagues, when the sports writers dreamed up a few new handles (the one that seemed to stick was "Penetang Phil"). Even today, when I go back home most of the people I meet on the street call me Babe.

My parents had a hard time of it raising me and the rest of their large brood—my older brother Norbert (who somehow picked up the nickname "Pivot"), kid brother Francis (called "DeeDee" by everyone in town) and our sisters, Madeleine, Viola, Jeanne and Elizabeth. For us and for almost everyone we knew, money always seemed to be in short supply.

A plumber and tinsmith, my father was a hard-working man who never seemed able to get ahead. Often the work he did for rich Torontonians on their Georgian Bay summer cottages went unpaid, a common occurrence in Penetang in those days. The fact that so many of the cottagers tried to take advantage of the local workers by paying them half of the agreed wage or by drawing out the payments over months or years caused a lot of hardship and lingering resentment among the people of the town. I know it made a lot of them leery about ever having anything to do with the big city.

Mom and Dad would scrimp and save, doing the best they could. I remember being sent to the grocery story with ten cents in my pocket to buy a whole cow's liver, just about the cheapest cut of meat you could find. Every fall my father and one of his brothers went on a fishing trip and came back with dozens of lake trout, which he stored in kegs of salt brine in the basement. We would eat every scrap of meat on those fish, including the heads.

When times were toughest, during the early years of the Depression, my mother took in washing. All of us kids tried to contribute by finding part-time jobs whenever we could. For years I delivered the *Toronto Star*, racing across town after school to meet the train from Toronto and pick up my papers.

For all the hardships, I remember those years as happy times. My brothers and sisters and I had the usual squabbles, but the white frame house at 49 Maria Street was mostly filled with laughter. For this my mother deserves all the credit. Called Liza by her friends, she was a wonderful woman who was loved by everyone. Often she helped deflect my father's quick temper to keep peace in the family.

In this my mother needed all the skills of a diplomat, because my father could be tough. If we got one step out of line he was sure to kick our behinds. We were always careful around him, afraid of setting him off.

During the Great War my father played cornet in the regimental band of the 157th Battalion, a unit raised from among men of the district, and for many years after his return he led the town band. But his real passion was the volunteer work he did for the Penetang fire department. He started out as a lantern boy, and by the time he died at the age of seventy-three he had been with the brigade for fifty-eight years, thirty-five of them as its treasurer.

My memories go as far back as the days when the brigade had horse-drawn fire reels. The ringing of church bells would send word of a fire. No matter what he was doing, when my father heard those bells he was off and running.

Penetang's volunteer firemen provided us with one of our most popular entertainments when they competed against brigades from Barrie, Orillia, Elmvale and other district towns in annual skills competitions. Cheering crowds would line the street to watch them determine who was fastest at unreeling and hooking up their hoses, or most accurate at dousing and knocking over targets.

I always felt the people of Penetang were like a big family. Everyone knew everyone else and there were never any serious issues, religious or otherwise, that divided the town. A good Catholic boy like myself, who faithfully attended Ste Anne's Church, even accepted an invitation to participate in the Orange Parade one year.

Although my mother and father weren't regular churchgoers, every Sunday they made us kids put on our best clothes and march off to mass. Built in 1886, Ste Anne's was, and still is, Penetang's tallest, most imposing structure. The limestone church was a landmark for sailors and fishermen out on the bay. To a young boy, it seemed only logical that God would choose to live in the most beautiful building in town.

Maybe the biggest reason Penetang seemed like such a warm, friendly place to me was that many of the people living there actually were my family. I had aunts and uncles in town and throughout the area, as well as dozens of first and second cousins to play with. Almost everywhere I went I was near kin. That's a great feeling of security for a kid to have.

A growing boy couldn't ask for much more. In the summer we would fish and swim in Penetanguishene Bay, and the winters seemed to offer just as many opportunities for fun. One of our favourite winter sports was to ski down the sidewalks of the steep side roads leading to Main Street. Sometimes when we were older we would make the same run in a four-man bobsled. I swear we must have reached speeds of eighty miles an hour. We held on tight and prayed we wouldn't hit a horse-drawn sleigh or an automobile on the streets we crossed on our way. When we got to Main we had to brake suddenly and veer right, trying desperately not to crash into the sheet-metal fence that rimmed the far side of the street.

We were rough-and-tumble kids who would do just about anything on a dare. We'd climb to the top of Ste Anne's and ring the bell, bringing the priests running out to try to catch us. By carefully planning our escape route down a side or back wall we always managed to get away.

Every year Halloween provided a perfect excuse to raise hell. Most people in Penetang still had outhouses back then, and one year a few of us lifted up an old man's privy and moved it several feet away. When he heard us, he came running out and fell right into the old slop hole. We felt so guilty about that prank we never did anything nearly so bad again.

When I got to high school I quickly earned a reputation as one of the town's best athletes. The school gym seemed like heaven to me. Equipment for basketball, lacrosse, baseball and other sports was there for everyone to use, or at least for those good enough to make the school teams. Most of the kids in town had never had a chance to play these games because our parents simply couldn't afford to buy us the equipment.

Hockey, of course, had always been the exception. The game was so much a part of life in Canada in those days that even the poorest among us managed to find hand-me-down skates and a battered old stick to play shinny with out on the ice in the bay after school and all day long on weekends and Christmas holidays.

I signed on for every sport going. I was a flashy, speedy forward on the hockey team, and a halfback and the punter on the football squad. I even went out for the lacrosse team, but quit after being viciously slashed in the face with a stick in my first game. I didn't like lacrosse enough to put up with that.

One of my proudest accomplishments was winning top prize in the school's field day one year. I still have the little bronze trophy. There were competitions in pole vaulting, the hundred-yard dash, and a variety of other track events. I had ten first-place finishes that day, and I did it all on an empty stomach. It was a particularly hard time for my family right then and there hadn't been anything for me to eat when I left the house for school that morning.

As I said, it was in high school that I got the opportunity to play baseball for the first time. I'm not saying I hadn't heard of the game or had never played a casual game of catch. But baseball wasn't a priority among the kids I hung out with when I was younger. We had so many other things to do in the summertime. And again, we couldn't have found the money for bats, balls and gloves even if we had been interested in playing.

Our baseball team wasn't in an actual league, but instead played a series of exhibition games against other schools. I started out as a catcher because no one else wanted to go behind the plate. Then our coach, Mr Wendling, asked me to pitch when he noticed that I was throwing the ball back to the pitcher faster than he was throwing it in.

The first time I pitched in an actual game was at a fair held near Collingwood where our team was competing in a tournament. I had absolutely no idea of what I was doing out there.

No one was able to give me any advice, including the coach, who didn't know any more than I did.

What a start. I had the daylights scared out of me when I beaned Archie Thompson of the Barrie team; who's difficult to forget because he was the only black kid in the entire district. The ball bounced off his head all the way to second base. I thought I'd killed him. But Archie didn't even go down. That tough kid just stood there and called for me to throw him another pitch.

At this stage my favourite sport was definitely football. I was playing for the school as well as for the town's intermediate squad, which competed against rep teams from throughout the district. As the punter for both teams, I averaged kicks of about 50 yards.

Our school played a home-and-home series against St Michael's College, a Toronto private Catholic school, that I'll never forget. It was snowing so hard for the first game in Penetang that instead of trying to clear the snow off the field, we decided to pack it down with rollers. We won 7–0 on a decoy play when I took the snap instead of the quarterback, then threw to a receiver near the sideline who was pretending to head for the bench.

In Toronto, after the second game of that series, I was approached by a priest who was a coach with the St Mike's football team. He offered me the chance to attend Grade Twelve the next year at the school on a sports scholarship.

I hadn't been in the big city often, but often enough to know that the opportunity to spend an entire school year on the St Mike's campus in the heart of downtown Toronto was too exciting to pass up. Besides, the move would actually save my parents money. St Mike's was going to pay for everything, including the not insignificant expense of keeping a hungry teenager well fed.

The experience didn't turn out exactly as I'd hoped. St Mike's allowed its students almost no freedom, so my hopes of getting to know the city came to nothing. It was study and more study, with a few hours a week off to participate in school sports.

Eventually I became so bored that on two or three occasions I climbed the school fence at night and escaped to a nearby tavern for a beer, some place where they weren't too fussy about checking for ID. I was joined on these outings by a novice priest who was beginning to question whether he really did have the calling.

The football was fun, though I rode the bench more than I would have liked. St Mike's had such a strong team under coach Bill Storen that they could afford to break me in slowly. We made it into the play-offs of the Ontario Rugby Football Union's senior series. One of our stars was Johnny Metras, a big, friendly guy who went on to coach the University of Western Ontario Mustangs to several college championships. Years later I was pleased to read an interview with Metras in which he said I might have made a pretty fair footballer if I'd kept at it.

We played the final game of our season at Maple Leaf Stadium, which sat at the foot of Bathurst Street near the lake. The 20,000-seat park was the home of baseball's Maple Leafs. If you had told me then that in just a few years I'd be pitching for the Leafs on my way to bigger things, I would never have believed it possible. I was a serious, often moody kid who didn't let himself dream such things. I'd already learned that life could be pretty tough.

I can't say I was very disappointed when St Mike's decided to stay out of senior competition the following year and ended my scholarship at the end of Grade Twelve. I was more than ready to get back to my friends and family in Penetang.

In 1932 I began playing baseball for the Penetang Rangers, the town's entry in the tough North Simcoe Intermediate League, which included teams from Barrie, Orillia, Collingwood and Midland. As usual, I was surrounded by family. My first cousins Marius and Jimmy Bald were the catcher and first baseman on the team.

Today in Penetang there are carefully groomed fields for both softball and hardball, complete with lighting for night games. But it was a lot different back when I played. Our home field was literally a cow pasture out on the outskirts of town, across from where the Coca-Cola plant is now.

Games were often interrupted when cows wandered onto the field. Conditions were especially treacherous for outfielders, who had to navigate around the cow pats while chasing down balls. Finally we put up a snow fence to stop the interruptions, and worked to get the field in reasonable shape. A screened backstop went up, wooden bleachers were built, and the worst bumps were smoothed out of the infield.

At this stage I still had almost no clue about what I was doing on the mound. I hadn't yet met anyone who could teach me about the mechanics of pitching. So I would just rear back with my right arm and throw with every ounce of strength I had in my 5'11", 170-pound body.

Later on in the majors it was estimated that my fastball travelled about ninety-five miles per hour. The movement on it was so distinctive that it became known around the American League by the name "Johnny Jump-Up."

I developed a three-quarter, slightly sidearm delivery. Occasionally, I dropped down into a lower sidearm release much like the one Dan Quisenberry used so effectively a few years ago for the Kansas City Royals. For some reason that escapes me now, I discarded that pitch before I got to the majors. I should have kept it. Hitters used to hate it when they saw me drop down.

My curveball came around only after many hours spent experimenting with a variety of grips and deliveries until I found one that worked. When you throw as hard as I did, the fastball is always going to be your best pitch. But on a good day my curve had a wide downward break to it that made it almost as effective as my heater. Because I gripped the ball tightly, my curve was only slightly slower than my fastball, which made it even more difficult for batters to tell what was coming.

I practiced my pitches every chance I got with a pal and team-mate of mine, Andy Vaillancourt, who worked in the bar-ber shop on Main Street. Whenever there were no customers, we would go back into the alley-way behind the shop, shoo the dogs away and get down to work.

Pretty soon I was routinely striking out ten to fifteen batters a game. I also swung a hot bat. There was nothing I liked better than to get up there and take my hacks. I was among the top hitters in the league, usually batting fourth in our batting order.

In my second season we made it to the league finals before being eliminated by Barrie, who eventually went on to the Ontario semifinals.

When we started winning, the people of Penetang got caught up in the excitement. The town would shut down for an important game and everyone would head out to the ball field.

I found myself becoming a local hero. "Great game, Babe!" people called out to me as I walked down Main Street. "Go get 'em Saturday, Babe. We're counting on you." The weekly newspaper, the *Penetang Free Press*, often gave the team front-page coverage.

Our biggest year was 1934, when we easily won our league championship. Then, in the first round of the Ontario play-offs, we beat North Bay in two extra-inning games as I struck out twenty-nine batters in twenty-two innings. The second round, against Meaford, was supposed to be a best-of-three series, but it went to five games when two were called because of darkness after several extra innings had already been played.

After pitching every game for our team throughout the season, I was running out of gas as the play-offs dragged on. We didn't believe much in relief pitchers in those days. I was the best we had so I went out there game after game.

A team from Chatham composed mostly of blacks beat us in the finals in four very close games. Ferguson Jenkins' home town was producing some pretty fair ballplayers even back then. We played the last game in an October snowstorm and even though we lost, I felt mostly relief that the season was finally over.

By now I was a grown man, almost twenty-one at the end of the 1934 season. I was beginning to wonder what the future held for me. But the idea of a career in baseball never entered my mind.

Like every other city and town in Canada, Penetang was hit hard by the Great Depression. Permanent jobs were almost impossible to find. All I managed was the occasional odd job, and summer employment at a foundry that produced wood stoves. Knowing that most of my townspeople were in the same situation didn't make being out of work any easier to take.

The next baseball season turned out to be my last in Penetang. My leave-taking was set in motion when a senior team from St Mary's came to town for an exhibition game. They were full of confidence, bragging that they were going to clobber us hicks.

I shut them down 2–0 and hit two long home runs.

A fellow named Kitch Jeffers was the catcher for St Mary's. A few months later he signed on to play the next season in Creighton Mines, a town near Sudbury where International Nickel operated a mine and sponsored the Cubs, a team in the senior-level Nickel Belt League. Jeffers thought enough of my performance to recommend that his new bosses sign me up.

International Nickel offered me a permanent job at the mine and the opportunity to play a calibre of baseball one step up from the intermediate competition I'd been facing.

My first choice would have been to stay in Penetang. I enjoyed being close to my family and friends, and I liked the life. I knew I'd miss football, hockey on the bay, and rowing the two miles out to Whiskey Island with a bunch of my cousins on a hot summer day, then swimming and downing a few beers. I knew I'd miss it all.

I decided to go around to the leading businessmen in town and tell them about the offer from Creighton Mines. These fellows all claimed to be big civic boosters and supporters of our ball club. Maybe I was being big-headed, but I felt certain someone would come through with a permanent job for me if they knew the alternative was losing their star pitcher to another team.

I didn't receive a single job offer. Some of my friends told me afterward that no one thought I would actually leave. I was too much of a home-town boy, they said. I'd be in Penetang until I died.

Mostly what I remember about Creighton Mines is that there were rocks everywhere. They gave me one of the most coveted jobs, out in the sun handling the timber they used to stope the mines. Then for a while I ran the cage that took the guys underground. The cage would fill up with thirty to forty men, and then down we went. My stomach would drop out from under me as we plunged 2,500 feet in a matter of seconds.

The money wasn't bad—about fifty dollars a week when I was working above ground and a little more when I operated the cage. The hardest thing to get used to was the rotating shifts. I never could adjust to sleeping during the daytime.

Believe me when I say there was almost nothing to do in that town. The boarding house I lived in was right next door to the mine. For a while I casually dated a nurse who was the daughter of the people who ran the general store, but she left for the bright lights of North Bay. Mostly what we did in our off-hours was shoot game after game of pool.

At the time, though, I was reasonably content in Creighton. People didn't expect as much out of life during the Depression. I was happy just to be getting a regular paycheque.

Stepping up into baseball's senior ranks proved an easy adjustment for me. Pretty soon I was pitching every game for the Cubs, routinely striking out ten or more, and hitting a ton of hits. One game I drove in seven runs, connecting for a grand slam in the ninth inning.

The league included teams from Coniston, Copper Cliff, Sudbury and Frood. Those were mean towns. The miners, many of them big Swedes and Norwegians, would turn out by the hundreds after their shifts ended to watch the games. They'd scream every insult you could imagine at us. Nothing was sacred. "You god-damned frog" and "stinking mick" were two of the milder taunts constantly thrown at me.

We once played an exhibition game against the House of David, a famous barnstorming team whose gimmick was that all their players wore long beards. The rumour was that their whiskers were meant to disguise certain members of the team who had been thrown out of organized baseball. The great

Grover Cleveland Alexander spent some time with them after he was through in the big leagues, playing for booze money.

This was the first professional team I'd faced. We won as I shut them out over the first six innings.

I played in the Nickel Belt League for three seasons, from 1936 through 1938. The last two of those years we won the league championship. In 1938 I set a league record by striking out 275 batters in the twenty-five regularly scheduled games of our season, and we made it into the Ontario senior baseball finals before losing to Strathroy two games to one.

Sometime in July of that year I got a telephone call from Jim Shaw, who had coached our Penetang team for a while and was involved in amateur baseball in Port McNicoll. Shaw was a fishing buddy of Dan Howley, the manager of the Toronto Maple Leafs. Apparently he kept telling Howley what a great prospect I was, that Howley was nuts if he didn't have a look at me.

There was going to be a Leaf try-out camp in Barrie in a couple weeks. Shaw told me I owed it to myself to go down there and show Howley what I could do. He said this was my big chance.

I wasn't so certain. Despite my success in Penetang and then in Creighton Mines, I wasn't all that confident of my ability to go any further in baseball. Most of the teams I'd been facing had two or three decent hitters at best. Besides, I was twenty-four by now, kind of old to be getting started in professional baseball.

But all my friends told me to go. They seemed as confident as Shaw that I was good enough. Figuring I had nothing to lose, I asked for a week's holiday and borrowed the keys to a buddy's Dodge coupe. After pitching in a play-off game, I drove all night to get to Barrie in time for the try-out the next day.

There were dozens of hopefuls on the field when I got there, almost all of them a few years younger than me. Clyde Engle, a former major-league outfielder and a Toronto scout, was in charge. He divided us into two teams and then began rotating different players into the game.

I struck out the side in order when it came my turn to pitch. The following inning I did it again.

A few years later, after I'd made a name for myself in the big leagues, newspaper and magazine profiles written about me gave a variety of descriptions of what happened during that try-out. One had Dan Howley sitting under a shade tree when the game began, but then moving behind home plate once he saw me pitch to a couple of batters. "He had to get a better look at such blazing speed," the article said.

When I came out of the game after two hitless innings, Howley was supposed to have said to Engle, "Don't let that fellow get away. He's a major-leaguer if I ever saw one."

Somehow I doubt those quotes are absolutely accurate. All I know for sure is that after my stint on the mound was over nobody said anything to me. Not a word. I waited around for a while, then got in the Dodge and drove to Penetang, where I spent the rest of my week's vacation.

I figured my stuff just hadn't been good enough to impress Howley. I didn't know what he looked like, so how was I to know if he'd even been paying attention when I was out there? He probably thought anyone could strike out the kids I faced in Barrie.

You can imagine how surprised I was when, a few days after I got back to Creighton, Howley showed up in town. "What the hell happened to you in Barrie?" he wanted to know. "We looked all over for you."

A large, bluff man known as Dapper Dan, Howley started in telling me that I had all the necessary tools to make it with the Leafs. There were a few fundamentals I needed to learn, but that would be easy. The main thing was that I had a natural, God-given talent to throw a baseball harder than most other men. An arm like mine, he said, was a rare gift.

Howley offered me a $500 signing bonus and a try-out with the Leafs the next spring at their training camp in Florida. He told me he was almost certain I'd make the team. It's a good thing I didn't know then that Howley was notorious for getting high on prospects who subsequently failed to pan out.

He was also known as a combative manager with a special knack for developing young pitchers. Howley managed the Leafs to pennants in 1918 and 1926, then led the major-league Browns and Reds for three seasons apiece before returning to Toronto.

There was no way I could say no to his proposal. If I didn't go, I'd always wonder what might have been. Anyway, my foreman at the mine told me my job would be waiting if things didn't work out in Florida.

My only regret is that I didn't get the cheque for $500 up front. The Leafs never did pay me that money. It wasn't the last time I felt cheated by management during my time in baseball.

I worked at the mine until February 1, then enjoyed a month's holiday in Penetang before boarding a Florida-bound train in Toronto on a ticket sent to me by the Maple Leafs. I rode a day coach all the way. It was the first time I'd ever been outside of Canada.

CHAPTER
3

LIFE AS A LEAF

I had plenty of time to think on the train taking me to my first spring training camp with the Maple Leafs in 1939. I wasn't so much nervous as anxious to get on with it, to finally see how good I was against men who really knew how to play the game.

One thing that did worry me was the fact that I was twenty-five years old. Even I knew that I was six or seven years older than most players invited to their first professional camp. In baseball you're a prospect until the age of twenty-two or twenty-three. After that people automatically wonder what's wrong with you, why you never made yourself known before.

In my case, the answer was easy. I'd been hidden away, first in Penetang and then in Northern Ontario. The Leafs were stepping up their efforts to locate local talent by conducting try-out camps like the one I went to in Barrie, but major-league scouts rarely ventured into Canada and they certainly never made their way to the Nickel Belt League. If it hadn't been for the persistence of my old friend Jim Shaw in insisting that Dan Howley take a look at me, I would never have gone further as a baseball player than the Creighton Cubs. Of that I'm certain.

So I did the only logical thing. From that point on I became three years younger than I actually was. For years afterward baseball reference books listed my year of birth as 1916 rather than the correct 1913.

Dan Howley wasn't about to blow the whistle on my little lie. Even before I got to the Leaf camp in the central Florida town of Avon Park, he was boasting to the Toronto reporters about his sensational new find. He was more than willing to convince himself and others that I was a fresh-faced kid who under his guidance was about to set the International League on fire.

At least part of the reason Howley and the newspapers were giving me such a big buildup was that I was a Canadian. A handful of native sons had played for the Leafs before, and they were always popular with the Toronto fans.

Of the several other Canadians invited to that camp, two eventually joined me in the majors. A fellow whose potential you couldn't miss was 6'4" string bean Dick Fowler, an outgoing seventeen-year-old whom Howley had discovered pitching in Toronto's Catholic Youth Organization league.

When Fowler was invited to try out in Florida, the guys in his Stanley Park neighbourhood collected thirty-five dollars and presented it to him, along with a suitcase. The kid still had money left when he got home from training camp. Fowler was sent down to the lower minors that spring, but by the end of 1941 he was pitching alongside me in Philadelphia.

Left-handed pitcher Frank Colman from London, Ontario, was demoted along with Fowler. After hurting his arm, Colman switched to the outfield and played six seasons with the Pirates and Yankees before a knee injury put an early end to his big-league career.

When Dan Howley moved up into the office of general manager during the off-season, Jack Burns became the Leafs' new manager. A player-manager who played a slick first base, Burns was a gregarious, friendly guy who had spent seven seasons in the majors, mostly with the St Louis Browns, before arriving in Toronto.

Soon after welcoming me to the team, Burns put me in the care of one of his coaches, Johnny Heving, a former catcher. Heving took me out to the mound and showed me a few fundamentals, such as how to push off from the pitching rubber with more power. He also gave me some pointers on working from the stretch position.

I kept waiting for him to tell me something really important, like how to smooth out the awkwardness in my delivery. I'd always known my pitching motion was rough, but I didn't have a clue about how to fix it. Neither, apparently, did Heving. Or else he just didn't think it needed fixing.

Unlike today, when every aspect of pitching has become a science, back then most pitching coaches pretty much left the player on his own. They didn't worry about fine-tuning your release point or most of the other things modern players are taught when they're still teenagers. Those were the dark ages for pitchers. Even the now-standard practice of icing down a sore arm after a workout didn't gain wide acceptance until the 1960s.

None of the veteran pitchers in camp came forward with any advice. Guys like Billy Weir, Earl Caldwell and Carl Fischer had all pitched in the big leagues and were now trying to stretch their careers out another few seasons in the minors. We became friendly later, but in spring training they saw me as a potential threat to their jobs. I was lucky if I got so much as a hello from any of them.

After a few days in camp I began to see why some of these fellows felt threatened. As unseasoned as I was, I had more stuff than almost anyone there. Howley was already chortling "I told you so!" to the writers.

At first I was shocked that things were going so well for me at this level of competition. By this time I knew the International

League wasn't the big time, but rather Class AA ball, one step down from the major leagues. There were two other AA leagues, the American Association and the Pacific Coast League.

Though it wasn't the majors, there were a lot of players in the International who had either been up there already or were about to make it. Most teams had at least two or three players who went on to make names for themselves.

The Buffalo Bisons, for instance, possessed a double-play combination that was promoted to the Cleveland Indians intact before the season was through. Shortstop Lou Boudreau and second baseman Ray Mack were two of the smoothest infielders I've ever seen. The Bisons also had a young pitcher, Sal Maglie, who became a famous star known as "the Barber" for his lethal brush back pitches.

In an era when some big-league clubs owned eight hundred players and there were forty-two minor leagues all feeding just sixteen big-league teams, playing in the International League was a hell of an accomplishment.

I knew for certain I belonged after we travelled to Lakeland to play an exhibition game against the Detroit Tigers on April 3. This was my first look at a real, live big-league team. The Tigers were one of the best squads in baseball, with stars like Hank Greenberg, Rudy York and Charlie Gehringer.

I held my own for three innings. Then Greenberg strode to the plate. What a giant he was, 6'4" of solid muscle. The previous season he had threatened Babe Ruth's record when he hit fifty-eight home runs. Now he stood there at the plate holding the bat up and high in that way of his, giving me the famous Greenberg glare.

Naturally, I pitched him carefully. When I'd worked the count to three and two, I uncorked a wicked curve. Greenberg ducked back as if the pitch were going to hit him, and the ball cut in and clipped the corner of the plate for strike three. I can still remember the look of surprise on his face. After the game he and Rudy York told the writers they'd been impressed by "that Marchildon kid." They predicted it wouldn't be long before I was pitching in the big leagues.

Dan Howley was ready to offer me a contract. "How does $350 a month sound to you?" he asked, leaning back in his office chair at the training complex. I should have told him it didn't sound very good at all. That wasn't a lot of money even back then. I also should have asked him for the $500 bonus he promised me back in Creighton Mines. But what did I know? He was offering more than I'd been making up north at the mine, and I hadn't yet proven myself as a professional. I signed.

My baptism of fire in the International League came in our very first game of the season, a 5–2 loss on a bitterly cold day in Syracuse. I retired six batters without giving up a hit in two innings of relief work. That earned me a start against the Baltimore Orioles, the predecessors of today's major-league club. In Baltimore I was unceremoniously knocked out of the box in the third inning after surrendering three runs.

Burns gave me the ball again on April 30 in Jersey City in front of 30,000 rabid fans. At that time Jersey City was the most successful franchise in the minors, outdrawing many teams in the big leagues. I'd never seen a crowd like that before. By the time I walked out to the mound to start the second game of the doubleheader I was sky-high with excitement.

Which may explain why I threw two wild pitches in the first inning, allowing a run to score. I shut them down the rest of the way, but we still lost 1–0. The Leafs' record now stood at 2–7.

My performance in Jersey City convinced Howley and Burns to name me the starting pitcher for the home opener at Maple Leaf Stadium on May 4. They wanted to showcase their Canadian phenom. I was only the second native-born pitcher to get the opening day assignment since the Leafs had moved into the stadium in 1926. (The first was Charles Stainton "Steamer" Lucas in 1935.)

Howley and Burns expressed complete confidence in me to the Toronto press. "Asked whether an opening-game assignment might not be too large an assignment for an untried youngster like the Penetang Babe, Howley and Burns roared definite negative assurance," reported the *Globe and Mail*. "There was a crowd of nearly 30,000 at Jersey City Sunday when Phil pitched the second game," Howley said, "and aside from a nervous start, he acted as good as a veteran of ten years—only he was much better."

I was thrilled at getting the assignment. Opening day at the Stadium was always a special occasion. The Maple Leafs may have technically been in a minor league, but even then Toronto thought of itself as a big-league city and put on a show. There were elaborate pre-game ceremonies attended by the mayor and other dignitaries. People skipped work to be there. Springtime didn't seem to start in Toronto until the Maple Leafs were back playing ball.

My mother and father and most of my family promised to come down. As soon as it was announced I was going to start, a group of Penetang businessmen began making plans to charter buses to bring as many townspeople as could make it to the game.

The night before opening day, a "Meet the Ball Club" banquet was held in the Crystal Ballroom of the King Edward Hotel. The five hundred fans in attendance gave me an especially generous round of applause as I was introduced. Everyone seemed curious about me and proud that a Canadian was starting the game. The special guest both at the dinner and the on-field ceremonies the next day was Ed Barrow, president of the New York Yankees and a former manager of the Maple Leafs in the early years of the century.

Opening day began for me with an unusual wake-up call. I was sleeping late in my room at the Ford Hotel, where I was renting by the month, when I was awakened by a loud knock on the door. It was two plain-clothes police detectives who told me I'd been robbed in the night. Apparently two men had picked the lock on my door and made off with my wallet while I slept like a baby through the whole thing. A few hours later the police had recovered the wallet, intact except for fifteen dollars, when they arrested the thieves on another charge.

With my family and a hundred or so friends from Penetang looking on, I walked out to the mound to face the Syracuse Chiefs on that cold, breezy afternoon. The crowd of 8,500 clapped and called out encouragement.

I struggled the entire game as we lost 4–1. The next day the newspapers talked about my "obvious nervousness." Well, who wouldn't be nervous in my place? All afternoon my fastball kept missing by an inch or two. I was constantly in and out of trouble. Twice I left the bases full. Before I was lifted for a pinch-hitter in the eighth, I'd given up ten hits and walked five batters.

Despite the buildup I'd received from Dan Howley and the Toronto press, I was beginning to think that maybe I was in over my head. Looking back now, I know it was unreasonable to expect that I could come straight from the Nickel Belt League and be an instant success at that level. I had talent, but absolutely no finesse.

My biggest problem was wildness, especially in the early innings. I've always been high-strung, and it would often take me two or three innings to settle down out there. Later on in Philadelphia the writers sometimes called me "Fidgety Phil" for my mannerisms on the mound. I would fiddle with the rosin bag and paw the dirt, trying to get comfortable.

Another thing I hated was pitching in cold weather. This complaint struck my American team-mates as a good joke. Being a Canadian, I was supposed to be able to pitch through a raging blizzard. But I was never able to get a proper grip on the ball when it was cold. My hands were naturally dry, even in warm weather. In the cold there was no sweat at all to help me grip the seams on the ball.

I didn't make it through the fourth inning in my next start. After that game, Burns started using me mostly in relief. After a couple of decent outings he gave me another start on May 27, this one in Buffalo. Pitching against Sal Maglie, I only lasted into the third and we went on to lose 8–6.

Nothing seemed to be going right for the Leafs or for me. We were in last place and showed no signs of getting better. Howley began parachuting new players in almost weekly in an effort to shake things up.

The problem was that our defense was weak through the middle of the infield and we lacked hitting power throughout the lineup. We did, however, boast one bona fide superstar, right fielder Bob Elliot, who led the team with a .328 batting average on the season. Bob was called up by the Pittsburgh Pirates on August 31 and went on to play fifteen seasons in the majors.

Another familiar name on that Leaf team was Mayo Smith, our centre fielder. Mayo and I were team-mates again with the Athletics in 1945, his only big-league season. He then became a successful manager, taking the Tigers to a World Series title in 1968. Mayo is responsible for a famous baseball quote: "Open up a ballplayer's head and know what you'd find? A lot of little broads and a jazz band."

Despite the lack of run support from my team-mates, at this stage of my professional career I couldn't blame my troubles on anyone but myself. I was getting my share of strikeouts but I was wild as a hare. I was constantly pitching behind in the count, and there always seemed to be men on base. That was big trouble because I had no clue how to hold them on. My pick-off move was terrible. Runners were stealing on me almost at will.

Finally, I went to Dan Howley for advice. "I was never wild as an amateur," I told him. "I don't know what's wrong. Suddenly I can't find the plate."

Howley looked at me pityingly. "Forget it," he said. "Hasn't it occurred to you that you're pitching against the best hitters outside the big leagues? A lot of these guys will be in the majors next year or the year after. They know where the strike zone is. They're letting balls go by that amateurs would swing at. You're too far off the plate with your pitches."

The New York Yankees were scheduled for an exhibition game at Maple Leaf Stadium May 31. Given how badly I was struggling, I was shocked when Jack Burns told me I was starting.

Later on I heard rumours that Yankee boss Ed Barrow had asked Dan Howley to give me the start. Barrow had liked what he'd seen of me on opening day at the Stadium and now wanted a second look. There was talk the Yankees were interested in buying my contract from the Leafs.

People now speak of the 1927 Yankees of Ruth and Gehrig, or possibly the 1961 team with Mantle and Maris, as the greatest ball club in history. But the 1939 Yankees of DiMaggio, Henrich, Keller, Rolfe, Crosetti, and Selkirk must have been right up there. Every hitter in that lineup could kill you.

New York won four consecutive World Series titles from 1936 to 1939, completely dominating the National League's best teams while doing it; they won sixteen and lost only three Series games during that time. The 1939 squad placed nine men on the mid-season All-Star team. Then the Yanks romped home to win the pennant by seventeen games.

They did all this the year I faced them with the Leafs despite the fact Lou Gehrig was forced to remove himself from the line-up May 2, ending his "Iron Man" streak at 2,130 consecutive games. That's why I say the 1939 Yankees have to rank among the game's greatest teams. Imagine being able to lose Lou Gehrig and barely notice it.

Gehrig took infield practice with the other Yankees before the game, then sat in the dugout the rest of the day. He appeared to move a little slowly around first base, but otherwise he was still a big, handsome, healthy-looking man. At that point everyone assumed that at age thirty-six Gehrig had simply grown old. It happens that way sometimes. Some players lose their abilities almost overnight. It was still a couple of weeks before Gehrig checked himself into the Mayo Clinic and heard the news that he was dying of amyotrophic lateral sclerosis.

DiMaggio was injured and didn't play that afternoon either. Catcher Bill Dickey was also given the day off. I was both relieved and a little disappointed at not facing those two future Hall-of-Famers. Otherwise, most of the familiar Yankee names were in the lineup.

As was becoming usual for me, I had trouble getting into a groove and the Yankees hit me hard in the early innings. Tommy Henrich stroked a two-run homer over the right-field fence in the first, and by the fourth they'd scored two more. After that I settled down, allowing only one more hit before being taken out after the seventh inning.

I was reasonably pleased with my effort. Giving up four runs to the Yankees seemed a solid afternoon's work. The rest of our guys, though, felt humiliated. Not wanting to waste Red Ruffing, Lefty Gomez or another of their regular pitchers in a meaningless exhibition game, the Yanks started their batting practice pitcher, Paul Schreiber, who was making his first start in a Yankee uniform. Managing only six hits and losing 4–1 to a batting-practice pitcher, even one wearing pinstripes, was a little hard to take.

The Yankee player who received the most attention from the Toronto fans and press was George "Twinkletoes" Selkirk. Born in Huntsville, Ontario, Selkirk had been assigned the impossible job of replacing Babe Ruth in the Yank outfield in 1935. No one could make New Yorkers forget the Babe, but Selkirk won the fans over by putting together a string of great seasons. He topped the .300 mark five times and twice drove in more than a hundred runs. The speedy Selkirk was given the nickname Twinkletoes by a sportswriter who saw him stretch a single into a double.

In a ceremony at home plate before the game, Selkirk accepted a cocktail shaker and half-a-dozen glasses on behalf of his former townspeople. Among the dignitaries at the presentation were hockey stars Charley Conacher, Busher Jackson and Turk Broda, who were there because for them, just as for millions of other Canadians, George Selkirk was a national hero. He was a Canadian who had made it in big-league baseball.

The fact that Selkirk had spent only the first five years of his life in Huntsville before his family moved to Rochester, New York, where he learned to play the game, didn't seem to bother anyone. He was born here and that was good enough to make Canadians proud.

The fans at the Stadium loved every moment of each confrontation between Selkirk and me during the afternoon. When I struck him out in the third, they gave me a huge cheer. Selkirk may have been a national hero, but I was a Maple Leaf.

I find it interesting to think back on how eager Canadian fans were for local baseball heroes. One player who had a

devoted following in Toronto was little Goody Rosen, sometimes called "the Toronto Tidbit," who was born in the city
and played sandlot baseball there before making his way up to
the Dodger outfield in 1937. I first played against him two
years later when he was sent down by Brooklyn to the Montreal
Royals.

Every time Rosen came to Toronto it was an event. Like
Hank Greenberg in the United States, Rosen was acclaimed by
his fellow Jews for having overcome anti-Semitism to succeed in
sports. Goody made it back to the majors and in 1945 hit .325,
the third-best mark in the National League.

Another favourite of Toronto fans was Earl Cook from
Lemonville, a village just north of the city. Like Rosen, he
learned his baseball on local diamonds. In 1939 Cook was
playing for the Buffalo Bisons and was one of the toughest
pitchers in the league. The next season he pitched both ends of
a doubleheader for Buffalo, winning each game by the same
2–0 score.

The affection of the fans for me, Rosen, Cook and the handful of other native sons who played at Maple Leaf Stadium in
those days makes me wonder just how popular a Canadian
would be in baseball-crazy Toronto today if he were talented
enough to play regularly for the Blue Jays. None of the
Canadians the Jays have had on their roster over the years—
Dave McKay, Denis Boucher, Rob Ducey—were good enough
to stick. But if someone like Larry Walker, the young Montreal
Expo star from British Columbia, were to play there I think he'd
own the town. I hope it happens some day.

A couple of days after the Yankee game, Jack Burns called
me into his office in the clubhouse and told me I was being
demoted to Cornwall of the Canadian-American League, one
level down from the International.

"Don't let this discourage you," he said. "You've got great
stuff. We just want you to go down there and work on your
control. All you need is experience."

I was disappointed by the news but I can't say I wasn't
expecting it. Since opening day I had lacked consistency. I

would have one good outing followed by three or four bad ones. What worried me most was that I had recently developed some soreness in my pitching arm. Like my control, the pain came and went. One day the arm would feel fine and the next it would hurt every time I threw the ball.

The Leaf trainer, Tim Daly, who filled the same role for the hockey Maple Leafs, wasn't much help. The only thing he could think to do was give my shoulder a quick massage. In those days you were simply supposed to work through a sore arm. Anyway, I didn't want to complain too loudly about it. A rookie pitcher known to have a bad wing doesn't enjoy a great deal of job security.

Cornwall proved to be exactly the tonic I needed. My first start was an away game in New York state against the Gloversville Glovers; we edged them 4–3. Then it was back across the border to Cornwall, a small Ontario city on the north bank of the St Lawrence River about fifty miles east of Montreal.

I have only hazy memories of the city. What I do remember clearly is making a visit to a local dentist that turned my season around. Three or four years earlier I'd broken a front tooth playing football. Now it had become infected and the dentist told me the tooth had to come out.

Almost as soon as he pulled it my arm started to feel better. The poison from the tooth must have worked its way down into my pitching arm. That afternoon at the Cornwall Athletic Grounds, in a return match against Gloversville, I struck out sixteen Glovers and gave up three hits as we won 6–1. The Cornwall *Standard-Freeholder* called it "a tossing performance almost unequalled in Athletic Grounds records."

Over the next seventeen days I racked up six consecutive wins for Cornwall. On June 20 against the Ottawa Senators, I struck out seven and hit a 430-foot homer, a double and a single as we won 9–3. After the game I was told they wanted me back in Toronto.

The Maple Leaf club had changed dramatically in the three weeks I'd been away. In an effort to shake the team out of its losing ways, Dan Howley had brought in former New York Yankee great Tony Lazzeri as the new manager. Another famous star, outfielder Heinie Manush, had also been added after he was released by the Pittsburgh Pirates.

I was glad to see that Jack Burns was still with the team, although he was now strictly our regular first baseman. As for the other changes, I was happy enough with them. It's not often a guy has the opportunity to play alongside two fellows who are destined for the Hall of Fame, especially when he's still in the minor leagues.

Lazzeri had everyone's respect from the moment he walked through the clubhouse door. You had to be a little in awe of a man who had been a member of the Yankees' famed Murderers' Row and put up the kind of career numbers he had. A famous clutch hitter, "Poosh 'Em Up" Tony Lazzeri had driven in over a hundred runs seven times during his twelve seasons with New York and played on five World Series championship teams.

Lazzeri was still active as a player when he joined us. He sometimes put himself into the lineup at second base, and he did a fair bit of pinch-hitting. He didn't have the range he'd had when he was younger, but he could still play.

Mostly he tried to instill in us the same intensity to win that he had been known for when he was with the Yankees. I liked him a lot. He was a quiet, dignified man who led by example. Lazzeri wasn't one to chew you out in front of your team-mates when you made a mistake. He would take you aside in private and tell you where you'd gone wrong and how to improve yourself. We didn't use the term back then, but nowadays you'd call him a player's manager.

Heinie Manush was just as easy to like, as outgoing as Lazzeri was quiet. He was always joking and telling stories. After seventeen seasons in the majors he had a lot of them to tell.

In 1926, while with Detroit, Heinie edged out Babe Ruth for the batting championship on the last day of the season, stroking six hits in nine at-bats during a doubleheader for a .378 average to Ruth's .372. He twice led the American League in hits and retired with a .330 career average.

My favourite Heinie Manush story takes place in the 1933 World Series, when he was playing for the Washington Senators against the New York Giants. Manush made history in Game Four as the first player ever thrown out of a Series game. Enraged when umpire Charley Moran called him out, Heinie pulled on the umpire's bow tie, held in place by an elastic band, and when it was stretched out several inches let the tie snap back.

Lazzeri kept me cooling on the bench for a few days after I returned, then gave me a start at the Stadium July 1 against Buffalo. I held the Bisons to two hits as we won 4–1 in front of a Dominion Day crowd of 10,000, the biggest turnout of the season. It was my first victory as a Maple Leaf.

Lazzeri left the team to travel to New York for "Lou Gehrig Day," July 4, at Yankee Stadium. That was when the Iron Horse made his famous farewell speech: "Today I consider myself the luckiest man on the face of the earth." When he returned to Toronto, Lazzeri told reporters, "I tell you, I shed a couple of tears myself. I never saw such a change in a man in such a short time."

Under Lazzeri's guidance we began to win more often, but not enough to work our way out of the cellar. We'd dug ourselves into too deep a hole earlier in the season.

Although I was pitching better after my return from Cornwall, I was still plagued by wildness, especially in the early innings. In my next start I was knocked out of the box in the second inning. Then, slowly, my control improved and I started to feel more comfortable and confident on the mound. I began to challenge the hitters, defying them to hit my best stuff. Confidence is so much a part of a pitcher's success. No matter how talented you are, unless you feel you have the advantage over the hitter, that you're in control, you're never going to be a winning pitcher.

Lazzeri was trying to bring me along slowly, mostly using me in relief but occasionally giving me a start.

"It's going to take time, Phil," he told me. "You've got the talent. Now you have to learn how to be a pitcher."

Despite having only a couple of wins to my credit, I was attracting the interest of several big-league clubs who tried to buy my contract. "The kid has everything," Lazzeri was quoted in the *Globe and Mail*. The same article went on to say, "The Yankee organization is definitely interested in the young miner and would gladly give Lazzeri the infielder and outfielder he needs to raise the Toronto standard for next year, plus a pitcher and probably a fair bundle of cash."

The Yankees. It would have been something to play alongside DiMaggio, Henrich, Keller and the other famous names on those powerhouse squads the Yanks produced year after year.

As July turned into August it became more difficult to concentrate completely on baseball as war in Europe began to seem like a very real and immediate threat. Every day newspaper headlines repeated Hitler's latest rantings. The possibility of war wasn't yet a serious consideration for most of my American-born teammates, who were convinced their country would remain neutral. But as a Canadian I knew we were likely to jump in the moment England got involved. I wasn't thrilled at the idea of having to march off to fight, especially now when my baseball career was just getting started.

When Germany finally invaded Poland on Friday, September 1, it cast a pall on what should have been one of the most exciting evenings of my young career. That night at the Stadium, two hundred of my townspeople from Penetang showed how proud they were of me in a ceremony before the game against the Montreal Royals. Including some old teammates who wore their town baseball uniforms, they lined up along the foul lines and presented me with a beautiful leather club bag.

My friends from home had the Stadium almost to themselves. Only five hundred fans went through the turnstiles. People were staying home by their radio sets to listen for news of the fighting in Europe and to wait for England to declare war.

I wanted so badly to win that game. For seven innings I threw shutout ball. Then in the eighth the Royals, sparked by Goody Rosen's bases-loaded triple, got to me for five runs before Lazzeri walked to the mound and took me out. We lost 7–6.

Two or three more relief appearances and a complete-game victory over Buffalo's Earl Cook brought me to the end of my first season as a professional ballplayer. The year had been a disaster for the team. The Leafs finished in last place with a record of sixty-three wins against ninety losses.

It was more difficult to judge how the season had been for me. Pitching in twenty-nine games, I had won five and lost seven. In 124 innings I had allowed 115 hits while striking out 90 and walking 92. My earned run average was 4.50. Opposing batters had a collective .202 batting average against me, the second-lowest mark in the league.

Except for that last statistic, my numbers weren't all that impressive. Yet people were talking about me as one of the best pitching prospects in the minor leagues. I still wasn't totally convinced, but I was willing to hope they were right.

Cashing in on my new celebrity status, I accepted a job for the winter as a beverage manager at a downtown Toronto hotel. I was enjoying myself, living the life of a bachelor in the big city and hoping that, despite the war, things could go on just as they were.

CHAPTER
4

CALL FROM MR MACK

I f someone had told me at the start of spring training with the Maple Leafs in 1940 that I would be in the majors before the season was through, I would never have believed it possible. Not after winning a grand total of five games my rookie year in the International League.

I knew I still had a lot to learn. My pitching motion was rough, kind of "herky-jerky" as one newspaper reporter described it. Wildness in the early innings continued to be a problem. I also had trouble holding runners on base.

It was true that baseball people were touting me as a future star. During spring training at our camp at Avon Park in Florida, new Leaf pitching coach "Sad Sam" Jones called me the best pitching prospect he'd ever seen. Praise like this felt especially good coming from a man who had won 229 games in 22 big-league seasons.

Sad Sam was a great addition to the ball club. He was a gentle fellow who, in spite of his nickname, always seemed to be in a good mood. A New York sportswriter had dubbed him Sad Sam when he starred with the Yankees in the early twenties because he supposedly looked unhappy on the field. Sam explained: "I would always wear my cap down real low over my eyes. The sportswriters were more used to fellows like Waite Hoyt, who'd always wear their caps way up so they wouldn't miss any pretty girls."

Like Cy Young before him and Bob Gibson later on, Sam adhered to the theory that a pitcher had only so many pitches in his arm and it was foolish to waste any of them. He even refused to make pick-off throws to first base. The one time he did, the first baseman was so surprised he dropped the ball.

It's hard not to like a man who tells everyone who will listen that you're going to be the game's next pitching star. Sam was great for my confidence and, me being the nervous type, my confidence could always use a boost. But I don't remember that he taught me much about pitching. As I've said before, most pitching coaches in those days left you pretty much on your own. Maybe Sam was afraid of ruining whatever it was he saw in me.

Although I didn't realize it at the time, the most crucial factor in my making it to the majors in 1940 took place before the season even got started when the Maple Leafs signed a working agreement with Connie Mack's Philadelphia Athletics of the American League. The Athletics agreed to provide the Leafs with several players in exchange for the right to purchase any two Toronto-owned players for $7,500 each.

It was a fairly standard deal for the time. But I'm not so certain that sly old Mr Mack didn't get much the better of the Leafs. Philadelphia had finished last or next to last each of the previous five seasons. So what were the chances of the Athletics being able to provide players with even marginal talent to the Maple Leafs?

Later on I heard that the main reason Mack made the deal was to guarantee that I would become Philadelphia property. If that's true, then the Leafs missed out on a potentially huge return on their investment in me. The Yankees were supposed to be interested in my services. So were several other clubs. Toronto could have sold me to the highest bidder for maybe $50,000 or more. But all they ended up getting for me was $7,500.

None of this was in my thoughts during spring training at Avon Park. I was still a relatively unsophisticated country boy who was just happy to be there. When Dan Howley offered me a fifty-dollar raise, making my salary $400 a month, the best pitching prospect Sad Sam Jones had ever seen quickly signed on the dotted line.

The Leaf team that manager Tony Lazzeri took north at the end of spring training was significantly different from the one that had finished in last place the previous year. Our former manager and first baseman Jack Burns was gone, as were Heinie Manush, Mayo Smith and several others. Replacing them were Harley Boss at first, Dario Lodigiani at second, Fred Chapman at short, and Eric Tipton and Buddy Bates in the outfield. None of these fellows went on to become more than marginal performers in the majors.

If anything, we were even worse than the year before. Our defense wasn't any better and it seemed an even tougher struggle to score runs. I lost my first start of the season in Syracuse even though I gave up only six hits.

This time the opening-day start at Maple Leaf Stadium went to veteran Carl Fischer. I admit to feeling a little relieved. After having had my hotel room broken into and then going through the emotional wringer of pitching in front of my family and so many friends the previous year, it was kind of nice to sit back and watch all the hoopla from the bench.

Once the warm weather arrived in May the muscles in my arm began to loosen and I got into a comfortable groove. Throughout my career warm weather was like a balm to me.

Unfortunately, the team continued to struggle. In Buffalo on May 22 we lost even though I pitched three-hit ball for seven innings before being removed for a pinch-hitter. I was beginning to think I'd have to throw a shutout every time out to get a win with these guys behind me. My record was now 0–3.

Poor Tony Lazzeri. I think that season was the longest of his life. He was so intense, wanted so much to win. Success was all he'd ever known throughout his career with the Yankees. Now he was in charge of a team that was on its way to racking up 101 losses.

"What's wrong with this team, Phil?" he asked me before a game one day. "Is it me? Am I to blame for the way we've been playing?"

I felt uncomfortable being asked for advice by someone of Lazzeri's stature in the game. I told him the truth. That it wasn't his fault we were playing so badly. The team was just plain bad.

By this point not all of the players shared my affection for Tony. Some felt that, having been a great star in the majors, he didn't have much respect for most of the minor-leaguers he was now managing. "If we hit the ball over the fence," one anonymous Leaf told a reporter, "Tony just shrugs. His attitude seems to say: 'Well, why shouldn't you knock it out of the lot? The pitcher is only a minor-league pitcher, throwing a minor-league hook.'"

Through June all anyone in Toronto talked about was news of the war in Europe. After the defeat of Poland and during the so-called "phony war" of the winter, it had been possible to hope that a peace settlement might be reached soon. Then in May and early June the Nazi armies swept through Western Europe to the British Channel. It was now clear the war would last for several years. That month the government introduced conscription for home defence and recruitment drives began in earnest for more volunteer troops to send overseas.

Although I consider myself to be as patriotic as the next guy, I wasn't even slightly tempted to enlist at this point in the war. I figured I'd be hearing from the government when they really needed me. Until then I intended to keep on playing ball.

Lazzeri was still using me both as a starter and in relief. That was common in those days even when you were taking a regular turn in the rotation. The top pitchers in the game were expected to appear in relief whenever their teams needed them. During my best years with the Athletics, Connie Mack would sometimes trot me out in crucial late-inning situations. Of Bob Feller's 570 career appearances, 86 were in relief. When Dizzy Dean won 30 games in 1934, he also relieved in 17.

Like most pitchers, I much preferred to start. From the time I first began pitching for the town team in Penetang I had been the guy expected to go nine innings or however long it took to win. I enjoyed that challenge. Pitchers who worked almost exclusively out of the bullpen were generally thought to be second rate, not good enough to start. It wasn't until Joe Page came along in the mid-1940s and starred as a short man for the Yankees that managers began to appreciate the advantages of having a full-time "closer."

My first win of the season didn't come until June 3 in Newark. But the pace quickly picked up after that. By July 1, after celebrating Dominion Day by shutting down Buffalo and hitting a triple during a relief appearance at the Stadium, I counted six victories to my credit, three of them coming in the previous seven days. But the team was ten games under .500 and still sinking.

There's a statistic that neatly sums up how difficult it was for that Leaf team to score runs. Of the sixteen homers we hit during July, all but two were solo shots.

In an effort to increase attendance and generate fan enthusiasm, the Booster's Club staged a series of player competitions between games of a doubleheader with the Montreal Royals at the Stadium July 17. These types of promotions were common back then in both the minor and major leagues.

Selected players from both teams competed in everything from sprints to egg tosses and wheelbarrow races, with small prizes going to the winners. Modern players would probably think such shenanigans beneath their dignity, but we didn't really mind. It was usually a lot of fun. That day I beat the Royals' Bert Haas in a hundred-yard dash.

It was right about now, after I'd had several good outings and won a few games, that I began to consider seriously the possibility that the Philadelphia Athletics might purchase my contract at the end of the season. My team-mates all seemed to think I'd be the first one taken. "How I'd love to have his stuff and his chance," said our relief pitcher Joe Mulligan, who had played fourteen games for the Red Sox back in 1934.

The hype surrounding me continued to build as the season moved into August. International League president Frank Shaughnessy called me the "nearest approach to a Bob Feller in the minor leagues," and added that I possessed "probably the sharpest curve in any league short of the majors."

Fans in the cities we visited started to pay closer attention to me. Because of my French-Canadian heritage, I was a box office attraction in Montreal. My start there August 4 was heavily advertised in advance. After I shut the Royals out 2–0, the French press eagerly gathered around my locker only to be disappointed to discover I could barely speak a word of their language.

The reception I received in Montreal made me sorry for the first time in my life that my parents hadn't made us learn to speak French when we were kids. Several Montrealers told me that if I'd been bilingual I would have been able to get a terrific off-season job in the city. Like the citizens of Toronto, Montrealers were always looking for a baseball hero to call their own.

I learned later that Philadelphia scout Lena Blackburne was following the Leafs around during this period specifically to report back to Connie Mack about me. Apparently Blackburne, a former Toronto manager who was later rehired to replace Lazzeri, gave me a glowing review.

The news I was waiting for came through on August 28. Dan Howley walked over to my locker and said, "We just got the call, Phil. Mr Mack wants you in Philadelphia at the end of our season."

The International League schedule concluded in mid-September, followed by a series of play-offs. The Leafs had long been out of contention, so the plan was for me to join the Athletics for the last two weeks of the American League season.

I would probably start or relieve in two or three games to give Mack and his coaches a look at what I could do against big-league hitters.

Howley offered some advice I never forgot. "You've worked hard for this," he said. "Now to stay in the majors you're going to have to work even harder. Getting there isn't half as tough as staying."

My record at that point in the season was 10–11, the best on our staff. Admittedly, ten wins doesn't sound like a lot for a guy headed for the majors. But with a better team I would easily have had six or seven more victories.

After our final game I said goodbye to my team-mates and rushed to Union Station to catch a train for Cleveland, where the Athletics were playing an Indian team that was fighting the Yankees and Tigers for the pennant.

I was as excited and nervous as you'd expect, as well as a little awestruck, as I walked into the visitors' clubhouse in Cleveland on September 15, 1940. Someone, I can't remember who, introduced me to a tall, thin man with a sweet, grand-fatherly face. Connie Mack reached out and shook my hand with a firm grip. "I've had good reports on you, Marchildon," he said. "Welcome to the team."

By the time I met Mr Mack, as he was always respectfully addressed by his players, the seventy-seven-year-old had become the most beloved figure in the game, the living symbol of America's national pastime. He had been born during the Civil War, played in the majors as a catcher starting in the 1880s, and helped found the American League in 1901.

As an owner-manager Mack had built two Philadelphia dynasties, first in the early teens and then in the late twenties and early thirties. He was the last manager permitted to wear civilian clothes in the dugout, favouring a black or grey suit, a high, stiff collar and, by the time I arrived, a soft fedora with the brim turned down. Earlier photographs of Mack show him in the more familiar derby hat or straw boater.

The best description of Mack was provided by the famous sportswriter Red Smith: "He could be as tough as rawhide and as gentle as a mother, reasonable and obstinate beyond reason, and courtly and benevolent and fierce. He was kind-hearted and hard-fisted, drove a close bargain and was suckered in a hundred deals. He was generous and thoughtful and autocratic and shy and independent and altogether lovable."

Mack was all these things, but for me the "hard-fisted" part too often overshadowed his better qualities. There were times during the next few years when I almost hated him for being such a miser, and wished he would trade me to any team where I would be paid something close to what I was worth.

Mack's chief lieutenant in the dugout was his son Earle, a short, nervous fellow who was in his early fifties when I joined the team but sometimes seemed almost as old as his father. I think being in Mr Mack's shadow for so long must have affected him. You could tell he was in awe of the Old Man.

Earle was his father's legs. Mack never left the dugout himself, sending his son out to argue with umpires or take a pitcher out of the game. Two other sons, Roy, the eldest, and the much younger Connie Jr., the product of Mack's second marriage (his first wife died in 1892), worked in the front office.

Many players from my era have bitter memories of the treatment they received from veterans when they broke into the majors. Established big-leaguers might deny them their cuts in the batting cage, make them the butt of practical jokes, or ignore them altogether. After the way the older pitchers froze me out during my first training camp with the Leafs, I expected the same reaction from the Athletics and was surprised when the regulars treated me as an equal from my first day with the team in Cleveland.

The great star Al Simmons, who had been a mainstay of the last Athletics dynasty and was now a thirty-eight-year-old pinch-hitter and coach, took me around the dressing room to introduce me to the guys. The team's top slugger, outfielder Bob Johnson, gave me a big hello and a slap on the back. Another hard-hitting outfielder, Sam Chapman, who later became a good friend, said he had heard about the hop on my fastball. Pitcher Johnny Babich told me to try not to be nervous, and that if he could help in any way, to just ask.

I was also introduced to Earle Brucker, a thirty-nine-year-old catcher who, like Simmons, was now primarily a pinch-hitter and coach. Serious and soft-spoken, Brucker was in charge of the pitching staff. He would become the most important influence in my career. More than anyone else, I owe my later success to him.

The warm welcome I received from these veterans may have had something to do with the fact that the Athletics were a lousy team on their way to a last-place, 54–100 finish. Simmons, Johnson and the rest probably didn't feel they had the right to lord it over even a raw rookie after the season they'd had.

Putting on a big-league uniform for the first time is a special event for every player. Today the uniform of the Oakland Athletics is a garish green and gold. But when I joined the team the heavy, flannel outfit was white at home and grey on the road, with blue lettering on both. A stylized "A"—not "A's"— was sewn over the left breast and on the cap. Before heading onto the field I lingered a moment to admire myself in the small mirror attached to my locker. From what I could see, it looked like a perfect fit.

Just a couple of months before I'd been called the closest thing to Bob Feller in the minor leagues. That afternoon in Cleveland I got a look at the real Feller in action and I can tell you he was an awesome sight. Feller retired the first twenty-two of our guys he faced in the opening game of a doubleheader, finally settling for a two-hitter and a 5–0 win. The Indians took the second game 8–5.

Seeing the man they called Bullet Bob in action your first day in the majors doesn't do a lot for a rookie's confidence. After watching him you couldn't help but wonder whether you belonged in the same league. His fastball got up around a hundred miles an hour and had a natural jump, rising as it crossed the plate. His curve was almost as fast and just as unhittable.

Feller was also just wild enough to keep hitters from getting comfortable and digging in at the plate.

Throughout the afternoon each of Feller's pitches seemed to explode into the catcher's mitt with more force than the one before it. There was nothing particularly graceful about his delivery. He just wound up with a high leg kick and fired with deadly efficiency. Only twenty-one and already in his fifth season with Cleveland, Feller led both leagues in 1940 with 27 wins and 261 strikeouts.

That Cleveland team was famous as "the Crybabies." Towards the middle of the season all twenty-five players had presented a petition to the team president demanding that their abusive, acid-tongued manager, Oscar Vitt, be fired. Management publicly supported Vitt and ordered the players to concentrate on playing ball. When the Indians finally lost the pennant by one game, it was said by many that they would have won if they hadn't been such crybabies. Too late, Vitt was fired and replaced by Roger Peckinpaugh.

The day after my arrival we split a doubleheader with the Indians, with Johnny Babich, the A's top pitcher that year with a 14–13 record, winning the second game. Mack had earlier announced that I would get my first big-league start the following day against the Tribe.

Suddenly I was the central figure in a controversy fuelled by reporters in New York and Detroit, who charged that Mack had no business starting an untested rookie pitcher against a team involved in a pennant race. Starting me in such a crucial game might give the Indians an unfair advantage.

Personally, I was more than happy to wait and pitch against another team. I was nervous enough and didn't need any extra pressure. I thought the arguments against using me made perfect sense.

So, in the end, did Mack. In my place he used veteran Bill Beckman, whose victory dropped the Indians to a half-game out of first behind Detroit. "I don't want anybody to think we're not trying to win," Mack told reporters. He said he would also pitch regulars against the Tigers in the series starting in Detroit the next day, waiting to experiment with rookies until the Athletics got around to clubs that were out of the running.

What I remember most about the series with Detroit was the sight of mighty Hank Greenberg belting three homers as we split a doubleheader our first day there. Greenberg exuded such strength and confidence at the plate. He seemed to live to drive in runs. "Get him over to third, for God's sakes," he would say to Charlie Gehringer, who batted in front of him. "I'll drive him in."

Greenberg brought home a big-league-leading 150 runs that season and hit 41 homers to carry the Tigers to the pennant. In the World Series, which Detroit lost to Cincinnati in seven games, Greenberg batted .357 with six RBIs. It was his last hurrah before being drafted into the Army early the next season, becoming the first big star to get the call.

The Athletics finally headed home to Philadelphia, where I was scheduled to start Sunday, September 22 against the Washington Senators, who were just ahead of us in the standings. My opponent would be hard-throwing Ken Chase.

Home field for both the A's and the National League Phillies was Shibe Park, which was baseball's first concrete-and-steel ballpark when it opened in 1909. I fell in love with the place the moment I saw it. To my eyes, Shibe was everything a ballpark was meant to be.

As with many of the old stadiums, the dimensions were determined by the streets of the surrounding neighbourhood, in this case North Philadelphia, about three-and-a-half miles from Independence Hall. The park's left- and right-field walls met at an almost perfect right angle in centre field, 468 feet from home plate. Distances down the left- and right-field lines were 334 and 329 feet respectively. Best of all from a pitcher's perspective, the distance between home plate and the backstop was about 90 feet, allowing more room than in almost any other big-league ballpark for the catcher to run down foul pop-ups.

Shibe was the type of old-fashioned stadium that Baltimore's Camden Yards has tried so hard to imitate. The main gates, at the corner of Lehigh and 21st Streets, presented a handsome, red-bricked face to the public, complete with a domed corner office tower. Inside the park, a roofed, double-decked grandstand enclosed the entire playing field except for right field. Seating capacity was about 33,000.

People said there was no better-maintained park in all of baseball. Workmen were always busy cleaning and painting. The grounds crew worked around the clock through the season to keep the infield and outfield grass in perfect condition.

This type of professionalism and attention to detail was something I noticed from the moment I was called up to Philadelphia. Everything seemed bigger and better at this level. Although the Athletics were among the poorest organizations financially, we never scrimped on anything. We stayed in the best hotels, rode first class on the trains and had better uniforms and equipment than I was used to in the minors. It was true what they said. Once you'd had a taste of life in the big leagues you never wanted to play anywhere else.

I didn't look like someone who'd be sticking around for long in my start against Washington. "Phil Marchildon, recruit right-hander from Toronto, started for the Athletics, but was removed after three innings," read the wire service report on the game. "Obviously nervous, Marchildon was nicked for six of the seven Washington hits, and all their runs. He walked three men and made two wild pitches to suffer his first big-league loss."

There's not much more to say. I was so wound up with tension I just couldn't get loose.

"Don't worry about it, Marchildon," Mack said after the game. "You'll get another chance in a few days." Earle Brucker came over and said a few encouraging words, then added, "Your delivery is awfully rough. Until now you've been getting by on the sheer strength of your arm."

So tell me something I don't already know, I thought. At that point I figured Brucker for just another do-nothing pitching coach.

Next to arrive in town were the fourth-place Boston Red Sox, giving me my first look at two of the greatest hitters in the history of the game. Ted Williams, in only his second season, was a tall, gangly, kind of goofy kid who was intent on becoming, as he often said, "the greatest hitter who ever lived." Nothing else seemed to matter to him. Instead of concentrating on the game when he was in the outfield, he sometimes pretended to be at bat, swinging at imaginary pitches with his arms.

Bill Dickey of the Yankees later told a story that illustrates the flaky arrogance of the young Williams. "One day I decided to try a little psychology on him," Dickey remembered. "First time he came to bat, I said, seriously, 'They tell me you can't hit to left field, Ted.' 'That's not so,' Williams answered. 'I'll show you I can.'

"Well, he popped up to the shortstop four times in that game as he tried to prove he could hit to left. Of course, I had the pitcher throwing inside to him, and he wasn't getting any power into the blows."

When Williams was taking batting practice before the game, I noticed that players on both teams had slowed down or stopped what they were doing to watch. Ted's swing was flawless, a beautiful thing to see. He sent ball after ball crashing into the outfield seats. You found yourself shaking your head. Where did that skinny kid get such awesome power?

On September 24, Jimmie Foxx hit the five hundredth home run of his career as the Sox swept a doubleheader from us. Red Smith once described a Shibe Park blast by Foxx, who had come up with and starred for the Athletics: "It looked like a low line drive streaking over the infield, but it was still climbing when it clipped the very peak of the roofed upper deck in left and took off for the clouds."

A friendly man fondly known as "the Beast," Foxx was in his sixteenth season when I first saw him, and he was still probably the strongest man in baseball. He used to cut the sleeves out of his uniform to show off his biceps and intimidate pitchers. "How much air do they hold, Jimmie?" asked Ted Lyons, the veteran White Sox right-hander. "Thirty-five pounds," answered Foxx. Lefty Gomez said Foxx "wasn't scouted—he was trapped."

There's a famous photograph of a young, shirtless Ted Williams comparing his muscles with a similarly undressed Foxx. It was obvious from the photo where Foxx's strength came from. Williams's home-run power could only have been a gift straight from God.

After a few days of watching my new team-mates, I was beginning to get an idea of the team's few strengths and all too many weaknesses. What did impress me was the outfield trio of Bob Johnson, Sam Chapman and Wally Moses.

Indian Bob Johnson, so-called because he was half Cherokee, hit 31 homers with 103 RBIs, the sixth of seven straight seasons he drove in over 100 runs. Johnson's misfortune was in coming along just as Mack was dismantling his last great team in the mid-1930s. Quiet Sam Chapman, a former All-American football star with the University of California, was great defensively and, like Johnson, hit for power, batting .276 with 23 homers in 1940. Fleet-footed Wally Moses topped the A's with a .309 batting average, the sixth consecutive season he had hit better than .300. (Moses had originally been spotted by a Giants scout who had orders to find a player who would appeal to New York's Jewish community. "But I'm Irish, Scotch and English," Moses told him, and he never saw the scout again.)

Apart from those three, I don't think the Athletics were much better than the last-place International League team I had left behind in Toronto. The infield was weak defensively and didn't offer much pop at the plate, although first baseman Dick Siebert did contribute seventy-seven RBIs. The pitching, except for Johnny Babich, was downright awful. Of course, working in front of that infield didn't help. With fourteen victories, Babich was the only pitcher to win in double figures.

Playing for such an untalented team became pretty discouraging after a while, and you took your fun where you could find it. Most years during my career the few truly meaningful games we played came towards the end of the season when we met teams involved in a pennant race. It was easy to get up for those games. You wanted to be the spoiler, to prove that playing the Athletics in tough situations didn't mean an automatic win.

Enthusiasm was never a problem when we met the Yankees, who arrived in Philadelphia on the heels of the Red Sox. Anyone who beat the famous Bronx Bombers knew they'd taken the best team in baseball.

After a slow start in the early weeks of the season, the Yanks charged down the stretch and stood just two-and-a-half games back of Detroit at the start of our doubleheader September 26. DiMaggio and company had won their last eight in a row.

They made it ten straight at our expense. But the next day our personal Yankee-killer, Johnny Babich, was brilliant in a 6–2 victory that eliminated New York from the race. As we congratulated one another, the Yankees walked grimly off the field after losing their first pennant in five years.

There was no question that Babich, who beat them five times that season, was largely responsible for the Yankee defeat. A former minor-leaguer in the New York system, Babich felt he had never been given a fair chance to make the big club and always seemed to save his best games for them.

Yank manager Joe McCarthy was reported to be disgusted with the loss after the game. "Johnny Babich!" he said aloud in the clubhouse. "Who ever heard of Johnny Babich?"

Joe Gordon, his All-Star second baseman, answered: "It's a cinch our scouts haven't."

Babich hated all Yankees, but he had a particularly bitter feud going with Joe DiMaggio, who kept getting fooled by Johnny's high outside slider. The dislike between the two reached a head the next season during DiMag's fifty-six-game hitting streak.

We travelled to Boston for the final weekend of the season and my last chance until spring training to show Mack I belonged. The Sox creamed us in both ends of the Saturday doubleheader, 16–4 and 8–1. Ted Williams had five hits that day. I was to pitch the second game of the next day's twin bill to close out the schedule.

The barrage continued in the opener as the Red Sox won again, this time 9–4. I felt shell-shocked before even taking the mound. Lasting into the eighth, I walked five and struck out four. After what we'd been through, my 4–1 loss seemed almost as good as a win. Ted Williams, by the way, hit two singles off me, both on curves. That was the book on Ted. Don't let him beat you on a fastball.

The difference this time out was that I was able to control my nerves, although I admit to having been a little rattled and embarrassed in the sixth inning when the Sox pulled a triple steal. Boston playing manager Joe Cronin was dancing around on third with the bases loaded when, with two out and Dom DiMaggio batting, he raced for home and slid in safely before I could react. Bobby Doerr advanced to third and Johnny Peacock moved to second. Welcome to the big leagues.

After the game Earle Brucker came over to my locker. "I've figured out what you're doing wrong," he said. "We'll get your delivery smoothed out in spring training."

Naturally, I asked what he'd seen. "No, I don't want you thinking about it all winter," Brucker said. "Go on home and relax. I know what we have to do."

I went home to Penetang and tried to take his advice, spending the winter sleeping late, skating on the bay and chumming around with my old friends. But I don't think I ever totally relaxed. I was too anxious to get to spring training and find out what Brucker had in mind.

CHAPTER
5

FABULOUS '41

Baseball fans immediately identify the 1941 season with the heroics of Joe DiMaggio and Ted Williams, who combined to make it probably the greatest season in history. It was the year DiMag batted safely in fifty-six consecutive games and Williams hit .406. In the fifty-plus years since then no one has come close to equalling either of those feats.

I count myself lucky to have been on hand to see both men play when they were at the peak of their abilities. I pitched to DiMaggio at Yankee Stadium in game forty-six of his streak, and was there in Philadelphia the final weekend of the season when Williams came to town gunning for .400.

For me the 1941 season was special from the start because it was my rookie year with the Athletics. My job was to go out and prove to Connie Mack that I belonged in the big leagues. My entire future in the game was on the line.

Just being able to play ball that summer seemed like an incredible luxury. I knew it was just a matter of time before I'd be called into the armed forces, although the chances looked good that I wouldn't have to go in for at least another year or two yet. I was twenty-seven at the start of the season and helping to support my family in Penetang. I figured there were still a lot of younger fellows back home without dependents to get through first.

But in those days nothing was guaranteed. The war was going badly in the spring. By May Hitler had pushed the Brits out of Greece and Rommel was creating havoc in North Africa. If the defeats kept piling up I knew I could be tossing warm-up grenades by the fall.

By now Americans were beginning to realize that the war was also getting closer for them. President Roosevelt was hinting strongly about intervention and a peace-time draft had been introduced requiring all eligible males over twenty-one to register. Hank Greenberg got his notice and joined the Army after hitting two farewell home runs May 6 in his last game.

Some people have credited DiMaggio's hitting streak with providing a kind of emotional release for American fans from the worries of the approaching war. It was amazing how involved everyone became in his streak as it continued on into the summer. You would hear radio stations begin news breaks with DiMaggio updates: "The Yankee Clipper had two hits today to extend his streak to…." Newspaper sports pages charted his progress in comparison with Dick Sisler, who had set the modern record by hitting in forty-one straight games in 1922, and with Wee Willie Keeler's all-time mark of forty-four straight, established way back in 1897. In July Les Brown's orchestra released a bouncy little tune entitled "Joltin' Joe DiMaggio" that became an instant hit.

Like the fans who filled the parks wherever he played that summer, I was in awe of DiMaggio's talents. There didn't seem to be anything he couldn't do on a ball field. He hit for power and average, ran fast and smart on the base paths, and played a great centre field, possessing one of the most powerful arms in the league. You would never see DiMaggio dive to make a catch. He never had to. His instincts seemed to guide him effortlessly to wherever the ball was heading.

Most of us who played against him thought Joe D. was the greatest player in the game. No less an authority than Connie Mack, who had seen them all, put only Ty Cobb ahead of DiMaggio on his all-time list.

Ted Williams, another guy who knows what he's talking about, has said that "there isn't a record in the books that will be harder to break than Joe's fifty-six games. It may be the greatest batting achievement of all."

It's certainly difficult for me to imagine any of the modern players making a serious run at DiMaggio's record. Players today don't have the discipline he always showed at the plate. In 1941 he posted power numbers of 30 homers and 125 RBIs, yet, incredibly, struck out only 13 times. Today's free swingers might whiff that often in a bad week.

People have asked me if at the time we players knew we were living through a season that would come to have such lasting significance. I can't say we did. We appreciated that DiMaggio was accomplishing something that had never been done before, but Williams' drive for .400 didn't seem nearly as important then as it does today. The .400 mark had been attained several times in the 1920s and as recently as 1930, when Bill Terry hit .401. There was no reason to believe it wouldn't soon be reached again.

Something else I didn't fully appreciate at the time, and which few Canadian fans are aware of even today, is the fact that a record nine Canadian-born players were in the big leagues that year. Almost no mention was made of this in the many stories written in this country marking the fiftieth anniversary of the 1941 season. Maybe I'm slightly prejudiced, but I think it's a shame so little is known about the Canadians who played in the past. Most of the younger fans seem to think Fergie Jenkins was the first of us ever to make it.

It's true that three of the nine Canadians had the advantage of learning their baseball in the States. I've talked about George

Selkirk, who was then in his next-to-last season with the Yankees before retiring. Another Canadian who moved to the United States as a small child—as a one-year-old, in fact—was Jeff Heath, born in Fort William, Ontario.

Whether or not Heath can fairly be called a Canadian ballplayer, there's no denying that for fourteen seasons he was one of the most feared sluggers in the game. He was a huge, powerful man who, like Jimmie Foxx, cut the sleeves off his uniform to show off his muscles. Heath enjoyed a career year in 1941, hitting .340 with 123 RBIs, 24 homers and a league-leading 20 triples. Early in the season he blasted a homer into the top deck of cavernous Municipal Stadium in Cleveland, way up where no one had ever hit one before.

Heath was a bit of a loose cannon. Bob Feller tells the story of the day a heckler sitting behind the Indians' dugout was riding Heath after he struck out. Heath reached across the top of the dugout, grabbed the guy by the hair and knocked him out with a single punch. The kicker to the story is that the heckler turned out to be on probation from prison. He was charged with disturbing the peace and sent back behind bars.

Sherry Robertson, a light-hitting utility infielder from Montreal who was a nephew of Washington Senators owner Clark Griffith, also moved to the States at an early age and learned his baseball there. Robertson managed to stick around for eleven years in the majors, all of them with Washington except for a few games he played with the Athletics in 1952, his final year.

The rest of us were pitchers who grew up in Canada. Until coaching improved in recent years, almost everyone who played baseball here before going on to the majors was a pitcher. Position players simply didn't get the opportunity to hone their skills and play enough games during our short season. Pitchers have always had the advantage of being able to practice as much as they want, throwing to a friend or against a wall.

Over the years, at various baseball functions in the Toronto area, I've gotten acquainted with Oscar Judd from Rebecca, Ontario. In 1941 he was a thirty-three-year-old rookie who was

0–0 in seven games for the Red Sox. Judd went on to win forty games in eight big-league seasons.

I should explain that the reason Judd and I didn't get to know one another until after our playing days were over was that fraternizing with opposing players wasn't tolerated by our coaches and managers. Nowadays you see players greeting each other like long-lost relatives during batting and infield practice, and laughing and cracking jokes with each other when they're on base during the game.

Back then players on the other teams were our enemies. We would catch hell from a coach if we said much more than a quick hello. As far as going out of my way to acknowledge players who were fellow Canadians, the thought never occurred to me. They were enemies, too.

Another Canuck I had only a nodding acquaintance with was Montreal's Joe Krakauskas, who posted a 1–2 record with the Indians and was 26–36 in seven seasons between 1937 and 1946 with Washington and Cleveland. Earl Cook, who I had faced in the International League, pitched two innings in one game with Detroit, his only big-league appearance. The only Canadian in the National League was Auldon Wilkie, a rookie southpaw from Zealandia, Saskatchewan, who compiled a 2–4 record mostly in relief for the Pittsburgh Pirates. Wilkie won eight games in three years with the Pirates.

Late in the season, Connie Mack purchased the contract of Dick Fowler from the Maple Leafs and brought him up for a look. In those last games of 1941 and again the next year, as well as after the war, both Dick and I were in the A's starting rotation. Two Canadians in the same big-league rotation on a regular basis is something that had never happened before and hasn't happened since. And although I would love to be proved wrong, I think it's a safe bet that it will be a long time before it happens again.

In the early 1940s the Athletics held their spring-training camp in California, with the pitchers and catchers reporting to the small coastal town of Carlsbad for early training, and then moving on to Anaheim two weeks later when the rest of the team arrived. It took me three long, boring days on the train from Penetang to get out there. I remember being held up for several hours at the border by Canadian Customs officials who were convinced I was trying to leave the country to dodge the draft.

All I could think about during the train ride, the thing that had been on my mind all winter, was what Earle Brucker had said to me after my last game the previous September: "I've figured out what you're doing wrong."

He let me in on his secret the first day of camp. "You're completely off-balance when you throw," Brucker said as we stood on one of the practice mounds. "That's probably the biggest reason you're so wild. Your left foot is coming down slightly to the right of your body. When you follow through, your whole body is straining against the leg, locking your hip. With your awkward delivery it's amazing you haven't blown out your arm by now."

Brucker drew a straight line toward home plate from the pitching rubber. "Now try stepping to the left, bringing your foot down on the line. This will straighten out your delivery and stop the strain against the leg."

Son of a gun if I didn't feel a difference right away. After about an hour on the mound with Brucker I even began to notice that my pitches seemed to have more movement on them. "That's because you're following through properly now," Brucker said. "The ball is even coming off your fingers faster."

Brucker told me I would have to keep working on my new delivery until it became second nature. He and Mack decided I wouldn't even see action in inter-squad games until they were certain I had absorbed all of Brucker's lessons.

Every day for the next month or so, while the rest of the team worked at various training exercises, I went out to a mound with a rookie catcher and practiced my new delivery. Afterwards I would join my team-mates for calisthenics and do at least a half-hour of hard running, then head back to our hotel for a mineral bath.

The natural sulphur springs located in Carlsbad were the main reason Mack decided to hold his early training camp for the pitchers there. Nothing was so soothing for your aching arm or back than to slide into one of those baths. The next day you felt absolutely great, with no soreness at all.

I have to give the Old Man full credit for knowing how to run a camp. Everything was always perfectly organized. His coaches had very specific duties and made certain everyone worked hard. Players who came to us from other teams said our camps were among the best in the big leagues.

A newspaper article out of spring training that year commented on what a hard worker I was, calling me one of the most dedicated players on the team. Sure I worked hard. I did whatever the coaches told me and more. But I didn't consider any of this work. Playing ball for a few hours a day in a sunny resort town beside the Pacific Ocean beat the heck out of working in the mines back in Creighton.

Spring training in California was an interesting change from the Florida camps I had attended with the Leafs. Once we got to Anaheim, which was then not much more than a small suburb of Los Angeles, our social lives picked up considerably. It would be another seventeen years before the Dodgers and Giants moved to the coast, and even the local celebrities seemed to appreciate having Connie Mack and his big-leaguers in their midst, even if we did have a habit of finishing in last place. We attended a couple of parties at Hollywood mansions, and the cowboy star Leo Carillo once invited the entire team out to his hacienda-style ranch house for a barbecue.

While in Anaheim I went bobcat hunting for the first and only time in my life. A couple of local businessmen invited me and fellow pitchers Luman Harris, Tom Ferrick and Porter Vaughan to join them on an expedition into the hills outside the city. It sounded like an interesting bit of local colour, so we decided to go along. At around 6 p.m. we met them and started climbing up into the hills, enjoying the scenery. Before long their hunting dogs picked up the scent of a cat and quickly had it treed. Then we headed back to our hotel.

But a reporter for *The Sporting News,* the publication known as "the Bible of Baseball," heard about our outing and decided to invent his own spectacular ending to the story.

The hunt "was great fun," he wrote, "until Marchildon suddenly lost his footing and started to slide down the crumbling incline. He tumbled, turned a somersault, landed on his shoulders and kept rolling, grabbing at twigs on the way. Tom Ferrick attempted to help, and he started sliding himself. Fortunately Marchildon found a bush that held his desperate grab. He came to a sudden stop and Ferrick grabbed his leg. Marchildon was laughing until Ferrick, peering sharply into the darkness, called his attention to what might have happened if they had rolled a few more feet. The mountain cut off sharply, just behind Phil, and there was a 200-foot drop."

What *The Sporting News* ending shows is how some reporters in those days made up stories and quotes to suit their own purposes. I'm not picking on that publication in particular. Over the years the *News* gave me generous and almost always flattering coverage. I appreciated that because it wasn't easy getting recognition when you pitched for a last-place club.

Looking back through the old clippings, I can find many more examples of things I'm supposed to have said or done that never actually happened. My family thought they had almost lost me when they read the bobcat story after it was picked up by the Toronto papers.

Several weeks into spring training Brucker finally felt I was ready to pitch in an exhibition game. Against the Hollywood Stars of the Pacific Coast League, I struck out four and allowed four hits in three innings. My new delivery was feeling more natural every day.

Around this time Mack said in an interview that there was a chance I would have to go back to the minors for more seasoning. Looking around at the other pitchers in camp I didn't think that was likely to happen. No one was throwing any better than me. Al Simmons came up to me one day after a few other rookies had been released. "Don't worry about anything, kid," he said. "You're a lock."

The team Connie Mack broke camp with had several new faces. Most promising of the newcomers was rookie Pete Suder, a twenty-three-year-old third baseman who had hit .301 for the Binghamton Eastern League club. Speedy outfielder Eddie Collins Jr., son of the great Athletics/White Sox second baseman, came up from Baltimore. During the winter Mack made a deal with the White Sox for veteran hurler Jack Knott, who would be our big winner in 1941, going 13–11. Joining me from Toronto was right-hander Les McCrabb, winner of nine games for the Leafs the previous season.

Otherwise it was much the same group that had managed to lose a hundred games in 1940. Almost all the pre-season forecasts called for us to finish in the cellar once again.

We barnstormed our way back east from California via the southwest, with stops in Arizona, Oklahoma and Texas. In every town we passed through, even if it was just to change trains, crowds turned out to see the famous Connie Mack in the flesh.

Not counting the president and a few movie stars, I think Mack's must have been one of the most familiar faces in America. People loved him. At a stop somewhere in Texas we were met by hundreds of cowboys, Indians, cattlemen, railroad workers and soldiers. The scene looked like something out of a John Wayne western.

We opened the season April 15 in a packed Yankee Stadium with a 3–1 win over the Bombers. Chubby Dean, who also won the 1940 opener against the Yanks, duelled with Red Ruffing until Sam Chapman iced it for us with a homer.

Chubby was one of the game's great eccentrics, and one of the few men I've ever known who could make Mack visibly angry. A southpaw who seemed to have all the talent in the world, he never managed to win more than eight games in any of his seven big-league seasons.

The man was a natural rebel who insisted on doing things his way, sometimes in spite of himself. Earle Brucker warned him one day before a game with the Yanks, "Whatever you do, don't throw DiMaggio a change of pace." So of course Chubby threw DiMag the fattest change-up you ever saw, and the Clipper parked it into Yankee Stadium's upper deck. In early May a fed-up Mack suspended Chubby for missing a game; he finally sold him to the Indians in August.

This was my first visit to New York. The city was too big, too dirty and too busy for a small-town boy like me. But Yankee Stadium—now there was something I could appreciate. If anything it was even more beautiful than Shibe. You felt dwarfed by the place as you stood out on the field surrounded by those famous triple-decked grandstands. The outfield was huge, 490 feet straightaway from home plate to deepest centre field. So much history had been made in that park. No matter how often I played there, I never stopped feeling excited every time I walked through the gates.

We split the final two games of the series with the Yanks and then headed to Philadelphia for our home opener, which we dropped to the Red Sox. While we were in town the Athletics front office helped me find a place to live. I certainly wasn't looking for anything fancy. In spring training I had signed a contract for $3,800 for the year, which was about standard for a big-league rookie but not a lot of money even in those days.

It would have been more than enough to get by on considering a steak dinner went for about three bucks and a pack of cigarettes for fifteen cents, except that the Canadian government only let me spend twenty-five dollars a week. The rest I had to put into a Canadian bank account. This was their way of guaranteeing I'd come home when called for military duty.

They even made Connie Mack post a bond of several thousand dollars to prove he would release me when the time came. While my forced savings plan helped me build a tidy nest egg, it didn't allow for much more than the bare necessities of life. I could barely afford to go to a movie once a week. The next year, after I complained that I couldn't make ends meet, my allowance was increased to a princely thirty-five dollars a week.

Along with utility infielders and fellow bachelors Crash Davis and Fred Chapman, I moved into the comfortable home of a middle-aged couple who were big baseball fans and did everything they could to make us feel welcome. We bought most of our meals out but made our own beds and even helped clean the place.

By the end of April our record was 4–8 and Mack still hadn't put me in a game. Just before our home opener he told a reporter he planned on using me mostly in "lost causes for experience." He said I had "speed but no control or finesse."

Even this early in the season we had already seen more than our share of "lost causes." I wondered what Mack was saving me for. Brucker told me to be patient and to keep working on my new delivery. When my turn finally did come it wasn't a mop-up job after all but a Saturday afternoon start against the Tigers in Detroit on May 3. Brucker must have convinced Mack I was ready. Either that or the Old Man figured I couldn't do any worse than some of the guys he'd been using.

For seven innings, nineteen-year-old Hal Newhouser and I locked up in a close one. "Prince Hal" had wicked stuff even then although, like me, he was often wild. Newhouser was pulled in the eighth when we bunched three singles together, but the Tigers held on to edge us 4–3. I went the distance, surrendering six hits and seven walks and striking out two.

It was an impressive enough outing for Mack to give me the ball again a week later in Washington, where I finally notched my first big-league win. This time I took a big lead into the seventh inning before tiring and being relieved by Nelson Potter, a veteran whose repertoire included a screwball, a slider and the occasional spitter. Nellie held the Senators until the ninth when they rallied for four runs and almost gave me a heart attack before he got the last out for a narrow 8–7 victory.

Mack seemed to have confidence in me from that point on and I was in the starting rotation to stay.

The City of Philadelphia declared Saturday, May 17, "Connie Mack Day" in honour of the Old Man's fifty-fifth year in big-league baseball. The celebrations began with a morning reception at City Hall and continued with a ceremony at Shibe before our game against the Tigers. There were at least two dozen famous names on hand, including baseball commissioner Judge Kenesaw Mountain Landis and former Athletics stars Jimmy Dykes, Eddie Collins, Lefty Grove and Ed Rommel.

Part of the plan was to surprise Mack with the renaming of the park to Connie Mack Stadium. But he nixed the idea when he got wind of it, saying the change would be disloyal to the memory of Ben Shibe, his longtime business partner and the park's namesake. Mack didn't agree to the name change until 1950 when he finally stepped down as manager.

For once Mack didn't take his customary walk up the players' ramp. Instead he entered the field through the grandstand, accompanied by Landis and American League president Will Harridge. After shaking the hands of hundreds of fans, Mack came onto the grass through a lane made by the players of both teams. There were three bands playing in the outfield and on the right-field wall was an impressive display of the nine American League and five world championship pennants won by his clubs.

Song-and-dance man George M. Cohan led the crowd in a rousing rendition of "The Grand Old Man of the National Game," a song he'd written especially for the occasion.

> *The grand old man of the national game,*
> *And every fan of the national game,*
> *Has a feeling of pride for Connie,*
> *There are cheers far and wide for Connie,*
> *The USA all rooting for him,*
> *The big brass bands all tooting for him,*
> *Today in baseball's Hall of Fame,*
> *Connie Mack is a grand old name.*

You could see that Mack was getting choked up by all the attention. During the ceremony at home plate, when all his accomplishments were being recounted, he had tears in his eyes and kept nervously buttoning and unbuttoning his coat and tugging on his high white collar.

The whole day was an education for me. I knew Mack was a baseball legend, but I wasn't completely aware of all he had done for the game and what a successful franchise the Athletics had once been. Remember, I was the guy who just three years before thought the Maple Leafs were in the big leagues.

Listening to his story was a crash course in the history of baseball. Born Cornelius McGillicuddy in East Brookfield, Massachusetts in 1862, one week after the Civil War battle of Fredericksburg, Mack played the early variations of baseball still popular in New England when he was a boy: one-hole cat, sting ball and round ball.

This wasn't something they talked about during the ceremony, but I later learned how Mack, a man who became famous for his honesty and integrity, had invented new ways of cheating during his playing days as a catcher. He became an expert at making a slapping sound that sounded like a foul tip when the batter swung and missed, a handy talent at a time when a caught foul on any strike was an out. Mack also learned how to ruin a hitter's swing by reaching out and just slightly tipping his bat.

He was known as the game's biggest chatterbox, "the talking catcher." In his distinctive high-pitched voice he would needle a batter about some error he'd made in the field, or about his big nose or bald head.

It was hard to imagine all the changes the game had seen during that one man's lifetime. Mack once recalled how in the days when he played "...the catcher took the ball on the bounce. The pitcher was forty-five feet from the batter... and would take a hop, step and a jump, swinging his arm in a wide circle and letting the ball go with his hand below his hip, in a sort of underhand delivery."

Never much of a hitter, Mack was able to stick in the National League, then the only major league, on the strength of his powerful throwing arm and because he was known as one of the most intelligent players in the game. He studied the habits of batters and learned to position his fielders where, as he said, "the fly balls would drop in their hands." Later on, as a manager, he was famous for painstakingly moving his players around by waving his scorecard as he sat in the dugout.

Mack was happy to admit that he sometimes overdid it. He told the story of a game against the Yankees with Babe Ruth at the plate. "I waved my outfield round, and they moved where I motioned, but still I wasn't satisfied and finally had to climb out of the dugout to place them and direct the defence. Meanwhile the pitcher was waiting in the box, and Babe was standing at the plate. After about three minutes' wigwagging, I got everyone set. You can guess what happened. Babe hit the first pitch over the fence."

Considering what a penny-pincher he was as an owner, I thought it was a little ironic that Mack was one of the leaders of the players' revolt for higher wages that led to the formation of the short-lived Players' League in 1890. He invested his life savings buying stock in the Buffalo franchise and lost it all.

Mack managed the Pittsburgh Pirates for two years starting in 1894 and then jumped to the Milwaukee club in Ban Johnson's Western Association, where he managed and ran the front office. When Johnson organized the American League in 1901 Mack, with the financial backing of sporting-goods magnate Ben Shibe, was able to acquire the Philadelphia franchise.

A lot of people said the new league would never fly, that the Philadelphia team was a "white elephant" and that investing in it was a waste of money. To thumb his nose at the critics, Mack made the white elephant the team's symbol, putting it on uniforms, jackets and pennants.

As part-owner and manager, Mack built two of the greatest dynasties in the history of the game. The first, in the early teens, featured the famous "million-dollar infield" of Stuffy McInnis, Eddie Collins, Jack Barry and Frank "Home Run" Baker; the second, the Athletics of the late twenties and early thirties, showcased such stars as Al Simmons, Jimmie Foxx, Mickey Cochrane and Lefty Grove.

Complaining that he couldn't afford to give them the raises they demanded, Mack sold off most of the stars on both of those teams. To him baseball was first and foremost a business.

"It is more profitable to have a team that is in contention for most of the season but finishes about fourth," he once said. "A team like that will draw well enough during the first part of the season to show a profit for the year, and you don't have to give the players raises when they don't win."

I thought it was this attitude that explained why only about 15,000 Philadelphians showed up at Shibe that day to pay tribute to the Grand Old Man of the national game. Rain threatened in the morning but by game time the sun had come out. Many people were amazed that the stadium was more than half empty for such a well-publicized event.

Though Mack was loved everywhere else in the country, I think many Philadelphians held a grudge against him for so cold-heartedly dismantling those great teams of the past and giving them years of cellar dwellers in their place. When I came up with the Athletics, Mack was in the middle stretch of a big-league-record nineteen consecutive seasons managing in the same league without a championship.

Finally the Old Man stepped up to the microphone. "Thank you, thank you all," he began. "To you fans, you loyal supporters of our club, win or lose, I want to express my thanks for helping make baseball what it is to me—my life."

With that, Sam Chapman and Chubby Dean, who was probably trying to get back in Mack's good books, hoisted him on their shoulders and carried him to the dugout, closing the ceremonies.

Then we went out and lost 8–5 to the Tigers.

SUMMER OF THE STREAK

Maybe it was the inspiring sight of all those championship banners hanging on the outfield wall during the Connie Mack Day celebrations. Whatever the reason, after that day we started on a tear that took us to what was for us the heights: the bottom of the first division. We occupied fourth place in the eight-team league by the end of July.

On May 25 we beat the Senators 7–3 at Shibe for our seventh win in eight games, putting us sixth in the standings, ahead of Washington and St Louis. When you get on a roll like that the enthusiasm is infectious. Everybody shows up at the ballpark with smiles on their faces, anxious to get out on the field.

Suddenly, even when common sense tells you differently, you believe there isn't a club in the world, including the Yankees, you can't beat.

"This ball club thinks it's better," said Earle Brucker. "These kids feel they're better than a tail-ender. How much better they haven't quite decided, but they've got ambitions."

"Confidence does it," added Al Simmons. "We're just breaking out of the second-division complex or cellar blues, whatever you call it. These A's aren't whipped because the schedule says Cleveland, the Yankees or whoever. They've got to be licked on the field."

The big difference was that suddenly we were putting runs on the board. Five of our guys—catcher Frankie Hayes, outfielders Wally Moses and Sam Chapman, second baseman Benny McCoy and first sacker Dick Siebert—were hitting over .300. Bob Johnson was struggling, but you knew his bat would come alive any minute.

The guys backed me up with twelve hits when I threw a three-hitter in Boston May 27 to notch my second career win. It was my best outing yet and an important victory because we were fighting the Red Sox for fifth place and they had taken the opener of the doubleheader. Johnson showed definite signs of breaking out of his slump by hitting a three-run homer into the left-field screen, his eighth of the year. Sam Chapman also homered as we ran up the score to 11–1.

We moved into fifth the next day with an 8–6 win over the Sox.

On June 2 word came that Lou Gehrig was dead at the age of thirty-eight. Even though we had all known his death was inevitable, that didn't seem to lessen the shock among his fellow players. I had only seen Gehrig that one time in Toronto, but even I was depressed by the news. I think it made us all aware of our own mortality. If such a rugged athlete, a man so hardy he never bothered to wear a topcoat during New York winters, could be taken away like that then it might happen to any of us.

Baseball writers commented that Gehrig's death all but completed a changing of the guard in the game. Most of the great stars of the 1920s were either gone or slowing down. Al Simmons was reduced to pinch-hitting for us, and Jimmie Foxx enjoyed his last productive season in 1941, driving in over a

hundred runs for the thirteenth consecutive year to tie him with
Gehrig for the record. Lefty Grove, another member of the last
Athletics dynasty, who was now playing for the Red Sox, won
his three-hundredth and final game July 25.

Fans were focusing their attention on young turks like
Williams, DiMaggio and Feller, all still in their early to mid-
twenties and already the game's greatest stars. The 1941 season's
banner crop of rookies included "Pistol Pete" Reiser, winner of
the National League batting title in his first full campaign; Stan
Musial, who hit .426 after making his debut as a September
call-up for the Cardinals; and Phil Rizzuto, a daily worker of
miracles as shortstop for the Yankees.

On the day Gehrig died, Joe DiMaggio singled and doubled
off Bob Feller in Cleveland to extend his hitting streak to nineteen straight games. At that point no one was paying much
attention. But by the time the Yanks arrived at Shibe for two
games June 27 and 28, DiMaggio had hit safely in thirty-eight
straight and millions of fans were wondering how long he could
keep it going.

I'd won my fifth game the day before the Yanks got to town,
going the distance as we beat the Tigers 8–4. Bob Johnson, now
one of the hottest hitters in the league, came through again, driving in six runs on a couple of two-run homers and two singles
in five trips to the plate. The homers brought Johnson up to sixteen for the season so far, tying him with DiMaggio for the
league lead.

The opener with the Yanks was an old-fashioned dust-up.
Yankee catcher Buddy Rosar got into a screaming match with
Earle Mack, who rushed to the plate to protest a close call. Later
in the game New York utility man Frenchy Bordagaray took a
relay throw from our second baseman Benny McCoy smack in
the head while trying to score. Bordagaray stumbled and then
fainted dead away as he crossed the plate. We finally won it 7–6
in the ninth when Siebert doubled home Johnson.

DiMaggio wasted no time in extending his streak by rap-
ping a single to centre field his first time up on the first pitch
thrown to him by our starter, Chubby Dean. In the seventh he

added a 450-foot homer that landed deep in the left-field bleachers.

By this stage of the streak a growing gang of reporters was following DiMaggio from city to city. Before the next day's game he admitted he could feel the pressure building with each day as he approached Sisler's modern mark of forty-one straight and Keeler's all-time record of hitting in forty-four consecutive games.

Like the fans, many players were checking the box scores every day or listening to the radio to see if Joe had gotten his hit. We wished him luck as long as he was playing someone else. When it came their turn to face him, most pitchers wanted to give DiMag a fair shake and get him out with their best stuff. Ending the streak on a succession of cheap walks just didn't seem right.

Most of us felt the same way as St Louis Browns right-hander Bob Muncrief, who surrendered a single that extended the streak to thirty-six straight. "It wouldn't have been fair to walk him—to him or me," the rookie said. "Hell, he's the greatest player I ever saw."

One pitcher who wasn't fussy how the streak ended, just as long as he was the one to end it, was DiMaggio's old nemesis Johnny Babich, our starter in the second game. Babich told reporters he intended to stop DiMaggio by either walking him intentionally or giving him nothing but junk to hit. Though the rest of us may not have agreed with what Babich intended to do, nobody said anything. We figured the feud between him and DiMaggio was their private business.

True to his word, Babich walked the Clipper in the first inning, then threw him three straight balls in his second trip to the plate. McCarthy flashed the hit sign and DiMaggio slammed a liner on another outside pitch that went right through Babich's legs on its way into centre field for a hit. Johnny fell to the mound getting out of the way. DiMaggio, who almost never showed emotion on the field, stood on base with a smile on his face, having now hit safely in forty straight.

After winning the game 7–4, the Yanks were on top of the standings, one game up on the Indians and getting ready to run away from the pack. They went on to clinch the pennant September 4, the earliest date ever, and finished the season with a seventeen-game lead over second-place Boston. In a World Series made famous by Mickey Owen's dropped third strike in Game Four, the Yanks took Brooklyn in five games.

My life should have been just about perfect right then. I was pitching well, the team was winning, and chances still looked good that I wouldn't be drafted for at least another season yet. On June 22 Hitler turned his armies against Russia, a move that took some of the pressure off Britain and her allies.

But my family had found out that my mother, who was then age fifty-six, had stomach cancer, and the doctors weren't holding out much hope of a recovery. It seemed impossible to think about being without the woman who was the glue that held our large family together. My oldest sister, Madeleine, was back home taking care of her. I wrote and told her to take some money out of my bank account to rent a cottage on Georgian Bay for the two of them. In all her life I don't think my mother had ever had a vacation. I wanted to give her one before it was too late.

Fortunately, I was able to put any negative thoughts out of my mind when I took the mound and concentrate completely on the job at hand. No matter how big and noisy the crowd, I was hardly aware they were there. Looking back on my career, especially the years after the war, I sometimes think I was too intense for my own good.

Because I didn't pay any attention to the fans, it always surprised me when other players let their taunts bother them. The most thin-skinned of all was Ted Williams, who would turn around and yell back at the bleacher fans in left field. I remember a game at Shibe around this time when Williams and the fans had at it and suddenly fruit, newspapers and scorecards started raining down on him. Finally a detachment of police was sent out to the bleachers to restore order.

Everything was working perfectly for me July 1 in Philadelphia against the Senators. I threw no-hit ball into the seventh and finally settled for a four-hit, 10–1 win. Sam

Chapman drove in five runs with a homer, a triple and a bases-loaded walk.

On the same day DiMaggio collected two hits against the Red Sox to equal Keeler's all-time mark, and the next day passed Wee Willie in style with a fifth-inning homer against Red Sox pitcher Heber Newsome, who won nineteen games that year.

I got my shot at stopping the streak a few days later in New York, where I was scheduled to start the opener of a three-game series on the Fourth of July holiday. Rain postponed that first game so I had a whole extra day to figure out how to prevent DiMaggio from making it forty-six straight at my expense.

Most pitchers tried to keep the ball in tight at belt level against him. And you had better hope that was exactly where you threw it. Get it up high and DiMag would see the ball too well and murder you. Put it out just a little over the plate and he was able to extend his arms in that long swing of his. That was something you definitely didn't want to happen.

Maybe I had too much time to think about what to throw him. Saturday afternoon DiMaggio hit my first pitch into the left-field runway leading to the Yankee bullpen for a 420-foot homer. It was a curve I left up just a little too high. Things only got worse after that. Rolfe and Sturm hit solo shots and Keller parked two into the stands as the Yanks won 10–5. Mack left me to suffer out there the entire game, either to save our bullpen or teach me a lesson in humility, I'm not sure which.

Sunday was a big day in the history of Yankee Stadium as 60,948 New Yorkers turned out for the unveiling of the monument to Lou Gehrig in centre field. The ceremony took place before the start of the doubleheader, with the players of both teams gathered around the mounted bronze bust after we had marched out like a closing fan from the infield foul lines. Front and centre were New York mayor Fiorello La Guardia, Joe McCarthy, Connie Mack, Gehrig's old room-mate Bill Dickey, and his widow Eleanor Gehrig. Lou's parents were seated in the stands.

"This monument to Lou Gehrig from his Yankee friends is our expression of esteem and friendship for the greatest first baseman of all time," said Bill Dickey when it was his turn before the microphone.

Chosen, I suppose, to speak on behalf of all of baseball, Mack called Gehrig "one of the greatest players to ever put on a baseball uniform. Not only was Lou Gehrig a great player but he was a real sportsman, a gentleman whom we all admired. I know of no more appropriate recommendation than to advise our youth to follow in the footsteps of Lou Gehrig."

The Yanks took both games from us as DiMaggio got six hits that day: three singles, two doubles and a triple. Joe must have hated to see us leave town. He hit .524 in the five games he played against the Athletics during his streak.

In a way I don't really mind having given up that homer to DiMaggio in game forty-six of the streak. He was such a great player, and the streak has come to have such an important place in the history of the game, that it's an honour just to have been part of it. Anyway, that's what I've kept telling myself for over fifty years.

The man who did get the credit for finally stopping the streak at fifty-six games, on July 17 in Cleveland, was Ken Keltner, the Indians' slugging star and the best third baseman in the league. Not many months before his death, Keltner was among the guests at a dinner I attended in Toronto to commemorate the fiftieth anniversary of the 1941 season.

"DiMaggio hit two bullets down the line," Keltner remembered, adding that he was playing on the line well back of third because he knew DiMaggio almost never bunted. "If I had been playing a normal third base they would have been sure doubles. But I was able to stop them and throw him out. They were pretty good stops, but I've made better. The way they tell it now, I robbed DiMaggio of two sure hits. That wasn't quite the way it happened."

Keltner said he thought it was actually Cleveland shortstop Lou Boudreau who was responsible for stopping the streak. In his last at-bat, DiMaggio hit a ball to short that took a bad bounce and hit Boudreau in the ear. "I still don't know how he made the play," Keltner remembered. "But he did and threw to second for the start of a double play."

Despite the setback in New York, we played solid ball the rest of the month and on July 27, after taking two from the Tigers and seven of our last eight games, we were tied with the White Sox for fourth, behind New York, Cleveland and Boston. On the last day of July we beat the White Sox at Shibe and had fourth place all to ourselves. The Athletics hadn't been in the first division so late in the season for ten years.

You would have thought we were chasing the Yankees for the pennant the way our fans reacted. Every seat at Shibe was sold and 15,000 more fans were turned away when Bob Feller and the Cleveland Indians came to town August 3 for a doubleheader. Feller was looking for his twentieth win of the season and got it in the opener, beating us 6–3. We edged the Indians in the nightcap 4–3.

It just goes to show how desperate our fans were for a winner. Philadelphia is a great baseball town but in the years just before I got there the city had seen a lot of bad teams. The A's hadn't finished better than seventh since 1934, and the National League Phillies since 1932. Our fourth-place club must have seemed like the second coming of the Athletics of Foxx, Cochrane, Dykes and Simmons.

There's one game in particular I remember from those days in early August when we were in the first division. Pitching under the lights against the Yankees at Shibe in front of another big, enthusiastic crowd, I was easily handling DiMaggio and everyone else in that famous lineup—with the lone exception of Charlie Keller, the man they called "King Kong," who had hit two homers off me the last time we met. Keller feasted off me my entire career. The Yanks had seven hits that night, with Keller accounting for four of them on three doubles and a single.

Naturally, the Yankee players were razzing me from their bench every time he came to the plate. His last at-bat someone yelled, "What're you going to pitch him this time, Phil?"

I had to laugh. I waved the ball in the air to signal time out to the umpire, and then rolled it to my catcher.

We won the game 5–3, but I can still hear the sound of Keller's three doubles thudding against the right field wall.

I don't know why Keller gave me so much trouble. No matter how I pitched him—and I tried everything—he always got his hits. The writers called him King Kong because of his heavy beard and bushy eyebrows. Keller hated the nickname, and you were wise not to use it around him. I just call him one of the best hitters I ever faced. In 1941 he was another of those guys having career years. Keller ended the season with 33 homers, 122 RBIs and a batting average of .298.

One more thing I remember about that particular game was that Red Ruffing was supposed to start for the Yanks but talked McCarthy into holding him back until the next afternoon. Ruffing hated pitching under the lights. He could get away with this because he was a star, and because night games at the major-league level were a fairly recent innovation that accounted for only a handful of games in the schedule of each team.

Many minor-league clubs had been playing night ball for ten years by 1941. The games were a way to attract fans who wanted to see a ball game after finishing work for the day. Toronto's Maple Leaf Stadium was equipped with lights, so playing at night was nothing new to me. Once the summer heat came I much preferred pitching after dark. A few degrees' difference in temperature meant a lot on a blistering day in St Louis or Chicago, when my heavy flannel uniform got sopped with sweat and I felt like I was suffocating from the heat. My pitches also seemed to have more movement on them when we played at night, probably because of the change in air pressure.

Some hitters felt they could follow a pitched ball better when they didn't have to contend with the sun bouncing off all those white shirts in the centre field bleachers. Yankee Stadium was one of the worst parks for that. Unlike Ruffing, most players either preferred playing after dark or didn't care one way or the other.

The first night game in the big leagues was played at Cincinnati's Crosley Field in 1935. By 1941 there were seven other stadiums equipped with lights, including the American

League parks in Chicago, Washington, St Louis, Cleveland and Philadelphia. Shibe's lights had gone up in 1939.

Now it seems obvious that night ball helped increase attendance and made the game more popular than ever. But at the time many die-hard traditionalists, including Ed Barrow of the Yankees, fought the change, predicting that night games would be the ruination of baseball.

It was America's declaration of war following the attack on Pearl Harbor that helped overcome the last resistance to night baseball. When the government requested that more games be played after working hours to accommodate millions of war workers looking for entertainment, scheduling games at night became an act of patriotism on the part of the owners.

I wish I could say the Athletics were every bit as good a team as our fans hoped that year and that we managed to stay in the top half of the standings for the remainder of the season. But by the second week in August we began a rapid slide that didn't end until we were once again firmly lodged in the basement.

Looking back, the only conclusion I can come to is that we had been performing over our heads all along. That and the fact that after New York and Boston, who finished in the top two spots, the quality of the teams in the league fell off quickly. Third-place Chicago played only .500 ball on the season. So maybe our rise to fourth place hadn't been such a big accomplishment in the first place.

The truth was that we had trouble scoring runs when it counted, our middle infield was terrible, we had absolutely no speed on the basepaths (Sam Chapman led the team with six steals), and by season's end our pitchers surrendered more runs than any other staff in the league and possessed the highest team ERA.

What I found most frustrating was playing in front of such a weak infield. Nothing drives a pitcher nuttier than when in a tight situation—say, with men at first and third and no outs or one out—he gets the batter to hit it on the ground but his infielders can't turn the double play. As a team, we committed two hundred fielding errors, more than any other club in either league. Second baseman Benny McCoy and shortstop Al Brancato often resembled a comedy team when trying to make even routine plays.

Playing in front of a bad infield affects your entire thinking process when you pitch, making you cautious exactly when you should be challenging the hitter. You figure you have to go for the strikeout in a tough spot instead of being able to focus on a hitter's weakness and not worrying about the guys behind you doing their jobs.

I mentioned that we had trouble scoring runs. On August 21 when we scored in the fourth inning of the opening game of a doubleheader with the St Louis Browns, the run broke a string of thirty-six consecutive scoreless innings.

We stopped off in Toronto for an exhibition match against the Maple Leafs on the last Friday of August. Mack was kind enough to let me have the day off to travel to Penetang and visit my mother at the cottage on Georgian Bay. It broke my heart to see how frail she looked. She died just a little over three months later, on December 4.

Two days after my visit home I was on the mound in Boston, where I threw a three-hitter in the second game of a doubleheader for my tenth win of the season. The Red Sox won the opener 5–3 as Ted Williams hit a three-run homer, his thirty-first, off Jack Knott in the sixth inning. It was his only hit of the day.

Mack just about made certain of that by having me intentionally walk Williams three times. The Old Man let me pitch to Williams in his only other at-bat, but Ted popped one up to catcher Frankie Hayes. The poor guy saw his average drop two points that day, all the way down to .407.

Our 3–2 win evened my record at 10–10, not bad for a rookie. With a month to go in the schedule I figured I was good for another three, four, maybe even five wins.

But ten wins it would stay, while I racked up five more losses. At least two or three of those games I might have won with a little run support. There was a 3–2 squeaker against Washington, a 2–0 eight-hit loss to the White Sox, and another 3–2 game in Detroit. That season I lost seven games by one run. My ERA was a respectable 3.57.

Not that I hadn't often contributed to my own downfall. In too many games I got myself in trouble by putting men on base with walks. Even with my new, improved delivery, wildness continued to be an almost constant problem. My total of 118 walks was the fourth highest in the league. At least I was in good company. The fellows ahead of me were Bob Feller, Hal Newhouser and Bobo Newsom.

So no complaints, not really. Except for the worries about my mother, I was happier than I'd ever been. Life in the big leagues was pretty sweet. It was fun travelling to new cities, staying in the best hotels, and watching little kids get excited when they recognized me. Signing autographs was no burden to me. I felt lucky to be asked.

By September I had been around the league a couple of times and decided that Chicago was definitely my favourite city. We stayed at the Del Prado, a hotel a short distance from downtown on the shore of Lake Michigan. The combination of being by the lake and the hotel's park-like grounds made us feel like we were holidaying at a resort.

Best of all for a young bachelor, a nearby hotel was a favourite place for airline stewardesses to stay when they were in town. As soon as we checked in, the stews would call to invite us over to their place for a party. Some of those bashes lasted all night. Then we would have to try to sneak back into our own hotel without getting caught by Mack or the coaches.

One day in July of that year I was nursing a terrific hangover after my room-mate Bill Beckman and I had stayed out until dawn with the girls. I didn't feel too guilty because I wasn't scheduled to pitch until the next day and figured I could snooze all afternoon out in the bullpen. But Mack must have found out what we'd been up to because when we got to Comiskey he told me I was starting. He probably wanted to teach his rookie the importance of clean living.

With my head throbbing, I proceeded to shut out the Sox on three hits over the first seven innings. Every time I looked into the dugout, Beckman was shaking his head in disbelief at what I was doing. He told me later he had taken bets with our team-mates that I wouldn't last past the second inning.

Although I finally tired in the eighth, I would have won that game if not for crucial errors by Benny McCoy and Dick Siebert. Mack finally took me out and Chicago went on to beat us 4–2.

After dropping into the cellar behind Washington and St Louis in mid-September, we were just playing out the string. As he had done with me the year before, Mack brought up several rookies from the minors for a look. One of them was Dick Fowler, purchased from Toronto where he had been one of the top pitchers in the International League.

Unlike me, Fowler looked great in his first start, holding Chicago to seven hits at Shibe September 13 for a 3–1 win. The big, friendly kid —he was still only twenty years old—seemed to have ice water in his veins. Nothing bothered him. Fowler was no longer the string bean I'd first met, having filled out to 215 pounds and gained another half-inch in height. He threw hard and had a nasty curve. Right from the start it was obvious he belonged.

By the last week of the season all eyes were on Ted Williams. As I've said, back then reaching .400 wasn't considered the unique accomplishment it is today; nobody imagined that it might not ever happen again. But it was still recognized as a considerable feat and the newspapers and fans were paying close attention when Williams, sporting a .401 average, arrived in Philadelphia for a three-game series on the final weekend of the regular season.

"The Splendid Splinter," "Teddy Ballgame," "the Kid"— choose your handle—had already permanently put his mark on the season by hitting a ninth-inning homer off the facing of the third deck at Detroit's Briggs Stadium to win the All-Star Game. No matter how many times I see it, it's still a sheer joy to watch the old film of that moment and see Ted laughing, clapping his hands and jumping like a young colt as he circles the bases.

Almost as soon as he was off the train, Williams was out at Shibe with a catcher and a coach, taking extra batting practice. He said he was a little worried because the shadows were bad at the park that time of year, especially in the late afternoon. In the slanting light and long shadows, even a mediocre pitcher could be almost unhittable.

Asked if he might sit out any of the games to protect his average, Williams said, "I want to hit over .400, but I'm going to play all three games here even if I don't hit a ball out of the infield. The record's no good unless it's made in all the games."

The Red Sox won the opener of the series on Saturday as Williams was held to one hit, dropping his average to .3996. Rounded off, that comes out to .400, which is how it would have gone into the books.

Red Sox manager Joe Cronin asked Ted if he was sure he didn't want to sit out the doubleheader the next day. "Hell, Joe, I want to play," Williams answered. "If I'm going to be a four-hundred hitter, I want to earn it all the way."

That night a nervous Williams walked the streets of Philadelphia in the company of Johnny Orlando, the Boston equipment manager who had given him the nickname Kid. Williams later said they talked about a lot of things, but mostly about Dick Fowler, who was starting the opening game for us and who Williams had never seen, as well as the other pitchers he was likely to face.

I wasn't going to be one of them. Brucker told me Mack intended to go mostly with the new kids over the weekend. That was fine with me. After five consecutive losses I was ready to call it a season. I planned to put my feet up and watch the game out in the bullpen with the other pitchers. There were always more laughs out there than in the dugout near Mack and the coaches.

Williams, by the way, didn't consider it an advantage to be facing our rookie pitchers. His average dropped steadily during September, mainly, he said, because he was seeing a steady diet of youngsters whose pitching styles he hadn't had a chance to study.

Sunday dawned cold and miserable in Philadelphia. Considering the weather and the fact that the Athletics hadn't played a meaningful game since early August, the turnout of 10,000 fans at Shibe indicates the public's interest in what Williams was trying to accomplish.

Before the game, Mack stood in the centre of our locker room and told us to bear down against Williams. If he suspected anyone of letting up on Ted, he'd run that player right out of organized baseball.

You knew the Old Man had the power to do it, too. His stature in the game was so great that when he disagreed with an umpire's call, he'd send his son Earle out to tell the umpire he wanted to see him. Then the ump would walk over to our bench and listen courteously to Mack's point of view. I suppose that was one of the perks that came with being a founder of the American League.

Mack went on to say that while he expected us to try our best against Williams, he also wanted us to throw strikes and not cheat Ted of his chance at hitting .400 by issuing him cheap walks. "The man deserves a fair shake," Mack said. "We're going to give it to him."

Williams's six hits in the two games that afternoon surely represent one of the greatest pressure performances in the history of the game. He singled sharply off Fowler his first at-bat and slammed a homer 440 feet over the right-field fence his second time up. Then he rapped two singles off reliever Porter Vaughn, another September call-up from Toronto.

Facing yet another rookie, Fred Caligiuri, in the second game, Williams singled and smashed a drive off the loudspeaker horns of the public-address system in the outfield for a ground-rule double. His final batting average: the famous .406.

We took the second game of the doubleheader for a split on the afternoon and a record of 64–90 at the end of a season people now remember as the greatest in the history of baseball. For a wide-eyed rookie from Canada, it all seemed pretty wonderful and memorable even as it was happening.

CHAPTER 7

ACE OF THE STAFF

I n 1942, the first season played after the United States entered the war, I joined the ranks of baseball's top pitchers by winning seventeen games for an Athletics' squad that finished with nine more losses than our last-place club of the season before. Only Tex Hughson of Boston and Ernie Bonham of the Yankees won more games, and they had the advantage of playing for the league's two best teams.

Nobody had won that many for the A's since Johnny Marcum in 1935. Headline writers in Philadelphia began calling me "Connie's Crack Canadian Curver" and "the Fiery Frenchman." One columnist even compared me to the young Walter Johnson, an observation too ridiculous to be taken seriously by anyone.

Back home in Canada, I became a national celebrity. There were dozens of newspaper articles written about me, and people right across the country seemed to take pride in my success. I was an especially popular hero in Toronto, where I had played ball for the Maple Leafs. When I was there after the season fans were constantly coming up to me with congratulations or requests for autographs.

A taste of fame is a wonderful thing. I think my first serious brush with it came at the perfect time for me. During the 1942 season I was twenty-eight, old enough not to let it go to my head and smart enough to appreciate every moment because I knew it might not last very long.

For a few weeks after the Japanese bombed Pearl Harbor none of us were sure there was even going to be a baseball season in 1942. Commissioner Landis told Roosevelt that baseball would willingly do whatever the government thought best, including shutting down operation for the duration of the war. On January 16, 1942, Roosevelt sent Landis his reply, the famous "Green Light" letter. "I honestly feel that it would be best for the country to keep baseball going," the President wrote. "There will be fewer people unemployed and everybody will work longer hours and harder than ever before. That means they ought to have a chance for recreation and for taking their minds off their work."

Baseball continued through the war, but it wasn't the same. At the start of the 1942 season there were sixty-one big-leaguers already in the armed forces, including a few stars. Bob Feller signed on with the Navy shortly after war was declared and Hank Greenberg re-enlisted in the Army. Other familiar names wearing military uniforms included Washington's Cecil Travis and Buddy Lewis, Johnny Berardino of the Browns, Brooklyn's Cookie Lavagetto, Hugh Mulcahy and Billy Cox of the Pirates, Detroit's Fred Hutchinson and Mickey Harris of the Red Sox.

Some teams were hit harder than others. Remaining almost completely intact were the champion New York Yankees (although Tommy Henrich missed the final weeks of the season and the World Series), while Washington, after finishing thirty-one games behind them in seventh place, lost thirteen players for the entire year.

Next to the Senators, the Athletics suffered the most. We started the season without the services of seven players. Gone was our slugging outfielder Sam Chapman, who had hit .322 in 1941, with 25 homers and 106 RBIs. We were also without the middle-infield combination of Benny McCoy and Al Brancato. I may not have had a lot of respect for McCoy and Brancato as infielders, but they were the best we had and I knew I'd miss them.

Most of the game's headliners, including DiMaggio and Williams, were still playing and put in full campaigns. But with others leaving throughout the season and a total of a hundred rookies breaking into both leagues, a record at that time, there was no doubt that the calibre of play was down slightly from 1941. Just slightly. Wartime baseball's rapid decline started the following season. By 1944 almost 60 percent of pre-war big-leaguers were in the armed services.

Playing ball during a state of national crisis took a little getting used to. Americans were shocked by the sneak attack on Pearl Harbor and frightened that it might happen again. During spring training in Anaheim I used to go up onto the roof of our hotel at night and watch as the giant searchlights swept the sky looking for enemy planes.

However remote the possibility of another raid may have been, the threat was taken seriously. Just before the start of the season, the chief civilian protection adviser of the Office of Civilian Defense in New York ordered that in the event of an air raid the ball game should continue right through the bombing. "The ballplayers will be the soldiers in that situation," he said. "They must stay right there and take it, if it comes, up to a certain point. The show must go on. Otherwise it would be like actors rushing off a stage. If they show panic, you can see what might happen."

I'm just glad I never had to try to concentrate on pitching to Joe DiMaggio with shrapnel flying through the air and Yankee Stadium tumbling down around us. Though maybe in an air raid Charlie Keller would have gotten so rattled I'd finally have been able to get him out.

Connie Mack named me his starter for the opening game of the season in Boston. It was quite an honour to get the assignment in only my second season in the big leagues. I had looked good in spring training and Mack told reporters I was far and away the best pitcher he had. Actually, he was thoroughly disgusted with everyone else. "I thought I was taking some pretty good pitchers to camp," the Old Man said, "but I was wrong. They have acted like anything but pitchers up to now."

He may have had second thoughts about making me his choice after the Red Sox got to me for ten hits and six walks in six innings of work as we lost 8–3. Ted Williams homered in the first inning and drove in five runs on the day.

Ted looked set to make the most of what would be his last season until after the war. He took a lot of criticism because he asked for and received a temporary military deferment on the grounds that he was supporting his parents. Many people were so worked up with patriotism back then that they resented the sight of a healthy male playing ball when so many others were off fighting. They particularly resented high-priced stars like Williams and DiMaggio, who also felt the heat until he enlisted before the next season.

Controversy didn't seem to affect the concentration of either of them at the plate. Williams won the Triple Crown with a .356 average, 36 homers and 137 RBIs. DiMaggio batted .305, drove in 114 and parked 21 home runs in the stands.

My next two outings, both against the Senators, were much better. I threw a complete-game six-hitter at Shibe for my first win of the year. Then, in Washington, I held the Senators to four hits in another win.

Starting against me for the Senators in the second game was right-hander Buck "Bobo" Newsom, one of the most colourful players in the history of the game. He was a huge, barrel-chested man who had a habit of calling everyone Bobo, maybe because he seldom stuck with one team long enough to learn the names of his team-mates. In twenty years in the majors he pitched for nine different clubs, three times winning twenty games and ending his career with a record of 211–222.

Crazy Bobo had more rituals than any pitcher I've ever seen. Without fail he would spit in his glove when leaving the bench, touch the ground on either side of the foul line, pull a blade of grass from the infield, then handle the rosin bag. He hated even the smallest piece of litter on the pitching mound, and would hold up the proceedings until he had put everything just right. To throw Bobo off his game, and for the sheer enjoyment of watching him go berserk, opposing infielders sometimes dropped confetti on the mound as they headed to the dugout between innings.

Stories about Bobo are now part of the folklore of the game. My favourite might be the one about how, when he played briefly for the Red Sox in 1937, Bobo kept a hutch of rabbits in his room to keep him company. When he went on a road trip they destroyed the hotel furniture. Newsom was traded shortly after the hotel presented Red Sox manager Joe Cronin with a bill for the damage.

Bobo once told reporters that he had discovered Joe DiMaggio's weakness. The next time they met, DiMag smashed three doubles. After the game Newsom said, "Yeah, I know what his weakness is—doubles."

Then there was the game against Boston in which he took a wicked line drive in the head off the bat of Oscar Judd. Bobo fought off his dizziness and kept pitching even though he claimed he could hear music in the latter innings. After the game a sportswriter introduced Newsom to his wife. "A pleasure, madam," said Bobo. "Would you like to feel the bump on my head?"

Even though I held the Senators to four hits in the match-up with Newsom, I walked seven and was in and out of difficulty in the late innings of the game. I would be sailing along and then suddenly I'd lose sight of the strike zone. When I did get it across I was all but unhittable.

"If he cures that wildness he's going to be a sweet pitcher," Al Simmons said after the game. "He's asking for a lot of trouble with those bases on balls but, still, he's winning and you can't complain about it."

My next time out I had even more stuff, and this time I didn't hurt myself by issuing too many walks. Al Benton of the Tigers and I locked up in the second game of a Sunday doubleheader. We were both throwing shutout ball into the sixth when Pete Suder got our first hit of the game.

I batted next. Tigers third baseman Pinky Higgins was certain I was going to try to bunt Suder over to second and came charging in toward the plate. But I got the sign to swing away and whistled a scorcher past his ear for a single. Another single by our right fielder, Elmer Valo, brought Suder home. I made the run stand up the rest of the way for a two-hit, 1–0 win, my third of the year.

Despite my occasional lapses into wildness—a problem I was beginning to think I'd never be able to cure completely—I was getting stronger and feeling more in control with every start.

I'd worked out a pitching routine I felt comfortable with. The day after pitching I would rest my arm. I would throw in batting practice the next day, rest the following day, then pitch again.

I thrived on pitching every four days. Something I can't understand is why modern managers insist on going with a five-man starting rotation. How fragile can these young pitchers be? They've been better coached than we ever were. Fitness experts are employed by every team and the latest training equipment is found in their clubhouses. Medical experts are rushed in the moment a pitcher feels the first twinge of soreness in his arm. When today's pitchers do pitch, they're only expected to last six or seven innings before giving way to some high-priced bullpen help.

In this era of expansion baseball it's tough enough to find four good starters, let alone five. If a pitcher is in shape, going out there every four days should be no problem for him. Many modern players would probably welcome the opportunity. More starts mean more chances to win, and more wins translate into even more millions of dollars come contract time.

Another reason I was pitching so well early in 1942 was that by now I'd had over a year to absorb the changes Brucker had made to my delivery. At first I sometimes forgot and fell into my old habit of landing slightly to the right in front of the pitching rubber. Now the motion was becoming automatic and most games I didn't have to give it the slightest thought.

I was learning something new almost every day. In spring training Brucker asked veteran Jack Knott to take a hand in my development. Knott, a lanky right-hander with only average natural ability, survived eleven seasons in the majors by out-smarting hitters. We talked for hours about what I should throw in certain situations. How to keep the batter off-balance and guessing. What hitters couldn't handle curves. Which veterans to feed only fastballs because their bat speed was starting to slow down.

One problem that became obvious as the season progressed was my habit of giving away what pitch I was about to throw as I clenched the ball in my glove during my wind-up. My wrist was flat in the glove for a fastball and curved slightly outward for the curve. Every third-base coach around the league had a different word sign to warn the batter what was coming. It just goes to show what great stuff I must have had that season— I was winning even though the hitters were primed for my every pitch.

Once I discovered what was happening, the problem was solved by an easy adjustment and a bit of practice. I've talked about how sportswriters often used to create stories out of their own fancy and pass them off as fact. The Canadian scribe Dink Carroll told such a good one about my problem with telegraph-ing pitches that I almost wish it were true. He had Sad Sam Jones trying to help me out while I was still with the Maple Leafs, a good two years before anyone had picked up on my habit.

"Sad Sam, a great kidder, once told Phil to carry his glove around with him wherever he went and to practice holding it in front of the ball," Carroll started his story. "That way he would learn to conceal his grip from the prying eyes of the spies on the first- and third-base lines.

"Phil took the advice so literally that he appeared in the hotel dining room carrying his glove and a ball. While the head waiter was finding a table for him, he struck a pose as though there was a runner on first base, took a peek over his left shoulder at that imaginary runner on first, and then went through the motion of delivering the ball. The manoeuvre brought down the house."

Jack Knott also tried his best to teach me a change of pace, a pitch I never could get the hang of. The difficulty was that I was one of the few pitchers who threw with a stiff wrist. That had always been my style—tight grip, stiff wrist. A pitcher with a looser grip and wrist can let go of the ball suddenly just as he snaps his wrist, which slows the speed and makes for an effective change of pace. After Knott finally threw up his hands in exasperation at my lack of progress, I abandoned the change and concentrated on developing a slow curve.

I avenged my opening-day loss with a 2–1, five-hit win over the Red Sox at Shibe May 9. Boston got its run in the fourth on a single by Johnny Pesky, a walk to Williams, and a single by Jimmie Foxx.

The Philadelphia newspapers pointed out that by pitching three-and-a-third perfect innings to start the game, I had completed the equivalent of a nine-inning perfect game. In my 1–0 win over Detroit the previous Sunday, I had retired the last nineteen men I faced without anyone reaching base. Against Boston I got through the first ten men without a hit. Add it up and you've got twenty-nine men in order—two more than the number required to pitch a perfect game.

After the game with Boston Jimmie Foxx told reporters how impressed he was by me. "What a pitcher that kid Marchildon is," he said. "I reckon Dizzy Trout of Detroit is the fastest pitcher in our league since Bob Feller's gone, but Marchildon this afternoon was as fast as Trout and had more stuff. He was great.

"Marchildon's got the darnedest fastball I ever saw," Foxx continued. "None of the other fastball pitchers can make a ball twitch the way Phil does. It comes down the middle then sails away from a right-handed batter. What makes his curve more effective is you never know what he's throwing—fast one or a hook."

What a kick I got out of reading Foxx's comments in the newspaper the next day. Praise like that coming from a certain Hall-of-Famer meant a lot. If Jimmie Foxx thought I was that tough, then maybe I really was becoming one of the best pitchers in the league. His words of praise sent my confidence soaring.

When you're going as well as I was right then, the rest of the guys on the team tend to kid around with you more because they know you're loose and in a great mood. I think I was always well-liked by my team-mates, but any player's popularity soars when he's doing so much to help the team.

One of our greatest kidders was Al Simmons. A few days after my shutout over Detroit he walked into our clubhouse before a game and stopped in front of my locker.

"Say, Phil," he said, "did you get that suit?"

"What suit?" I asked.

"You're to get a suit for that Sunday game. Somebody heard it on the radio."

I might have fallen for Simmons' gag the year before when I was a rookie and shown up at some downtown shop asking to be fitted for my prize. As a promotional gimmick, clothiers sometimes gave out a hat or a suit of clothes to a player who had thrown a shutout or hit a grand slam. But I hadn't heard anything about a new suit and by now I'd been around long enough to know he was pulling my leg.

Simmons was such an important part of our ball club. From the moment I first walked into the clubhouse he'd been there with advice and encouragement whenever he thought I needed it, and he was the same way with every member of the team.

I think Connie Mack loved him the best of everyone he ever managed. The only photo of a player the Old Man kept in his office was one of Simmons at the plate in the famous stance that earned him the nickname "Bucketfoot Al." A right-handed hitter, Simmons raised his left foot up and away from the pitch toward the third-base dugout when he swung, a motion called "stepping in the bucket."

When Simmons reported to his first training camp with the Athletics, the veterans made fun of his stance and came up with the nickname. His style of hitting was thought to take away a hitter's natural power; it was also considered unmanly because it made him look like he was trying to bail out from tight pitches.

"Let that young man alone," Mack is supposed to have told the veterans riding Al. "He hit .398 at Milwaukee and .360 at Shreveport, and if he can hit like that it's all right with me if he stands on his head at the plate."

Mack never had cause to regret the $50,000 he had paid to purchase Al's contract. Simmons hit .308 as a rookie and drove in over a hundred runs in each of his first eleven seasons. In 1927 Al batted .392, and he was brilliant in the Athletics' three pennant-winning seasons, hitting .365 in 1929 and taking batting titles the next two seasons with averages of .381 and .390.

He was just as good in the outfield. "There never was a better left fielder when it came to going into the corner to cut off a sure double," said Bill Dickey. "He never threw to the wrong base and often dared the runners to challenge him."

They say Al was a swaggering, often overbearing man in his younger days. He roomed with Ty Cobb for two seasons when the Georgia Peach was finishing up his career with the Athletics, and he admitted some of Cobb's famous nastiness rubbed off. "Ty Cobb was my idol," Al said. "I tried to model myself after him, and maybe I was too successful in some ways."

Simmons played best when he was angry. "When I was hitting," he later remembered, "I hated pitchers. I wanted them dead. Them so-and-so's were trying to take the bread and butter out of my mouth.

"If I didn't get a hit, I thought the pitcher was a lucky stiff. There wasn't a pitcher in the world who could fool me, and even if he did, I had a good enough pair of wrists that I could alter my swing and slap that ball around at the last split second."

Al's bat was thirty-eight inches in length, the longest in baseball, and because he stood deep in the batter's box and his wrists and forearms were so strong, his bucket step didn't detract from his power. He even handled low outside curves, reaching out with his long bat and slashing them into right field.

He hated pitchers—and the nickname Bucketfoot. "As far as I was concerned, it questioned my courage," he said. "It sounded like I was afraid of the ball. After a while, they stopped calling me that because they knew it made me angry, and the angrier I got, the better I hit."

By the time I met him Al had mellowed considerably, though he could still work himself into a fine rage at the plate. Most of the old arrogance was gone. He was a thoughtful man who now wished he had done a few things differently.

His biggest regret was turning down a chance to play for those great Yankee clubs of the late 1930s. In the dismantling of his last championship squad, Mack sent him to the White Sox in 1933 for cash. After three seasons in Chicago, the Sox decided to sell him, letting him choose between the Tigers and the Yankees. Al chose the Tigers.

"It was the worst decision I ever made. If I'd gone with the Yankees, I'd have played on four consecutive pennant winners."

His last remaining career goal was to retire with three thousand hits, something he never achieved. "If I'd only known as a kid what I know now," Al said, "three thousand hits would have been so easy. When I think of the days I goofed off, the times I played sick and took myself out of the lineup because the game didn't mean anything, I could cut my throat."

Al tried to give all of us younger players the benefit of his experience. He told me to squeeze every last penny I could out of Mack. "Whatever he's paying you, it's not enough." In 1931 Al had successfully held out for a contract that gave him $100,000 over three years, refusing to report until the Old Man forked over the dough. After missing all of spring training, he smashed the first pitch he saw that year for a homer.

Although he believed a player was entitled to everything he could get, looking back Al felt it was almost impossible for a ballplayer to stay at his mental peak once he was secure financially. "When I finally decided I had it made, I was never again the ballplayer I was when I was hungry. The only man I ever knew who never lost his fire when he got rich was Ty Cobb."

Al once invited me to the racetrack with him on an off-day

in Boston. Playing the horses was his favourite way to relax on road trips. The sport didn't interest me, but there was no way I was going to turn him down. I enjoyed every moment of the day we spent together. It was an honour to be able to pal around with the great Al Simmons.

Everyone on the team felt the same way about him. Even though Al was reduced to coaching and pinch-hitting, Connie Mack still thought he was the most valuable member of our ball club. "I wish I had nine men like Simm," he told a reporter. "Just coaching there on third base, he does more for the spirit of this club than anybody else on the field."

My sixth win of the season came May 21 in Detroit against Dizzy Trout, the Tiger right-hander Jimmie Foxx thought was the league's fastest pitcher now that Feller was gone. A little of the hum was missing from Trout's fastball this day as we crushed the Tigers 11–3. The victory left us in fifth place with a record of 15–22, the high-water mark for us that season. On top of the standings, where they always seemed most comfortable, were the Yankees, a mere ten games ahead of us.

The most important rule to live by in baseball is to never take anything for granted. One day you can be on top of the world, one of the best players in the game, and then the next morning you can wake up with a sore arm or back and it's all over. This is especially true for a pitcher, who relies so completely on one vital appendage, his pitching arm. Any injury that prevents that old wing from doing what it's supposed to is cause for alarm because there's no certainty that it's ever going to get better.

There I was sailing along with a record of 6–3 in only the second month of the season when I stepped in a hole and sprained my back while doing my running in the outfield before a game. My entire body felt out of whack for weeks afterwards. Anyone who has ever had a sore back knows how debilitating it can be. I was feeling lousy, but I didn't want to let the team down. Already I had come to be considered our ace and I thought it was my responsibility to play through the pain.

That was a mistake. Going out and losing my next four starts didn't help anybody and only prolonged my injury. It's not as if I got any thanks for my effort. Even though I told our trainer I had a sore back, Connie Mack seemed mystified by my troubles. In those days a pitcher wasn't considered injured as long as he still had feeling in his arm.

On June 17, sitting in the grandstand at Chicago's Comiskey Park during batting practice before my next start, Mack speculated aloud to a group of writers about my recent problems.

"We thought for a while we were working him too much, but when we gave him a week's rest between starts he seemed wild and unable to win despite the rest," the Old Man said.

"So we went back to working him regularly and hoping he would find himself. His control improves with work, I believe. All we can do is wait for him to come out of it."

Fortunately, my back was finally starting to feel better and that afternoon I threw a five-hitter against the White Sox for a 4–3 win. I knew for certain I was back to normal four days later in St Louis when I beat the Browns by another 4–3 score to notch my eighth victory of the year.

Then on June 23, just when I was back on track and heading for what was once again looking like a sensational sophomore year, the telegram I'd been dreading for months arrived. I was to report for immediate duty in the Canadian Army.

Not at the end of the season, not in a month's time, but right away. I couldn't understand the rush to get me into uniform. I was in my late twenties and helping to support my family. No way was I convinced they had already gone through all the younger guys back home. I was willing to bet the reason I was being called this early was because of my high profile as a baseball player.

So far only one other Canadian professional had been conscripted—Ralph Hammond, a southpaw pitcher from Guelph who was on the Toronto roster and was several years younger than me. A little earlier in the season Joe Krakauskas had returned to Canada to enlist.

Luckily for me, we were on our way to Washington to play a series against the Senators. While we were in town I paid a visit to the Canadian Embassy to plead my case. I was ready to do my duty, but I wanted them to put off my induction until the end of the season. That didn't seem like a lot to ask.

At first the embassy official I spoke to was inflexible and said I would have to report as ordered. Only after a lot of discussion was I able to convince him I was telling the truth about my family's need for my financial support. He finally agreed to sign an order postponing my induction until the end of September.

Now, at almost the mid-point of the season, it seemed more important than ever to have a great second half. I wanted to leave Connie Mack with the memory of a pitcher at the top of his game so I would be in a strong bargaining position when I came back after the war.

We all tried not to think too much about what we were sacrificing on a personal level by entering the military. Everyone agreed Hitler and Japan had to be stopped at any cost. Millions of people were suffering and dying all over the world. Our own concerns were insignificant by comparison.

Still, I couldn't help worrying how my time away would affect my baseball career. Although the next year saw the tide of the war turn in favour of the Allies, most of the fighting was still to come and I knew I'd be gone for at least two or three years. At my age that was a lot. Even if I was lucky enough to survive the war, there was no guarantee I'd be able to make a successful comeback.

I had gotten such a late start in my professional career that at an age when many other players had been building up their salaries for seven or eight years, I was still earning peanuts. After I won ten games as a rookie, Mack had given me a raise of $500, bringing me to $4,300 for the year. Squeezing money out of the Old Man was like trying to get blood from a stone.

I don't think there was a player on the team who was satisfied with his salary. Bob Johnson was particularly bitter. "Get every penny you can out of the old bastard, Phil," he often said to me. "Don't let him cheat you."

After starring for the Athletics for ten years, Indian Bob was so fed up that at the end of the season he demanded to be sold or traded. The exchanges in the press between Johnson and Mack were almost comical.

From his home in Tacoma, Washington, Bob said he didn't want to play with "a team so poor as the Athletics," and that he might just stay in Tacoma and work in the shipyards.

"Well, I'm glad that Bob is really going to work," said Mack. "I will not sell Johnson, so he will either play with us or make good his threat of going to work. I feel we treated him very well and, as a matter of fact, I thought we paid him more than he was worth. Of course, I imagine he probably doesn't think so.

"As for the team being poor," the Old Man concluded, "I was well aware of that."

Mack was bluffing about not selling Johnson. He had always been happy to accept money for his best players, and in the end Johnson was sold to the Senators. After a year in Washington, Bob finished his major-league career with two seasons as a Red Sox.

An appearance in the upcoming All-Star Game at the Polo Grounds in New York would have been helpful in any future negotiations with Mack. There was talk among the writers in Philadelphia that I would be selected for the team. But I wasn't surprised to be passed over. Although my eight wins put me among the league's top winners, I'd had that recent stretch of bad outings. And in any case it was always easy to overlook a pitcher toiling for the lowly Athletics.

Among the changes ushered in by the war was the playing of two All-Star games in 1942. The usual confrontation between the leagues was held July 6, with the American League coming out on top 3–1. The next day in Cleveland, the victors took on a team of service All-Stars that included Hank Greenberg, Bob Feller, Johnny Berardino and Cecil Travis. Again the American League won, this time 5–0. The two games raised $100,000 to buy baseball equipment for American servicemen, and another $60,000 for Navy and Army welfare agencies.

Every one of the sixteen teams in the majors hosted a war-relief game during the season, with all proceeds going to service relief agencies. The most memorable of these matches took place at Yankee Stadium August 23, when as a special attraction Babe Ruth and Walter Johnson revived their old rivalry in front of 69,136 nostalgic New Yorkers.

Before the start of the doubleheader, Johnson took the mound and once again faced down the Babe.

"The Big Train" threw seven pitches before Ruth got hold of one and lofted a high fly that curved just foul before landing in the right-field stands, the part of the park they used to call "Ruthville." Knowing when to quit, the Babe dropped his bat and circled the bases while the crowd roared its approval.

After the game Johnson was asked if he'd been grooving the ball to Ruth. "The fans didn't come to see me strike anybody out," he answered. "They came to see Babe hit a home run."

But the best stunt of the season was completely unrehearsed and unexpected. Buddy Lewis, formerly of the Senators and now an Air Corps pilot, had been given orders to pilot his C-47 transport plane on the first leg of a journey to the Far East. Taking off from an air field near Washington, Lewis couldn't resist saying a last farewell to his old team-mates, who were in the middle of a home game. He took his plane in so low over Griffith Stadium that he could almost make out the letters on the players' uniforms, circled the stadium once, then dipped his wing in a dramatic final salute before gaining altitude and flying off to fight the Japanese.

Every starting pitcher breathes a little easier once he gets into the double figures in wins. My tenth victory came under the lights at Shibe on July 13 and started the Philadelphia writers talking about the possibility of my becoming the first Athletics hurler to win twenty games since Lefty Grove in 1933.

It wasn't the best game I pitched that season, but it was one of the most memorable. White Sox starter Johnny Humphries and I battled through the first five innings, with Chicago going out ahead 3–2. Then, batting in the sixth, I hit a long outfield fly that brought home our third baseman Lou Blair to tie the score.

Just as we were taking the field for the start of the eighth, everything went pitch black. You couldn't see your hand in front of your face. A spokesman for the Council on Defense came over the public address system to announce that this was a test black-out, Shibe's first, and that not even a match should be lighted. To show how glaring the flare of a match could be during an air raid, one of the park attendants, stationed in the score-board, lit one. It was amazing how that single tiny flame stood out like a beacon in the total darkness.

Play resumed and Humphries and I fought on into the eleventh. With two out in our half of the inning, I came to the plate and lined a single to centre. Humphries walked our next batter, bringing Elmer Valo to the plate. Valo drove a one-and-two pitch over second into the outfield, and I took off for home, beating the throw to the plate by several feet to win the game.

What made that win particularly satisfying for me was that I helped out with my bat. In the days before designated hitters, pitchers took more pride in their hitting ability and worked hard on improving their stroke in batting practice. One reason it was more important for pitchers to hit well was that managers weren't so quick to go to their bullpens, which meant starters got far more at-bats than they do today in the National League where pitchers still hit. Some pitchers, like Red Ruffing of the Yankees, were so good with a bat that their managers often used them as pinch-hitters.

Over the course of my career I must have helped myself win a dozen or more games thanks to my ability as a hitter. Just one week after my tenth victory, I singled with the bases loaded in the sixth inning off Detroit's Dizzy Trout to drive in the two runs that won the game. And in the start after that, I doubled in the tenth against Chicago and eventually came home with the winning run for win number twelve.

They say imitation is the sincerest form of flattery, so I like to think Joe DiMaggio would be pleased to know that I patterned my batting stroke after his. Though I had always been a strong hitter, I found I was having trouble handling major-league curves. The big stride forward I took when I swung didn't give me enough time to react to the pitch and left me off balance.

DiMaggio planted himself at the plate. He stood with his feet wide apart, the stride of his left leg barely perceptible. His swing had a spare elegance that eliminated any unnecessary motion. It felt natural right away when I tried it. I found I was able to wait on the pitch longer and that curves didn't fool me as often.

The publicity that had been building around me since I'd won my tenth game reached a head when, on August 4 in Boston, I became the first American League pitcher to record thirteen wins. I only allowed the Red Sox four hits, but it was kind of an ugly win as I walked six, hit a batter and threw two wild pitches.

Still, I was leading the pack and writers in every city we visited were starting to take notice. Most of them were amazed I'd managed to win thirteen for a team that at that point in the season had won only forty-two games. "Every other big-league manager would part with a couple of eye-teeth to have the Canadian-born ace of the Athletics on his side," wrote an American Press reporter. "In return for the pair of ivories, they'd be collecting one of the outstanding pitchers in the major leagues, even though he has been toiling in virtual privacy with the tenants of the American-circuit cellar."

Most writers said I would have been a lock to win twenty to twenty-five games if I'd had the good fortune to play for New York or Boston. I agreed and said so in the press without worrying that the other guys on the team would take offense. They had the same daydreams about playing for someone else.

"I don't see how I could miss twenty," I told a New York reporter who asked how many I might win as a Yankee. "It's not only their hitting—although a few runs would help—but it's that infield. Give a pitcher guys like Gordon and Rizzuto to grab those ground balls behind second, and he works with a helluva lot of confidence."

Most of the American writers didn't quite know what to make of a Canadian-born ballplayer leading the league in wins.

One St Louis columnist marvelled that baseball could even be played in my home town of Penetanguishene, "where they have eight months of winter and play baseball in between snow-storms. How Marchildon learned to play is a mystery."

During the 1992 World Series between the Toronto Blue Jays and the Atlanta Braves, Canadians took offence when the U.S. Marines carried our flag onto the field upside down during the opening ceremonies before the second game in Atlanta. They also didn't appreciate some of the pre-game shows on American television that showed clueless Canadian kids trying to play baseball with hockey pucks and goalie sticks.

None of that surprised me. I lived with American misconceptions about Canada throughout my career. When I started to win consistently the press circulated all kinds of wild rumours about my life in the northern woods. One of them had me staying in shape in the off-season by hunting timber wolves around my home town. Almost everyone assumed that, being a Canadian, I must have lived in a log cabin and worn snowshoes strapped to my feet most of the year.

I had to develop a thick skin. It wasn't always easy to be gracious when Americans automatically expected me to speak with an unintelligible French accent. "I thought I would find a typical French Canadian," wrote a dumbfounded Cleveland reporter. "One of those By Gar characters with an 'aire' on the tail of half his words."

Even the Athletics' own souvenir program promoted the French-Canadian stereotype, having me speaking pidgin English in a story about how Dan Howley followed me back to Creighton Mines after my try-out with the Leafs. Howley asked me why I left the camp, and I'm supposed to have said, "Nobody look at me, nobody speak to me, so I think I'm no good, so I left."

One of the nicknames pinned on me was "Froggy Phil," in reference to my French-Canadian heritage. While I preferred the more popular handle Penetang Phil, I didn't let being called Froggy get under my skin. Nicknames that today seem derogatory weren't taken quite as seriously back then. Joe DiMaggio's team-mates regularly referred to him with affection as "the Big Dago" or simply "Dago." If DiMag didn't take offense at Dago, then I figured I could live with Froggy Phil.

As the season progressed I found myself thinking more and more about my upcoming military service. News of the war was the major topic of conversation that summer now that the United States had become involved. After suffering through a Russian winter, the Germans were back on the offensive in the east, their Panzers pointed in the direction of Stalingrad. In the Pacific the Japanese suffered a major naval defeat at Midway, and fierce fighting was going on at Guadalcanal.

During my rookie season, despite the constant threat of conscription hanging over my head, it had been possible to push the war out of my mind for short periods of time while the Americans still remained neutral. There were a few players who wanted to discuss the latest battles described in the newspapers, but most of us preferred to concentrate on baseball. Not surprisingly, one player who had absolutely no trouble staying focused was Ted Williams, who later claimed that until the Japanese bombed Pearl Harbor he was hardly aware there was a war going on.

But in 1942, many of us still playing faced enlistment before the start of another season. In the clubhouse you heard players discussing whether to join the Marines or the Air Force, how long the war was likely to last, and where they hoped to be posted.

I wasn't sure what to do. After hearing my father tell so many horror stories about life in the trenches during the First World War, I hated the idea of joining the Army. Not much more appealing was the thought of being out in the icy North Atlantic as a sailor. The possibility that seemed most exciting was service in the Royal Canadian Air Force. I could imagine myself enjoying weekend passes in London between missions as a Spitfire or bomber pilot. The only problem with the Air Force was that I knew that at that point in the war their casualty rates were far higher than any other branch of the military.

I decided to postpone any decisions until I got to Toronto

after the season for my induction. In the meantime, my goal was to win twenty games, something that seemed within my reach with six weeks remaining in the schedule.

It figured that it would be the Yankees who pretty much killed my chances at making it by beating me in my next two starts. Charlie Keller was waiting for me in New York August 8, hitting a three-run first-inning homer to put me in a hole at the start. Bill Dickey and first baseman Buddy Hassett also homered as the Yanks handed me my ninth loss of the season. Six days later at Shibe, New York set a big-league record by turning seven double plays in an 11–2 win. Rizzuto and Gordon were as smooth as ballet dancers around second base, making a couple of plays that had us rubbing our eyes in the dugout.

When I lost a heart-breaking 2–1 seven-hitter to the Senators August 20, I knew winning twenty would have to be put on hold until after the war. The team was in a terrible slump, even for us. My fifteenth win of the year, a 3–2 squeaker over tall left-hander Thornton Lee of the White Sox at Shibe August 30, ended a nine-game losing streak. The last two victories I would enjoy for three long years came against the Red Sox September 5—a 4–3 complete game in which Ted Williams took me deep for his twenty-ninth homer—and in a relief appearance in Cleveland four days later, when I threw hitless ball for the last five innings of a thirteen-inning game.

It would have been satisfying to say goodbye with a win. But in the opener of a season-ending doubleheader at Shibe September 20, the Senators knocked me around for seven runs in the ninth and drove me from the box. The loss gave me a final record of 17–14 for the season.

The good news of the day was that the team came back to take the second game 2–1 in ten innings, an important win in the eyes of Connie Mack since it prevented a hundredth defeat, a final humiliation the Old Man had urged us to avoid. Our record of 55–99 left us forty-eight games behind the pennant-winning Yankees, who went on to suffer a rare defeat in the World Series, going down in five games to a Cardinal team led by Stan Musial and Enos Slaughter.

It felt funny cleaning out my locker after the doubleheader, not knowing when or even if I would ever be back in that clubhouse again. You could tell most of the guys were feeling the same way. Everyone was quieter than usual, going from locker to locker to shake hands, wishing good luck to the fellows they knew were going into the military.

I still had a bad taste in my mouth about blowing the first game of the doubleheader, but overall I had to be happy with my season. Winning seventeen games for a last-place club was something to be proud of. I was fourth in the league with 244 innings pitched, and third in strikeouts with 110. In a little over two seasons I'd come to be regarded as one of the best pitchers in baseball.

Although by this time I should have known better, I was foolish enough to hope that Connie Mack would call me into his office and offer me a bonus after the season I'd had. God knows he'd gotten far more than his money's worth out of me. But he never said a word. The Old Man didn't even have the courtesy to come over to say goodbye and wish me luck.

I still have trouble believing that. After I won seventeen games for him, the legendary Connie Mack couldn't take the trouble to shake my hand and say a few words to me before I left for the war.

There was a bright side, though. Mack's attitude made me so angry that the prospect of military boot camp suddenly seemed a whole lot easier to take.

Penetang Babe
about 1918.

Penetang captured the North Simcoe League championship in
1934. I'm second from left in the back row. Coach Jim Shaw, who
recommended me to the Maple Leafs, is third from left in front.

Leaf coach Sad Sam Jones touted me as a future star.

A fan favourite
in Toronto.

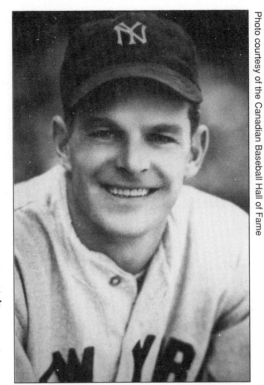

Yankee star
George Selkirk
was the pride of
Huntsville, Ont.,
and a hero to all
Canadian fans.

A product of
Toronto sandlots,
little Goody Rosen
had a huge following
in the city.

After less than two seasons as a pro, I was called up to the Philadelphia Athletics in September, 1940.

Connie Mack: a baseball legend and the biggest tightwad in the game.

A's pitching coach Earle Brucker taught me how to win in the big leagues.

CANADA'S STRONG-MAN GIFT TO THE MAJORS

Phil Marchildon - - Equally Adept at Pitching or Hitting

It's 1942 and people are starting to take notice.

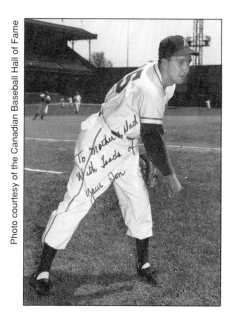

The other half of the Canadian Connection: Torontonian Dick Fowler and I combined for 31 wins in 1947.

The greatest hitter I ever saw: Ted Williams at ease before a game.

Movie star Leo Carillo invited the team to a barbeque at his ranch when the A's trained in California before the war.

Sport Stars Join Air Force.....

Royal Canadian Air Forces added two outstanding | outstanding pitcher in the American Baseball League
baseball and hockey stars to their long list of sportsmen | last summer with the Philadelphia Athletics. He gradu-

Hockey star Roy Conacher and I were inducted into the RCAF
together late in 1942.

Early in my Air Force training. I'm third from right
in the second row.

With my skipper Wynn Morgan, who didn't survive our crash.

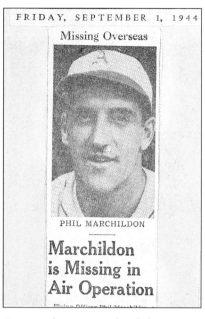

Missing Overseas

PHIL MARCHILDON

Marchildon is Missing in Air Operation

For weeks no one back home knew if I was dead or alive.

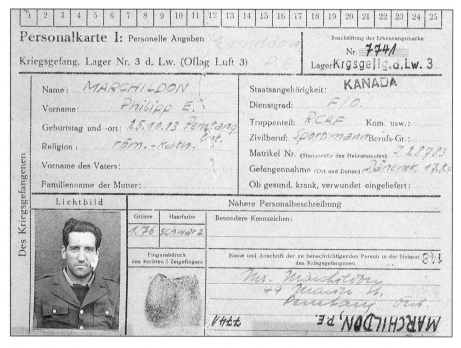

The identification card I was issued my first day at Stalag Luft III. The bandage hides an outbreak of boils.

Irene and me
on our wedding
day in 1945.

Back in Penetang
after the 1946
season, proudly
displaying Carol,
our "All-Star" baby.

Marchildon—Connie's Crack Canadian Curver

AT TORONTO — IN SERVICE — WITH ATHLETICS

Home from the war and happy to trade uniforms.

The Athletics of 1947, the year I won 19 games and the team became a winner. I'm on the far right of the last row. That's Dick Fowler beside me.

Hall-of-Famer
Al Simmons was
an inspiration
to everyone on
the club.

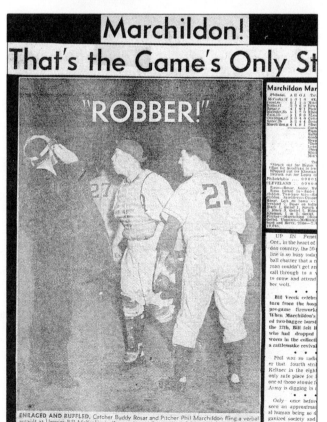

The "Robber"
caption says it
all — umpire
Bill McKinley's
bad call cost
me a shot at
a perfect game
in 1947.

How Wifey Feels When Hubby Strikes Out

By Sue Reckefus

WHAT wife hasn't suffered in silent agony as hubby's joke is greeted with blank looks at a party or wished she could sink under the table when the roast he is carving falls to the floor?

Those are tough moments for any little woman, but, fortunately, for the average wife they don't happen too often.

Imagine, if you can, the feelings of the spouse who must watch her husband perform before, say—30,000 people and fail!

Watching hubby strike out as the crowd boos is a familiar experience for ball players' wives, but after talking to them we found they aren't a breed apart—they feel awful, even as you and I.

We asked five wives of A's players just what their reaction was to a strikeout and whether or not they mentioned the heartbreaking moment when they got home. So next time you feel badly about something hubby did, console yourself with these answers:

MRS. Barney McCosky has developed a bit of ... since becoming the wife of a ballplayer. ... feel good when her left fielder strikes out, bu... for the silver lining.

"Oh, of course I do feel funny," she said slow... ing out is nothing to celebrate, but I try not to...

"After all there is always next time and I kee... he'll hit a homer then. So I really don't mind it...

But she agrees with the other wives as f... mortems after the game is over. For ball-pla... comments are taboo. "I never say anything ... about strike-outs," she said, "when the game ... it should be left in the park. What is the se... minding him of something no one can help ... thing about?"

She and Barney are living at 4630 H st. ... fan, Mrs. McCosky is rarely at home when t... bawls, "Play ball!"

"I rarely miss a game," she bubbled excite... the team going so good, I just couldn't stay aw...

MRS. Ferris Fain, wife of the A's first baseman, ... groaned when she heard the question.

"I feel badly every time," she said, "I never get over it. My heart is in my mouth every time Ferris gets up to bat. 'I know you can't help that sinking feeling when he doesn't get one. But," she added cheerfully, "I'm always sure that next time it will be a different story."

When Ferris gets home, Mrs. Fain never men... tions the strike-out. "He is restless," she said, "w... things go wrong and there would be no poi... in discussing what can't be helped."

The Fains, including a three-year-old daugh... ter and 4½ month old son, are living at 504... N. 9th st. during the home stand. Mrs. Fain is able to take night games. She obtains baby-sitters and she rare... ly misses the sport under lights. "I do want to take the little girl to a day game," she smiled, "so she will be able to tell the kids she saw Daddy play when she gets home."

I FEEL w... when he walks too many players," said Mrs. P... Marchildon, wife of the pitcher.

"Not that I feel good when Phil strikes out," she said, "but after all, pitchers are not expected to be sens...tional hitters. It is nice when he does have a hit... a crucial moment. I feel wonderful, then, but I can't say I feel miserable when he strikes out.

The Marchildons and the Savages—Bob is a pitch... er, too—are staying together at 300 Gilham st., dur... ing the A's home stand. Mrs. Marchildon has a year- old daughter and Mrs. Savage a seven-month young... ster to take care of, so they aren't able to go to many games.

"We get a sitter in the evening," explained Mrs. Marchildon, "after the children are in bed and then we go out to the park together. With both of us married to pitchers, we can sympathize about the same things. One of us doesn't have to feel sorry if the other's husband strikes out, because neither of us expects a high batting percentage."

Irene didn't appreciate being referred to as "wifey" in this article from a Philadelphia paper. Being the wife of a pitcher, she said she didn't worry when I struck out.

My battery mate Buddy Rosar was one of the best defensive catchers in the game.

Head table at the tribute held in my honour back home in Penetang after the 1947 season. My father is seated at the extreme right of the photo.

Demonstrating
my new forkball
for the press
in 1947.

Fishing with
Carol and
Dawna in
the 1950's.

Harry "Red" Foster welcomes me into Canada's Sports Hall
of Fame in 1976.

In 1983 George Selkirk and I were inaugural inductees to
the Canadian Baseball Hall of Fame.

Irene and me in a recent photo.

Still pitching.

CHAPTER
8

FLY BOY

With photographers on hand to capture the big moment, Boston Bruin hockey star Roy Conacher and I were welcomed into the Royal Canadian Air Force. Air Force public relations officials invited the Toronto press to the staged event and made certain photos and releases were distributed to newspapers throughout Ontario. Conacher, a member of Canada's most famous sporting family, was going to be a physical training instructor. I had enlisted for air crew duty.

Right from the start the Air Force seemed a natural fit for me. It was the branch of the military I'd been leaning towards all along, and I didn't need much persuading to sign on when two RCAF officers came courting me shortly after I'd arrived in Toronto at the end of the baseball season.

At that point I was a few days into basic training along with hundreds of other new recruits at the Canadian National

Exhibition grounds, a marshalling yard for men entering the services situated on the shore of Lake Ontario. The way it worked was that you were automatically in the Army unless you applied for and were granted a transfer to the Air Force or Navy.

I was still trying to decide what to do when these two fly boys showed up and started telling me how much happier I'd be in the Air Force. More excitement, better uniforms, the opportunity to see the world. "We'd also like you to play some ball," one of them said. "We could really use you."

That clinched it right there. It only made sense to try to keep my arm in shape while I was in the military. Coming back after the war would be that much easier if I could toss a few innings in a game every now and again.

I knew full well the consequences of my decision. At that time the Army was sending only volunteers overseas, a controversial policy that didn't change until the autumn of 1944. So I could have stayed in the Army and remained safe in Canada on Home Defense for at least a couple of years and maybe for the duration of the war.

But once I joined the RCAF, an all-volunteer force, they could send me wherever they wanted and give me their choice of duty. Call me crazy, but that was exactly the way I wanted it. I didn't want people saying that Phil Marchildon, the big-shot ballplayer, had taken the easy way out.

For the same reason, I later turned down the opportunity to become a fitness instructor and stay in Canada playing baseball for Air Force squads. I figured if I had to be in I might as well be in all the way.

In short order my transfer came through and I carried my kit bag the few hundred feet across the Exhibition grounds to Manning Depot, a building known in peace-time as the Coliseum and the annual home of the Royal Winter Fair. Almost 100,000 RCAF recruits went through the depot during the course of the war.

We still got the occasional waft of old animal droppings in the huge open space called "the bullpen," where hundreds of men slept in row after row of double-decker bunks. It was a miserable place for anyone who valued his privacy. I can still remember the sound of all those men snoring in unison at night. The din seemed to rise up and amplify as it bounced off the rafters. In the morning, all you could hear were men hacking as they cleared their throats and reached for their first cigarettes of the day.

Many of the recruits in the bunks around me were nineteen or twenty years old and away from home for the first time. Some asked me about life in the big leagues—what was it like to pitch to DiMaggio and Ted Williams? Others, especially the ones from rural districts, reminded me of myself at their age. They'd never heard of me and seemed barely aware that big-league baseball existed.

We spent most of our time marching, and when we weren't marching we were taught such vital lessons as how to give the proper military salute and the correct procedure for making a bunk. Doctors were forever poking needles into our arms. It's surprising how many grown men faint dead away at the first sight of a needle.

Most everyone there was hoping to become a pilot. The recruiting posters didn't depict navigators poring over maps or wireless operators in front of their sets. They showed dashing pilots at the controls of a Spitfire or a Wellington bomber. Being a pilot was widely thought to be the most glamorous occupation in the military.

The weeding-out process began almost immediately with a variety of written and physical examinations. After a few weeks of this, I was shipped to a base near the small town of Souris, Manitoba.

In Souris I was soon made a gunner. My tests showed that I had exceptional eyesight and depth perception. The officers also told me I was a little old to be starting out as a pilot. That seems so strange to me now. It's easy to forget how young we all were. Pilots posted to bombers were responsible for the lives of six other crew members, and yet most of them were barely out of their teens.

I enjoyed my new job. As a boy in Penetang, I'd done a little hunting so I was used to handling guns. My favourite drill was target practice from the rear cockpit of an old Fairey Battle, a light bomber that had seen action early in the war with the RAF before being shipped to Canada for use in air gunnery schools. We'd get a few thousand feet up and blast away at target kites towed by other planes.

While naturally I would have preferred to be back in Philadelphia playing ball, preparing myself to go into battle turned out to be fascinating work. The enthusiasm of the other fellows in training carried me right along. The greatest fear of most of them was that they'd be ordered to stay behind in Canada training others.

One of the proudest moments of my life came in Winnipeg on July 23, 1943, when I received my commission as a pilot officer. The same day I was given orders to proceed to Halifax for further training. En route I spent a few days' leave in Toronto, where the first thing I did after booking into the Ford Hotel was to visit a tailor shop on Yonge Street and put in a rush order for two new officer's uniforms. I think I was almost as excited trying on those uniforms as I was the first time I suited up for the A's.

Walking back to the Ford late one night I stopped at a restaurant on Bay Street for a coffee and spotted Ken Patience, a fellow air gunner I knew from Souris, sitting with a striking brunette. He introduced her to me as his sister Irene. As we sat and talked I found myself becoming more and more attracted to this lively twenty-one-year-old who worked as a bookkeeper in the Singer Sewing Machine office.

An article written shortly after Irene and I married said that when "Phil first saw Irene he took three strikes down the middle without lifting the bat off his shoulder." It was something like that. We made plans to meet the next day for lunch and after that spent as much time as we could together for the rest of my leave.

It must have been my charm that won Irene over—either that or my new officer's uniform—because at that point she wasn't a ball fan and had never heard of me. One day when we met she told me how excited her boss Jack Reinhardt, who is still a good friend, had been when she told him she was dating me. "I suppose now I'll have to keep going out with you," she said sweetly. "Otherwise Jack is liable to fire me."

Try as she might not to show it, I could tell she was impressed when we went dancing one night at the Hotel Embassy on Bloor Street and the waiters and everyone else made a fuss over us after I was recognized. I finally managed to convince her the whole thing wasn't a set-up. We danced the night away on a dance floor specially built on springs, a gimmick that, along with air conditioning, was the Embassy's big drawing card.

Despite all the fun we had, looking back now the memory of that leave in Toronto is a little painful for Irene because it was the last time she saw Ken, who was also being transferred to Halifax. A good-looking young man full of life and charm, Ken was killed when his plane was shot down over Belgium in 1944.

I stayed in Toronto two extra days to be with Irene. When I reported to Halifax late I got a reprimand, but I didn't regret a thing. Irene and I had decided to write regularly to one another and both of us were already hoping something permanent might develop between us.

While I was in Halifax I pitched a couple of games for the Air Force against a Navy team. Imagine how humiliated I felt when I lost my first outing 7-0. As a big-leaguer, everyone expected me to mow down the Navy batters. So did I. Even though I hadn't pitched for months, I was as surprised as anyone when those amateurs belted me all over the field.

I made certain I got a few hours of practice in before my next game, which we won 4–3 as I struck out sixteen Navy batters. This was more like it. I have to admit that for the few days between those starts I was worried that I might have suddenly lost it.

Despite the promises of the officers who had recruited me for the Air Force, those two games in Halifax were just about all the ball I'd played since my enlistment. Shortly after I'd signed on there had been a RCAF-Army exhibition match at Maple

Leaf Stadium in which Dick Fowler, who was now a soldier, and I battled to a 2–2 draw. I struck out twenty and Dick whiffed twelve of our guys. All proceeds from the game went to a British War Victims' Fund sponsored by *The Evening Telegram*.

I can still remember the photo of me they used in advertisements for the game. Dressed in my regular Air Force uniform, I posed with my right hand over my head in my pitching motion. Instead of a ball they superimposed an illustration of a ridiculously large grenade into my hand.

In July I was told the good news that I was being posted to England for further training and eventual combat duty. Like the rest of the guys, I was anxious to get over there and do my part. I had no desire to stay behind in Canada and miss out on the war now that I'd come this far.

Our group made the crossing to England aboard the Cunard liner Queen Mary, now stripped of all her luxuries to accommodate several thousand soldiers and airmen. Constantly zigzagging to fool any lurking German submarines, we made the crossing in five days.

The picturesque south coast town of Bournemouth was the first stop for all RCAF personnel arriving in England. A popular tourist destination in peace-time, the town now served as a holding station for bored and impatient Canadian airmen awaiting assignment to training units. It was here that many of us got our first look at the enemy. Individual German raiders made a habit of swooping down on the town in surprise attacks.

My initiation came as I was walking along the main street on a Sunday afternoon. Looking up I saw a German Me-103 plunge out of the sky, level off just above roof level and begin strafing the street with machine-gun fire several blocks ahead of where I stood. I knew it was a 103 because I'd spent long hours learning to identify German fighters during training back in Canada.

I watched, fascinated, as the fighter came towards me. Other pedestrians were scrambling into buildings all along the street.

Just in time I came to my senses and jumped into a doorway as bullets hit the sidewalk near where I'd been standing.

The next few months were a blur of boring training exercises at several bases scattered throughout England. Bomber Command was certainly in no rush to get us into combat, which was reassuring because we knew we had to be winning the air war if they could keep us on hold for so long.

In December we were put into permanent air crews. Once you were assigned to a crew, barring unforeseen accidents or transfers, these were the six other men you'd be flying with until you either were shot out of the sky or completed your thirty missions, the magic number that got you a ticket back home. In many ways your crewmates became closer to you than family. You listened to their troubles over beers at the local pub. You went on leave together. On every mission you counted on the specialized skills of each one of them to help keep you alive.

Our captain was Wynn Morgan, a likeable Winnipeger in his early twenties. We all came to trust him completely. The skipper set the pace for the rest of the crew. We may have grumbled sometimes but we appreciated it when he worked us hard during training flights. Morgan was constantly trying to learn more about his plane and improve his skills as a pilot. The only mild criticism any of us had about the skipper was that he always descended too quickly during landings, rudely bouncing us back into the air off the runway a couple of times before finally putting the airplane down.

Quiet, serious Scotty Moffat from Toronto was our other gunner, working from a mid-ship bubble on top of the bomber, while I was positioned in the rear turret. Another soft-spoken Torontonian, George Gill, was the navigator. Next to the skipper, he was probably the most important member of the team. George always hit our target and then got us home through even the thickest English fog.

The wild man of the crew was wireless operator Courtney Stewart from North Bay, who was constantly getting himself into scrapes as he tried to cram the maximum amount of fun into every moment he wasn't in the air. Flight engineer Bob

Young was a personable Englishman on loan from the RAF.

Finally, there was our resident brain and bombardier, Swiss-born Jacques Clerc, who before the war had been a lecturer at the University of Saskatchewan and the University of Toronto. Clerc, who spoke English, French and German, had refused the offer of a transfer to an intelligence unit. He'd carefully thought it through and concluded he could be of more use to the war effort aiming bombs.

Together the seven of us entered the final stage of our training: the Heavy Conversion Unit, known as "the finishing school." This was when we learned to fly the aircraft we would use on actual operations. We started out on a Wellington, the workhorse of Bomber Command, and later switched to a Handley Page Halifax, a no-nonsense aircraft with a box-like fuselage and square-tipped wings. We flew the Halifax on all but the first of our missions.

Our first mission, mid-way through finishing school on January 26, 1944, was a short hop over France to drop leaflets, a routine test given most new crews. Although the danger was considered minimal, we were a jittery group as we headed out over the Channel and saw the first bursts of flak come at us from the German shore batteries. After that baptism our nerves settled as we proceeded to drop our cargo of junk mail smack on target.

By May, when we were deemed ready to start flying real missions against the enemy, I'd been promoted one step up in rank to Flying Officer. With rank came certain privileges. Officers had their own rooms and enjoyed the services of a batman to do their laundry and other chores. Then there was the comfort of the officers' mess, where you could get a drink when you needed it and nervously wait out the bad weather that sometimes kept your plane on the ground for days at a time.

We were assigned to Squadron 433, known as "Porcupine Squadron," at a base near the Yorkshire village of Skipton-on-Swale, about twenty-two miles north-west of the city of York. The county of Yorkshire was home base for all of No. 6 Group, the RCAF wing of Bomber Command that had been formed

January 1, 1943 to the great satisfaction of all Canadians. Before that Canadians had been assigned to Royal Air Force crews. Now we served under our own officers and had an identity separate from the RAF, which had resisted the group's formation. At its peak there were fourteen RCAF bomber squadrons—with twenty planes per squadron—operating under Canadian command.

I thought I'd seen some bad weather in Canada, but the bone-chilling rains and almost constant fog of a Yorkshire winter were worse. Britain's largest county was a strange mixture of the dreary and the beautiful. Almost all the buildings were made of the same greyish-brown stone, and the mill towns and industrial cities were the most depressing places I'd ever seen. But then on a sunny summer day the hills turned a deep green and the moors had a wind-blown beauty that reminded me of parts of the Georgian Bay shoreline.

The natives sometimes didn't know what to make of the thousands of Canadians in their midst. Often it seemed like we were speaking a different language. Asking to use a toilet, we might be told that the "nessy," or outhouse, was in the back. If you asked for a cup of tea they said they'd "mash" it right way, which meant they'd make it. Women called us "loov" and everyone said "aye" for yes.

But we got along and most people we met were happy to offer directions or any other help they could give. In the pubs the local men were always ready to challenge us to a game of darts, with the loser paying for the beer. Of course, it helped that we were "Colonials" rather than Americans, who, the English liked to complain, were "overpaid, oversexed and over here."

Our first missions were "softening up" strikes on French targets in preparation for the invasion of the Continent that everyone knew was coming within a matter of weeks. We attacked railway marshalling yards in Boulogne, Le Clipon, Cherbourg and several other centres. The goal was to do as much damage as possible to the enemy's transportation system while killing as few French civilians as possible. Along with 111 other bombers from 6 Group, we took part in a raid on Le Mans on May 22 that was considered a model example of precision bombing. Two French civilians were killed as we levelled the railway yards and the nearby Gnome & Rhône factory.

All but a handful of our operations took place at night. The policy of night-time bombing was adopted by the British early in the war as a way of reducing casualties. Later on it was left to the Americans to conduct daylight raids into Germany in their Flying Fortresses. Between the Yanks and us, the Germans were getting it around the clock.

The popular image of a tail gunner is one of a fellow busily firing his machine guns at one swooping German fighter after another. That may have been true for the American gunners who operated in daylight and could see their targets, but most of us flying in the dark never once fired our guns in battle.

Most nights you could see a hundred yards at best. Even when we thought we could make out the shadow of a night fighter in the darkness we still didn't fire. We just prayed he hadn't seen us. Our 3.03-calibre machine guns were pea-shooters compared to the guns and canons the German fighters were equipped with. Taking them on was the last thing we wanted to do. Our job was to get to our target, drop our load, and get the hell home.

A tail gunner was almost automatically regarded as the most eccentric member of the crew. I suppose everyone figured old "Tail-End Charlie" just had to be a little nutty to be able to put up with crouching behind his guns for as long as eight or nine hours at a stretch, scanning the sky all the while for enemy fighters he prayed he wouldn't find.

My position in the rear turret, which looked like it had been stuck onto the butt end of the fuselage of our Halifax as an afterthought, completely isolated me from the rest of the crew. They were heading forward while I was looking back at where we'd already been. My turret was also the coldest spot in the entire airplane. My electrically heated flight suit usually kept me warm enough, but sometimes it was so cold the oil in the breech-blocks of my guns froze solid and they refused to fire. That made for a particularly nervous trip.

No one told us the invasion was on but we could see something was up when on June 5 Bomber Command threw every available plane into the air to hit targets in northern France. Early that evening on our way over the Channel I looked down through the glass of my turret and saw the invasion fleet heading for Normandy. I don't think anyone has ever seen a more awesome sight. There were so many transports, destroyers, battleships, barges, corvettes and other ships that you almost couldn't see the water between them. I called out through my head-set for the other guys to take a look at history in the making.

We kept on hammering German positions in France in the days following the Normandy invasion. On June 10 it was the Versailles-Matelots railway junction. In an attack on Arras the night of June 12, German fighters shot down six of the eighty-nine 6 Group aircraft on the mission. A note in my flying log estimated there were two hundred searchlights on the ground.

Getting zoned by one of those giant beams was our worst nightmare. Some of the searchlights were radar-controlled, and once one had you the rest were almost certain to lock on. After that the German batteries took aim like they were shooting clay pigeons. Your chances of survival were suddenly a matter of pure, dumb luck. Flyers who lived to tell of the experience said it was like having a flashlight shone directly into your eyes. Even on the darkest night everything went pure white.

During the pre-flight briefing on June 16, we were told our target in the area of Sautrecourt was of vital strategic importance. "Make certain of this one, chaps. There's a lot riding on you tonight." Some four hundred bombers were to take part in the raid.

It turned out that Sautrecourt was one of the launch sites of the Germans' new secret weapon, the V-1, or "buzz bomb." The first of them had fallen on London only four days before and their existence was still officially being kept secret from the English public. Propelled by a jet engine, the cigar-shaped V-1 packed a ton of high explosives. Hitler was counting on it as well as on several other new weapons still to come to help turn the tide of the war.

I learned for myself why the V-1 was called a terror weapon a few weeks later while I was on leave in London. Sitting in a crowded cinema, we suddenly heard the by-now unmistakable throbbing racket of a buzz bomb overhead. The projectionist turned off the soundtrack of the movie and we sat there in silence holding our breath. We knew that once the engine cut out, the bomb would nose over and plunge to earth. Seconds ticked slowly away. Then, when it was obvious the bomb had passed us by, the crowd erupted in a spontaneous cheer.

Leaves in London were a rare treat. Our Yorkshire base was about a day's journey from London by train, so the destination for most of our shorter passes was the local market town of Thirsk, or nearby York, a beautiful city dating back to Roman times. Usually in the company of Courtney Stewart, who was always up for anything, I spent many happy nights searching out the pubs along York's narrow older streets, where the upper stories of the buildings overhang so much that a person can reach out and shake the hand of someone in the house across the way.

A visit to wartime London was an unforgettable experience. I got a better appreciation of the type of damage we inflicted on the enemy when I wandered around the city and saw bombed-out buildings and work crews digging in the rubble for unexploded bombs. Air warfare was a fairly impersonal business. From 10,000 feet up or higher, all I could see when I looked down from my turret were faint orange flames and a few flak puffs. More often clouds obscured the target completely.

London's streets were filled with men and women wearing the military uniforms of a dozen nations. At night in the blackout you would hear the wail of air-raid sirens and then stumble into the nearest "tube" entrance for safety along with hundreds of Londoners who had long ago grown accustomed to sleeping on the stairways and platforms.

It would make colourful reading if I were able to tell of drunken brawls in service clubs and a romance or two with a lovely English girl. But the truth is that my wildest nights out consisted of drinking a few too many beers and maybe dishing out some good-natured ribbing about the results of a darts match. The fact that I was a few years older than most of the other fellows probably helped keep me out of trouble. I'd also already realized that my heart belonged to Irene back in Toronto.

When I did get to London on leave I counted myself lucky to be able to spend almost all my time with family. My younger sister Viola, her husband Adam McKenzie and their young son Wayne had been living in a North London suburb for several years. Adam, who was always called Mac, was brought over by De Havilland Aircraft before the war to work as an inspector, but mostly to play baseball in an industrial league then operating in the greater London area that was manned almost entirely by transplanted North Americans.

Mac had been playing for Barrie in a game against Penetang back in the North Simcoe League when he first laid eyes on my sister, who was sitting on a car roof cheering me on. Now, after a cosy family dinner, Mac and I would play catch in a nearby park. I'd been airing my arm out every now and again with some of the boys back at the base who wanted to be able to say they'd caught a major-leaguer. I felt pretty good and jumped at Mac's suggestion that I pitch in a series of exhibition matches against American Army squads.

"I want to have a little fun in the first game," Mac said. "Let's not tell anyone who you are. As far as the Americans are concerned, you're an English cricket bowler."

A more confident group of Yanks you've never seen. They swaggered onto the field, laughing and waving to their English girl-friends sitting on the sidelines. When I wound up and threw a sharply breaking curve to the first hitter, he stood there paralyzed. My fastball was next, then another curve that caught the outside corner for strike three. The poor guy hadn't lifted his bat off his shoulder.

After a couple of hitless innings the Americans were shaking their heads and muttering among themselves. "Geez," one of them said. "That limey could pitch in the big leagues right now. Are they all that good?"

A few strikeouts later Mac, who was playing second base for us, figured it was time to let the soldiers in on the gag. "Don't feel badly," he said to a batter who'd thrown his bat down in disgust after watching a called strike three to end an inning. "That's Phil Marchildon of the Philadelphia Athletics."

The Yanks took the news with mostly good grace. Two or three were angry at first, but soon everyone loosened up and started joking about how bad I had made them look. Some of them came over for autographs after the game.

I played two more exhibition matches after that. Mac passed the word that I'd be pitching and a crowd of four or five hundred turned out each time. Although I was rusty, my stuff seemed as good as ever. It wasn't smart to look any farther ahead than my next mission, but I was already starting to think about getting back to the Athletics.

You had to keep thinking positively, believing that somehow you'd beat the odds and survive your thirty missions even though at that stage of the war only about one-third of the men in RCAF bomber squadrons were making it through. You avoided developing friendships outside your crew because when they didn't come back it was a painful reminder of how slim your own chances were.

We were starting to hear talk that the war in Europe would be over by Christmas. The Russians were advancing steadily in the east, and our own troops were firmly ashore in Normandy. If my luck held I'd get my thirty missions in and be discharged in time for the opening of training camp the following spring.

Our dawn raid on Caen July 18 in support of the Second British and First Canadian Armies erased all thoughts of baseball, Irene and everything else except living through the next few minutes. That morning eight hundred bombers dropped 5,000 tons of explosives on German positions, all but destroying Caen in the process.

Accustomed as I was to flying at night, actually being able to see what was going on through my turret windows was a rare experience. We approached the target at about 5,000 feet, with most of the formation flying above us. Off to my right I watched as a bomb from a higher-flying Halifax sliced through the tail-wing of one of our aircraft. Somehow the plane managed to stay in the air. Seconds later I saw another bomb crash into the aircraft to our rear, sending it spiralling in flames towards the ground.

The realization dawned on me that the same types of accidents probably happened on many of our night-time operations. Flying in the dark, we had no way of knowing how many losses were the result of our own errors rather than enemy fighters and flak. I wasn't sure I wanted to know.

We flew on through an increasingly heavy barrage from the ground and dropped our bombs on a target almost entirely obscured by a giant cloud of dust and smoke. Instead of veering off out of the flak, the skipper continued flying straight ahead. By now the German batteries had us targetted and I could hear shrapnel thudding into the airplane.

"Turn, God-dammit!" I wanted to yell into my head-set, frustrated because I knew I couldn't. Over enemy territory I was under strict orders to maintain radio silence.

Just as I could feel Morgan finally begin to pull off to the left, the plane shuddered and I knew we'd been hit. I waited for the Halifax to falter and start to dive. But she continued to fly normally as we headed out over the Channel for home.

Back at base I learned that the skipper hadn't turned sooner because we'd been carrying a surveillance camera with a delayed timer. He was told to fly straight ahead until he heard the shutter click.

We counted more than thirty shrapnel holes as we walked around the battered Halifax, including a wide gash through one wing that missed the gas tanks by inches. That was the hit I'd felt shake the entire plane. If the skipper had waited another second to start his turn we'd have been goners.

That mission taught me to take absolutely nothing for granted. From then on the tension became more unbearable every time I climbed into my turret. Whenever I came back after a particularly rough mission my nerves were a mess. It felt so good to be back on the ground.

As the weeks slowly passed, ten, fifteen, twenty successful missions were noted in my log book. How long could our luck hold?

The worst part was waiting for take-off after we'd been through all the pre-flight briefings. First up was the commanding officer, who told us our target, the types of bombs we would carry, gas loads and other specifics. Then the intelligence officer described the positions and strengths of the German air defenses. Next came marshalling instructions and notice of take-off times. Finally, there was the weather briefing.

After all this we had several hours to kill until take-off. On sunny days we sat out on the runway and talked, or found a patch of grass and tried to snooze. I checked and rechecked the four machine guns in my turret, then checked them again just for something to do. As take-off approached I grew increasingly anxious, especially if I knew our target was going to be a tough one: maybe an industrial site in the heavily defended Ruhr Valley—"Happy Valley" we called it—or a large German city.

When the weather was bad we anxiously watched the sky for a white flare fired from the control tower, the signal that the mission had been scrubbed. The thought of a few beers and a game of darts that night in the cosy local pub was a lot more inviting than anything the Germans had waiting.

"Gentlemen, your target for tonight is a synthetic oil plant at Wesseling...."

"Your target is the submarine pens at Boulogne...."

"Tonight's target is Hamburg. Expect night-fighter activity as you approach the...."

My saddest memories are of a daylight raid we took part in on August 14 against German positions in the Caen-Falaise area, when some of our planes accidently bombed Canadian forces on the ground, killing sixty-five soldiers and wounding more than three hundred.

Allied troops were attempting to trap the Germans in the soon-to-be-famous Falaise Gap. Bomber Command provided 114 aircraft, all but 9 of them from 6 Group, for a strike designed to clear the way for the advancing ground troops. The mission went horribly wrong when Canadian soldiers set off yellow flares to indicate their positions to the advancing bombers. Some of our bombardiers mistook the haze from the flares for the dust of exploding bombs dropped by the aircraft ahead of them and began releasing their loads.

Thank God there was never any question that we were one of the crews at fault. Our bombardier, Jacques Clerc, was too smart to be fooled by a few flares. All crews had been issued stop-watches and ordered to hit a certain speed over the Channel, then time their approach to the target from the French coast. Other bombardiers blindly followed the example of those ahead of them, figuring that no matter what their stop-watches said the target must have been correctly identified. Not Jacques.

That was our twenty-fifth mission. Only five more to go. Just as ballplayers carefully avoid mentioning a no-hitter in progress for fear of jinxing their pitcher, none of us talked about how close we were to going home. We tried not to think about it. But that was impossible. Just *five* more.

CHAPTER
9

STALAG LUFT III

"Prepare to bail out," I heard our captain, Wynn Morgan, shouting through my head-set. Seconds earlier there had been a loud clang as we'd taken a hit from a night fighter and the Halifax made a sickening lurch.

Sitting in my rear turret I turned my head towards the front of the plane to see flames billowing back at me from one of the engines on the starboard wing. Obeying the skipper's order, I reached for my parachute and struggled to get it on over my bulky flying suit. "Keep this crate together just a few seconds more," I prayed. "Give me a chance to get out of here."

It was our twenty-sixth mission. Four more and I would have been on my way back home, back to Irene and my baseball career with the Athletics. We were so close.

At 9:27 p.m. on August 16 we had taken off on what was called a "gardening expedition," ordered to drop mines at the entrance of Kiel harbour, an important shipping centre in northern Germany near the Danish border. The battery-powered mines were designed to sit on the sea bed until they were activated by acoustic or magnetic waves from passing ships. Throughout the war they were a constant nuisance to the enemy; it is estimated that they sunk as many German ships as the Royal Navy.

The squadrons of 6 Group conducted a large proportion of Bomber Command's mining operations and were regarded as experts at the job. Our crew had been sent out to plant "vegetables" several times before. From the pre-op briefing, this mission seemed fairly straightforward and maybe even safer than most. While a group of over two hundred bombers were pounding the city of Kiel itself, and presumably attracting the attention of the German fighters, we and fourteen other planes would lay our mines.

What a German fighter pilot was doing patrolling the Baltic Sea when the heavy action was over Kiel is anybody's guess. We were still about fifty miles from our target when he struck. Scanning the darkness from my turret I never even caught a glimpse of him. All I saw out of the corner of my eye were the flashes of his tracer fire. Then I felt the lurch, turned and saw our engine on fire.

It's probably a foolish thought, but I've often wondered whether, if I'd had my mouth-set turned on and yelled a warning to the skipper the split second I saw the first flashes, he'd have been able to turn the Halifax quickly enough to save us. I hated that stupid radio-silence regulation. What was the point of having me back there constantly watching for danger if I wasn't able to tell the captain when I did see something?

By ignoring an even dumber regulation, one that must have been responsible for the deaths of hundreds of gunners during the course of the war, I almost certainly saved my life when it came time to jump. According to the book, my bail-out procedure was to climb out of my turret, grab my parachute hanging outside the turret entranceway, and then put it on as I worked my way the thirty feet or so through the narrow corridor to the door located at mid-ship.

All of that would likely have taken several minutes, assuming that I *had* several minutes and that the plane kept flying on an even keel. What if the ship was breaking up or spiralling towards the ground? There's no way I could have made it.

This was something that had been worrying me since our earliest missions. After talking it over with Morgan and getting his okay, I decided to keep my parachute, which was too bulky to wear in the cramped turret, within arm's reach, and then leave by the shortest route possible in an emergency—right out the turret's sliding glass doors. I'd prop my feet against my machine guns and then push off backwards into space.

Everything happened so quickly after we were hit. In no more than four or five minutes I'd managed to get my chute on and slide the doors open. I was just positioning myself when I heard Morgan's voice again. "Bail out!" he ordered, and then the intercom went dead.

We were probably about 17,000 feet up and doing 180 to 190 miles an hour when I pushed myself out of the turret. The air banged into me, blowing off my boots and hat. I'd had the ring of the parachute in my hand when I left the plane. Now the force threw my arm away from my body, opening the chute almost immediately.

As I floated down I watched the burning Halifax fade into the distance. Below me I could just make out the shape of another parachute.

I didn't know if I was over land or water, but wherever I landed I wanted it to be somewhere close to my crewmate. It's funny what goes through your mind at a time like that. Until that point I'd been reacting more than thinking. Now I remembered a Hollywood war movie I'd seen in which the hero managed to guide the direction of his parachute by tugging on either side of the harness straps.

Bad idea. When I pulled on one of the straps my speed picked up until I felt like I was free falling. That scared the hell out of me. Finally the chute resumed its soft descent and I decided to leave well enough alone.

It was about one o'clock in the morning and so dark that I still didn't know if I was going to have a wet or dry landing until I splashed down into the sea. In the winter I wouldn't have lasted ten minutes in the frigid water, but luckily it had been a hot summer. Compared to the cool night air, the water seemed almost warm.

I knew the first thing I had to do was get my parachute off before its weight dragged me under. Bobbing in the choppy water, I managed to work the harness off my shoulders. Then I began struggling out of the heavy pants of my electrical suit. Having no idea how far I was from land, I had to have my legs free for what might turn out to be a long swim.

After being in the water only a few minutes, I was already getting tired from my exertions. And I still wasn't through. Only half of my Mae West, which was supposed to inflate automatically, had filled with air. I had to blow up the other side myself.

I leaned my head back against the neck of my life jacket and tried to catch my breath. Almost immediately I heard a voice from somewhere in the darkness call for help. It was our navigator, George Gill. "Over here!" I yelled back. "It's me, Phil! Are you all right?"

George, who sounded no more than a couple hundred feet away, answered that he seemed to be in one piece, although he was a little groggy. The strap of his chute had hit him in the jaw and knocked him out when he jumped from the plane. He didn't come to until he was in the water.

I knew George couldn't swim, so I told him to try to relax and let the life-jacket do the work, to concentrate on keeping his head back to avoid swallowing salt water. George has always said that by helping him stay calm I saved his life.

We listened for the calls of any of our crewmates who might have dumped nearby, but we knew that with the plane travelling almost two hundred miles an hour when we were ordered to bail out they could be miles away. George thought he was the first one to leave the plane. I must have been second.

Gradually my eyes grew accustomed to the dark and I thought I could make out a faint horizon line in the distance. I called to George—I still couldn't see him—to try to paddle towards shore. George said he thought we were off the coast of the Danish island of Fyn. If we got ashore undetected, maybe we could somehow get in touch with local resistance leaders who would help us in our escape. It wasn't really much of a plan, but it would have to do for the moment.

At first we seemed to be making progress. Then the current got stronger and pushed us back. After struggling towards the shore for what must have been three or four hours we were frustrated and exhausted, and not much closer. The water had only felt warm for the first few minutes after we splashed down. Now we were numb from the cold. George and I both knew we couldn't last much longer.

Just when we were ready to give up hope we heard the sound of a boat engine. I must have been half delirious at that point because I remember actually wondering whether or not I should blow the whistle attached to my life-jacket to attract the boat crew's attention. I thought, what if it's a German patrol boat?

Thankfully, I came to my senses and began tooting away on my whistle. Better a prisoner of war than a corpse washed up on a foreign coast. I saw a light come towards me and heard the noise of the engine grow louder. The boat stopped to pick up George, then started towards me.

It wasn't a German patrol boat after all, but a Danish fishing trawler. Two Danes hauled me in and sat me on the small deck beside George. They put blankets over us and offered cigarettes. One of them patted my shoulder and smiled. "We are friends," he said in halting English.

I didn't find out until after the war that the two fishermen were actually members of the Danish underground. They planned to put us in a car once we were ashore and try to smuggle us by stages to neutral Sweden. After the German surrender those Danes were sought out by RAF officials for information about pilots who had been shot down in the area. One of them, Jorgens Hansen, got my address and wrote me a letter late in 1945 in which he told me of their plan. He said he and his friend had seen our burning aircraft and gone out searching for survivors. He also mentioned that even though we were only about a half-mile out when they picked us up, the current right there was so strong that we would never have made it to shore on our own. That much I already knew.

At the time we had no idea what the Danes had in mind for us. They likely wouldn't have revealed much even if their English had been better. It would have been foolish to take the chance of us somehow giving them away if we were captured.

Since the fishermen said they were our friends, I had an idea we might be going to make a run for it. I swallowed a couple of adrenalin tablets that were tucked away in a hidden compartment of my flight jacket.

As it turned out, all I needed was strength enough to raise my hands above my head and surrender to the two burly German soldiers who were waiting as the Danes brought their boat into the pier at the town of Assens. Maybe the Germans had also seen our burning plane. The Danes had no choice but to act as if they'd been planning to hand us over all along.

The Germans took us to the local hospital where a Danish doctor pronounced us in excellent shape considering what we'd been through. He poured out a shot of booze for each of us and told the nurse to take our wet clothes and have them dried.

That doctor must have been absolutely certain the German guard who remained to watch over us didn't understand English. "We hate these bastards as much as you do," he said, all the while smiling at the guard. "We'll get word back to England that you're safe."

George and I were taken to a nearby jail and locked in a cell. It had been a long night and even the adrenalin pills couldn't fight off my exhaustion. I collapsed onto my cot. There was no point in worrying about tomorrow. Whatever happened now was completely out of our control. Don't think about it, I told myself. Just sleep.

It was a shock the next morning to open my eyes and find myself in that small cell. For a moment I forgot where I was.

Then the events of the night before came flooding back. Thinking it through as I lay on my cot, I realized how lucky I was to be alive. Naturally, there was frustration in knowing that the end of my tour had been only a week or so away. But considering how close I'd come to dying, being a temporary guest of the Third Reich didn't seem like such a bad alternative.

So I was in reasonably good spirits when a German sergeant opened our cell door and told us that he and the corporal with him were to be our escort to the Luftwaffe interrogation centre near Frankfurt. The sergeant politely asked about our health and ordered some bread and soup brought to us before we left on our journey. He also sent the corporal off to find me a pair of pants and shoes.

The view through the window of our private train compartment was fascinating as we crossed the border and rode through the German countryside. I had expected the home of the evil Hun to somehow be different. For years newspapers and movie newsreels had been painting a picture of a cuckoo-land filled with goose-stepping fanatics. So far all I'd seen were farms that looked pretty much like the ones back home and civilians who wouldn't have been out of place on the streets of Penetang or Toronto. The small towns we passed through appeared to be mostly unscarred by the war.

As we entered the outskirts of Hamburg the situation changed dramatically. The devastation was almost unbelievable approaching the train station in the centre of the city, where we were to make a connection for Frankfurt. Germany's second-largest city had been reduced to rubble.

In late July, 1943, Bomber Command had made a series of massive attacks on Hamburg, an important centre for submarine production. The second of these raids destroyed more than three-quarters of the metropolitan area as incendiary bombs caused a fire-storm that created winds of 150 miles an hour. It was said that more than 50,000 people died. Some were swept into the air and smashed against buildings. Others were boiled to death when they dove into Hamburg's rivers and canals trying to escape.

Since then Bomber Command had kept up the pressure, hitting the city again and again. Our crew had participated in one of these raids less than a month before. Now here we were in the centre of our handiwork.

The morality of the massive bombing raids on Dresden, Hamburg, Berlin and other large German cities has been questioned in recent years. If we were supposed to be the good guys, then why did we conduct raids that killed so many innocent civilians?

Like most veterans, I haven't lost any sleep over the issue. I feel sorry for the Germans who died, but worse for all the civilians in England, France, Holland, Russia and several other countries who were killed by Luftwaffe bombs. Looking out at the ruins of Hamburg as we slowly made our way through the city, I thought the Germans had gotten what they deserved for starting the war in the first place.

The natives didn't quite see it that way. The sergeant was nervous at the prospect of taking us out onto the crowded platform of the station.

"These people hate you," he told us. "Don't say or do anything to attract attention. If you do, I cannot guarantee your safety."

For half an hour or more we sat silently on a bench while waiting to board our train. Most passers-by just stared. Some cursed under their breath when they saw us. An older man stopped directly in front of our bench and began shouting at the top of his voice. When a crowd began to form the sergeant stood up and roughly told him to move on.

The Luftwaffe interrogation centre was located in Oberursel, a town close to Frankfurt. When we got there in the late afternoon George and I were immediately separated. A few days later he was sent to Stalag Luft I, near Barth, where he was eventually liberated by the Russians. We didn't see each other again until we renewed our friendship in Toronto about ten years later.

My cell was a sweat-box about four feet wide, furnished with only a bare cot. It must have been a hundred degrees in there. Within minutes I was drenched in sweat. When I stripped down to my undershorts and tried to get some sleep, I was attacked by dozens of fleas that lived in the thin, filthy mattress of my cot. I swear those fleas were the size of beetles. By the next morning I had red welts all over my body from their bites.

This was my home for the next two weeks. Between the heat and the fleas I got almost no sleep. My diet consisted of two slices of dark bread in the morning and evening, and a bowl of weak, tasteless soup at noon. I was always hungry. By the end of my stay I'd lost about twenty pounds.

A few days after my arrival a young, friendly officer arrived at my cell and ordered a guard to take me away and get me cleaned up. After a shower I felt almost human again. I was brought crackers, a slice of cheese and a stein of beer as the officer and I sat and talked in a small room. I still remember how good that beer felt going down.

The officer was a Stuka pilot who said he had completed 180 missions and was awaiting reassignment. As he told his story I couldn't help feeling sympathy for German airmen. For them there was no such thing as a completed tour. Having the bad luck to be on the losing side, they had to keep flying to the usually bitter end.

His job was to prepare me for my interview with the Luftwaffe intelligence officer. "Be careful with this man," he said as I finished my beer. "He has a toothache today and is in a very bad mood."

Just my luck, I thought. I had already pictured a strutting Nazi with a monocle over one eye and a horsewhip in his hand. Now I had to face one with a sore tooth to boot.

Seated behind a table when the pilot and I entered the interrogation room was a stern-looking, middle-aged man who greeted me with a curt nod. A Luger was placed in front of him.

He got right down to business. "Let's speak as officer to officer," he said. "I already know which squadron you belong to, your base, and even the name of your commanding officer. You see, our intelligence is quite good. All I want from you is the serial number of your aircraft."

I saw no harm in telling him that I honestly didn't know the serial number of my plane. We'd used several aircraft during our twenty-six operations. I never bothered to memorize their serial numbers.

My answer didn't go over very well. "You mean to say the Allies have so many aircraft you use a different one each time?"

"Not each time out," I answered. "But fairly often. Anyway, I'm just an air gunner. There's really not much I can tell you."

He'd probably heard my answer about the serial number a hundred times before. By that point he and every other sane German had to know how overwhelming the forces against them were and that there was no hope of victory.

That was it. I was dismissed and taken back to my cell, where I sweated and scratched for several more days. By the end of my stay one of my feet had become infected from wearing the tight boots given to me after my capture. I'd also developed large boils on my face.

Civilians standing on a bridge pelted us with rocks as I was marched with about ten other prisoners to the nearby train station. I had trouble keeping up when we were ordered to quicken our pace. Boarding the train, a guard told us our destination was a POW camp in Upper Silesia.

"Marchildon Missing in Action" read the headline over a short Associated Press article dated September 1, 1944. "Flying Officer Phil Marchildon of the Royal Canadian Air Force, former star pitcher for the Philadelphia Athletics, has been reported missing in action overseas, Roy Mack, A's vice-president, said today.

"Mack said his father, Connie Mack, had been notified by the pilot's sister, Jeanne, of Penetanguishene, Ontario, his home town...."

For about two more weeks no one knew if I was dead or alive. But by that point in the war enough flyers had gone missing only to turn up in POW camps weeks and even months later that Irene and my family didn't give up hope. Thankfully, the Danish doctor who had promised to get news of our rescue back to England was as good as his word. By mid-September confirmation came that I was a resident of Stalag Luft III, one of the largest prison camps in Germany. Just six months before my arrival, the camp had been the scene of the famous Great Escape.

Located about 105 miles south-east of Berlin near the town of Sagan, then in Germany but now part of Poland, the camp held about 10,300 Allied airmen—Brits, Canadians, Australians and New Zealanders, as well as Americans, who had been put into their own compound by the time of my arrival. Luft III was set in a black forest of unusually ugly and scrawny fir trees. Around the perimeter stood a double row of barbed-wire fences about ten feet tall, with guard towers set at intervals of a hundred yards. A single warning wire two feet high was positioned ten yards before the inner fence. This was no-man's land. Step one foot inside and a guard was likely to shoot you.

I lined up with the other new prisoners to be deloused and then issued an identity card. A guard who had lived in Brooklyn before the war and even spoke with a Bronx accent wrote "Sportsmann" to describe my occupation. I was POW number 7741.

Prisoners called themselves Kriegies, short for Kriegsgefangen, which was German for prisoner of war. I was assigned to a bare wooden barrack in the East Compound housing eleven men, some of whom had been in camp for as long as four years. Because smoke and odours rise, new Kriegies were relegated to the upper bunks. A room full of men who didn't have much incentive or opportunity to bathe could get pretty ripe. We were allowed one hot shower a week and not everyone bothered.

There were other prisoners who knew of me and could confirm my identity, so I didn't have to undergo the usual interrogation by our own camp administration to prove I wasn't a spy placed by the Germans. If a new Kriegie said he was from Saskatoon, then he'd better know where the downtown streets met and maybe even the name of his Grade Ten math teacher. The interviewers prided themselves on their research.

The need for tight security went back to the heyday of the Escape Committee, when the energy and skills of most of the men in camp were concentrated on finding ways of breaking out and getting back to England. There were forgers to create passports and train tickets. From old uniforms and rags, designated tailors sewed passable civilian clothes and even German uniforms. Compasses were constructed from bits of metal, melted-down gramophone records and shards of glass, and bore the inscription "Made in Stalag Luft III."

After months of preparation the efforts of the Escape Committee had culminated in the breakout known as the Great Escape. On the night of March 24, 1944, seventy-six men made it out through a 336-foot-long tunnel dug from a barrack in the North Compound. Nicknamed "Harry," the tunnel was equipped with electric lights and even a primitive air-conditioning system made from kit bags and pieces of scrap wood that pumped air through a pipe of connected milk tins.

Only three escapees made it back to England. Hitler himself ordered that fifty of the recaptured POWs be shot. He was talked out of killing them all by aides who feared the Allies would take their revenge against German prisoners. Only one of the seven Canadians involved in the escape survived.

By the time I arrived in camp, all thoughts of further escape attempts had been put aside. The price paid had been too high and at that stage of the war it seemed foolish to take more risks.

It was strange to know that the possibilities of my life now extended no further than the barbed wire that surrounded the camp. The happiest prisoners were the ones who learned to be patient and accept the limitations of the situation. It was futile for a guy to drive himself crazy worrying if his wife had been faithful in the years he'd been away. Or to count on the war ending soon. There was absolutely nothing we could do but wait and take whatever happened.

The camp was a self-contained world. It even had its own monetary system, based on the cigarette standard. By carefully hoarding the smokes from their Red Cross parcels, and by supplementing their supplies with parcels sent from home, some men were able to become the equivalent of cigarette million-aires, possessing fortunes of three or more cartons.

With cigarettes you could barter with other prisoners for luxuries from their Red Cross packages. A Hershey chocolate bar might be purchased for two hundred cigarettes, while a can of Borden's sweetened condensed milk, considered the greatest of all indulgences, went for several times that. Even the guards could be bribed to smuggle in fresh eggs and other items in return for a few packages of Camels or Lucky Strikes.

Without the Red Cross parcels to supplement our diets, life at Luft III would have been much tougher than it was. Our hosts barely provided enough food to keep us alive: the daily ration of two slices of black bread that tasted like sawdust, the occasional grey potato, watery barley soup or, as a special treat, a "meat" soup with a few chunks of fat and maybe a pig's ear floating on top.

Shipments of the Red Cross parcels arrived like clockwork. For most of the time I was in the camp each prisoner received one per week. A parcel might include individual tins of corned beef, salmon and sardines, biscuits, marmalade, butter, salt and pepper, powdered milk, coffee or tea, cocoa and a package of cigarettes. Even with the parcels we never felt like we had enough to eat, but we weren't starving either.

Dinner, usually served in our barrack at around 8:30 p.m., was prepared in the block kitchen by the designated cook and waiter of the day, called "the stooge." The stooge's most impor-tant responsibility was to make certain, absolutely certain, that all the portions were divided equally. Fights threatened to break out when men thought they'd been given a too-thin slice of bread or corned beef.

A special treat might be a small cake made from delicacies saved from our Red Cross parcels. Some men set aside the sugar and raisins from their packages until they had enough to brew a disgusting-looking, sludge-like wine of legendary potency. The morning after a tasting they could barely walk. I never had the courage to try the stuff myself, fearing permanent damage to my stomach and liver.

Everyone was eager for news of the war, especially now that the end seemed so near. A short-wave radio had been constructed with radio parts smuggled in by guards in return for cigarettes. Every day a couple of men who knew shorthand took down the BBC news report word for word. Their notes were then written out and read in all the huts.

"Did you hear that? The Russkies are rolling up the Krauts. They're only a few hundred miles from here. Better brush up on our Russian, lads. They'll be knocking on our door in a couple of weeks."

As each broadcast brought news of another Allied advance, you could feel the spirit of the camp soar. Everyone walked around with wide grins. Men started talking about the thick, juicy steaks they were going to devour when they got back home, and bragged about how they'd keep their wives in bed for at least the first month. It was hard to tell which they wanted more, a T-bone or sex.

The guards who smuggled in the radio parts were fairly typical. Most of them were decent men forced to do a job they didn't want or enjoy. They saw no harm in making our lives a little easier provided we had something to offer in return.

One guard, a corporal who had been living in Montreal before the war, complained bitterly to me about his situation. "I came back to visit my family and then the fighting started," he said. "Before I knew it I was in uniform. I just want this war to be over so I can go back to Canada."

There were also a few die-hard Nazis who delighted in making our lives miserable. The worst was a tall, middle-aged tower guard whose face was twisted in a permanent scowl. A group of us were playing softball one day when someone missed the ball and it bounced under the warning wire into no-man's land near his post.

One of our players, a Canadian, walked to the wire and looked up at the guard. "Nicht schiessen, Posten!" he called, which meant "Don't shoot, sentry." The German waved him in. When the Canadian had no more than a foot over the fence he shot him dead.

I also heard the story of a prisoner who was laying on the grass one sunny day. A tower guard shot him when the POW yawned and stretched an arm back under the wire.

Despite the hardships of our life at Luft III, the camp was considered one of the best in Germany. Most Allied POWs had it a lot worse than we did. Our own camp administration was involved in the organization of everything from theatre groups to sporting activities. Morale was amazingly high, even among the men who'd been there for years.

Our spiritual needs were attended to by a remarkable Oblate priest from Quebec, Philippe Gaudreault, who conducted multi-faith services Sundays and is fondly remembered by everyone he came in contact with. This slim priest with piercing dark eyes chose to remain with us at Luft III even after the Germans offered to send him home to Canada.

Gaudreault had been on his way with several other recent graduates from the seminary to a mission in Basutoland in South Africa when his ship was sunk by a German surface raider. The priests were taken to Germany and given temporary assignments as chaplains in prison camps. As a non-combatant, Gaudreault was eligible under the terms of the Geneva Convention for repatriation. When the time came to leave he refused, believing his place was now with the men of the camp.

How could you not admire a man who selflessly turned down the freedom the rest of us craved more than anything? Although I attended his sermons, I didn't know him well. Those who did appreciated that he never tried to convert others to his religion, suggesting to anyone who asked his advice about such a switch that they wait and make their decision after the war when life was back to normal. Gaudreault suffered every hardship with us, right through to the bitter final days of the Death March. At a time when there were many reasons for men to lose their faith, his example helped some go on believing.

The Geneva Convention stipulated that officers could not be forced to work for their captors. Free from having to dig ditches or plant fields, many of us spent hours every day reading. Some used the time to begin working towards future university degrees.

There were three libraries in camp stocked with thousands of titles donated by the Red Cross as well as other relief agencies and relatives at home. One library was devoted to fiction, another was a literary reference centre, the third a technical library considered to be of a particularly high standard.

I'm proud to say that I managed to struggle through Tolstoy's *Anna Karenina* as well as several other impressive titles. I knew I'd probably never have the opportunity or the inclination to get back to them again.

Some men devoted their energies to the camp theatre. Here's what I wrote in a journal I kept during my stay at Luft III: "Theatre, in our block, 64, provides interesting performances in the evenings, besides musical concerts of classical and popular tunes, played over a sound system. Four plays have been performed during this year, the acting being of a high amateur quality, and the female impersonations are extremely good. One play put on by the prisoners was Bernard Shaw's *Pygmalion*. The POWs enjoy these very much. The chairs of the theatre are constructed of Red Cross boxes and are strongly made. The music is provided by records sent from home and also by a band made up of Kriegies who never played in an orchestra before and are considered amazingly adept."

But it was sport—almost every type of sport—that more than anything occupied the attention and time of the men. Thanks again to the Red Cross and donations from home, there was equipment for ice hockey, softball, rugger, soccer, basketball, cricket, field and track, volleyball, horseshoes, badminton, boxing, field hockey and gymnastics.

Almost everyone participated in at least one athletic league and most were in several. Basketball was by far the most popular sport in camp, with two leagues, four hundred participants, and play-offs between block champions. About two hundred men played in the soccer league. Softball, introduced by the Canadians, attracted three hundred and fifty players, including many Englishmen who claimed to prefer it to cricket. I was a heavy-hitting outfielder for the softball squad that won the camp championship 2–1.

There was even a crude nine-hole golf course the men had designed with "putting greens" of sand. Balls were made by cutting strips from the rubber soles of old running shoes and wrapping them around a marble until it was the size of a golf ball. Then a leather cover was sewed on. A well stroked ball travelled about a hundred yards. Some days they were whizzing all over the place—off walls, through windows. The curses you'd hear when someone hooked one of those precious balls over the fence and out of camp!

Reading and sports helped pass the time, but there was no escaping the fact that life in prison was an unnatural existence far removed from anything we'd ever known. I wondered if I would remember how to act in polite society. That world seemed so far away.

"Looks like I'll be missing another baseball season," I wrote to Irene on December 11, 1944. "We can only hope for the best now. I, for one, am praying for the day it ends and hope it will be soon. We seem kind of useless here and feel it deeply. We feel the people at home do not realize our predicament as fully as they might. It makes us angry at times...."

No wonder we felt the folks back home didn't appreciate our situation or the sacrifices we'd made. Abundant proof arrived in the mail bags. In my prison journal I noted the extracts the men had posted on camp bulletin boards from their letters. Most of them can still make me laugh out loud even after all these years:

First letter from a fiancée: "Dear Jack, you were reported missing for a month so I got married."

"Darling, in your May letter you asked for slippers. What colour would you like?"

"I hope you are not being extravagant with the pocket money you got."

From a fond mother: "I was at home when word arrived that you were missing, which you will agree is a blessing."

"Can you buy beer over there, or do they just sell wine?"

One fellow received a sweater through the Red Cross and

wrote to thank the donor. The following was part of the reply: "I am sorry you got it. I wish it had gone to someone on active service."

"Are the German girls good dancers?"

"I hope you are behaving yourself at the dances, and not drinking too much beer."

"Darling, I hope you are staying true to me."

"Take care of Andy when you are out drinking. He is so wild."

"Joe's in Stalag 8B. I hope you can drop around and see him soon."

A Kriegie wrote home asking for his bank balance. Six months later a reply came from his mother: "Guess." He made his guess. Six months later a reply stated: "Wrong. Guess again."

"I've got a grandmother in Germany. Have you met her?"

"I wonder if you are as tired as I am of this war?"

"Sorry not to write oftener. But I'm sure your life has more variety than mine."

"I understand that some of the boys are being taken out of camp on sightseeing tours. I hope you will be one of the lucky ones."

"A friend of mine who was a POW in the last war said that the Germans were lots of fun."

"I cannot help thinking that your present circumstances are a punishment for your enjoying blowing things up."

"You mustn't forget there's a war on."

I kept hoping the mail would bring news about the fate of my crewmates. Or that maybe I'd meet someone in camp who had seen one or more of them at the interrogation centre or another stalag. But the mail seemed to get home a lot faster than it came back. Though Irene and my family were writing regularly, I received only a single letter during the more than four months I was in camp. That was from Irene, telling me she'd be waiting when I finally got home.

The Christmas we had hoped would see us celebrating the end of the war came and went. Over several weeks an influx of hundreds of new prisoners arrived in camp, mostly American soldiers captured during the Germans' early successes in the Battle of the Bulge. For the first time air crew and soldiers mixed at Luft III. The Germans had taken so many prisoners that their regular Wehrmacht camps were overflowing.

Despite our growing impatience we managed a good measure of Christmas cheer. The theatre group presented an old-fashioned holiday pantomime that received thunderous ovations and, thanks to the fact that our Red Cross parcels were coming in faster than ever, there were more than enough Hershey bars and other holiday treats to go around.

We knew the war couldn't possibly last much longer. Early in January the German offensive in the Ardennes fizzled and the Russians were attacking along the German-Polish border. By mid-month advance units of the Red Army were only 150 miles from the gates of Luft III.

Soon we could hear the distant sounds of Russian guns in the east, faint at first but growing louder each day. Flashes of artillery fire were visible at night through the cracks in the shutters over our barrack windows. During the day we stood in the snow along the wire of no-man's land and watched as a growing stream of German refugees fled from the Russians on the highway that passed the camp a few hundred yards beyond the fence.

Any day now, almost any hour, we expected the Russians to burst through the gates and set us free.

We were asleep in our barracks just before midnight when the lights went on and a guard shouted, "Everyone up! We are evacuating the camp. You must be ready to leave in thirty minutes."

For a moment we lay there, stunned with disappointment. Then everyone was up and cursing at once. "The dirty bastards!" "What do they want us for? They've lost, for God's sake. Why don't they realize that?"

We soon forced ourselves to get busy throwing blankets, sweaters, toques—anything warm—into our kit bags. It was well below freezing outside and we knew we would be walking to wherever it was the Germans planned to take us. "Take all your cigarettes," someone said. "We might need them to trade with the Krauts."

A few practical thinkers rushed to the library and began ripping the pages out of books with the thinnest paper for future use as toilet paper. A fellow Canadian suggested we make sleighs to carry our supplies, an idea that made perfect sense to everyone except the two Aussies in our hut, who weren't quite sure what we were talking about. I made mine from a wooden box I found lying around the barrack, using a twisted sheet from my bed as a harness.

Midnight came and then several more hours passed as we waited—and wondered. Why were the Germans going to so much trouble to keep us captive? Maybe Hitler planned to hold all the POWs as hostages in order to get better surrender terms. We didn't know it at the time, but throughout Germany prisoners were being marched to the rear wherever the Allies threatened to break through. Everyone had a different theory. Maybe they were going to shoot us all. But that didn't seem likely— there were hundreds of thousands of us. Besides, the Allies could threaten to do the same to German prisoners.

It was early the next morning, January 28, before we were finally ordered from our barracks and marched through the camp gate. On the way out we were each handed a Red Cross parcel, part of a stash of thousands our own camp administration had hidden from the Germans for just such an emergency.

We headed west, trudging through the snow for as much as thirty miles the first day. Our line stretched out of sight back towards the camp. Already some men were suffering from exhaustion and frost-bite. None of us were used to this type of prolonged exertion after months and sometimes years of confinement. In front of me men were discarding items they didn't think they'd need or were too tired to carry. In the days ahead some even began throwing down cans of food from their Red Cross parcels. The few of us who'd made sleighs added them to our own supplies.

At night, if we were lucky, there would be a barn for shelter. Usually we were herded into farm fields where we slept out in the open, shivering under straw and our Army blankets. One night the guards shot a man who climbed a fence in search of firewood.

In the mornings I would look around me and see thousands of men jumping to get warm, slapping their arms and legs. It snowed steadily our first two or three days on the road.

After about a week we straggled into Spremberg, a busy railway junction fifty-five miles to the west of Sagan. There they loaded us into cattle cars and sent us off to several destinations throughout Germany. Many were taken to the huge stalag at Luckenwalde, where they remained until the Russians overran the camp in the last weeks of the war.

I spent two days on the train, with barely enough room to sit down. On the second day the guards gave us each a single cup of water that had been drained off the engine. At the town of Marlag, near Bremen, they opened the doors and marched us to an old, condemned camp. Men began collapsing all around me as we were kept waiting outside the gate for seven hours in the rain while the guards carefully searched each one of us.

From our safe vantage point a few miles outside of Bremen, I watched a massive bombing raid on the city a few days later. It was a clear morning, and I could see the vapour trails of hundreds of our planes in the sky. A huge cloud of dust and smoke rose up. I could actually feel the ground shake beneath my feet.

None of us watching were in any mood to feel sorry for the occupants of the city. Bomb them all, we thought. Just end this war.

In mid-February the Germans marched us out again, although this time no one, not even our guards, seemed to have any idea where we were heading.

In the days that followed, German troops sometimes rode in Red Cross trucks at the front and rear of our column in an attempt to hide themselves from Allied fighters. Everything that moved was being attacked in those days. Several times over the next few weeks we had to dive into ditches as the fighters swooped down and strafed us. A few of our men died in the attacks, leaving the rest of us with a feeling of helpless rage at our own pilots, but mostly at the Germans for keeping us on this pointless march.

We made a slow arc south-east from Bremen towards the Elbe River. There were rumours our guards had orders to shoot us if we didn't reach the Elbe by a certain date. Even if that were true I doubt they would have followed through. Our senior officers had warned them they'd be held accountable for their actions after the war.

Other than counting heads, the guards didn't bother us much any more. We were free to wander off and forage in fields for forgotten vegetables, and to trade our cigarettes and what little else we had with farmers. Life was generally becoming more bearable now that the weather was warming up.

One day another prisoner and I approached a farm house where, with the use of sign language, we got permission from the woman who opened the door to wash up at the outdoor water pump. We were standing there buck naked, lathering up with Lux soap from a Red Cross parcel, when she walked over holding a grainy, greasy-looking bar of home-made soap. She gestured to show the difference between her soap and ours. When we handed her the Lux she smelled it and began to cry. We got eggs, bread and a slab of mouldy cheese for that single bar of Lux.

A few days later, as our column straggled through a small town, a young boy passed by on his way home with a jug full of beer. I stopped him and offered a pack of Camels for the jug. The kid's face lit up and he grabbed the pack out of my hand. At that point cigarettes were about the only currency left in Germany.

After a few of us finished off the jug we went down the road in the direction he had come from and found the local tavern. Several packages of cigarettes kept the old man behind the bar pouring beer for the rest of the afternoon. In my weakened state even that wartime brew went straight to my head and for the first time since before the start of the march I felt genuinely happy to be alive.

We were on the move almost constantly, rarely stopping for more than a day or two in one place. Exhausted Germans trudged by on their way west to surrender to the Americans or British rather than the Russians. Tagging behind were refugees carrying everything they owned in baby carriages and wooden carts.

By the end of April we had marched back into northern Germany to farm land near the city of Lubeck, not more than two hundred miles from where we had begun the march three months earlier. They had put us through all that misery just to bring us back almost to where we started.

A guard told us President Roosevelt was dead. I read later that Hitler and Goebbels celebrated when they heard the news, believing it might be the miracle they'd been hoping for to stave off defeat. But it was obvious our guard and every other German we passed on the road had long ago given up hope.

The end had to be close now.

CHAPTER
10

LIBERATION

I was one of the first to wake up the morning of our liberation, May 2. I'd left the barn where we were sleeping to answer the call of nature. A severe case of dysentery had sent me on the same trip several times during the night. By now I was about thirty pounds under my normal weight and weak as a kitten.

On the way back I noticed that our guards had disappeared. Another fellow who had just gotten up and I decided to have a look around. When we had walked a few hundred feet along the tree-lined road away from the barn we could hear the sound of armoured vehicles. Then through the trees we saw what we thought were artillery guns.

"I think those are ours," I remember saying. The other fellow and I looked at one another for a moment, and then we both started shouting. "Over here! We're friends! Don't shoot!"

Seconds later several British soldiers emerged from behind the trees with big grins on their faces. We pumped their hands and slapped their backs as other Brits came out of the woods. The rest of the men who had been in the barn were awake by now and started streaming towards us. Everyone was laughing and embracing. A few were crying.

After things settled down the Brits, part of the 12th Armoured Corps, told us our guards had walked to their lines several hours before and surrendered. They were being held in a British prison camp closer to Lubeck.

One of the guards assigned to our group after the prisoners of Luft III had been scattered at Spremberg was the scowling tower guard who had taken such pleasure in shooting the Canadian who had gone into no-man's land for our softball.

"There's a score we'd like to settle with one of the bastards," a member of our group said to the British officer who was in charge of moving us to the rear. "Would that be possible?"

The fellow who'd spoken up was driven to the camp where the guards were being held. He told us later that after identifying our man he watched as the German was immediately taken out to a field and shot. Justice was swift in the last days of the war. We all thought that guard got exactly what he deserved.

Five days later, while waiting at an airfield for transport to England, I heard the news that the Germans had surrendered. I was happy, of course. But it all seemed anticlimactic. For me the war had ended back on that road near Lubeck.

At the RCAF hospital in Bournemouth I was put on extra rations, the same food and portions given to pregnant women. Although the dysentery stayed with me for a few more weeks, I slowly started to regain my strength and put on weight. It was flabby weight, though. I'd lost all my muscle tone during my time in Luft III and on the march.

The doctors said I was in fairly good shape physically, much better than many other prisoners. It was my nerves that were troubling me more than anything now.

"I'm sorry to have to tell you they're all dead," an RCAF records officer in Bournemouth told me when I requested information about my missing crewmates.

"Four of them drowned after bailing out. The body of Flying Officer Young was found in the aircraft."

Until that moment I'd forced myself to believe that somehow they'd pulled through like George Gill and I had. My first thought was that I knew why Bob Young, our young English flight engineer, hadn't jumped. Bob was deathly afraid of the water. When the time came he probably couldn't force himself out of the plane. Or he might have hesitated until it was too late.

The news of my crewmates sent me reeling. Maybe it was knowing that everything that happened had been a simple matter of chance or fate, whatever you want to call it. Why had George and I survived when they hadn't? If that Danish fishing boat hadn't come along when it did, we wouldn't have made it either. Over the next few days I kept thinking of the skipper, Courtney and the rest of them. About what great guys they'd been. I had trouble accepting that they were gone.

I decided to pay my sister Viola and her husband Mac a surprise visit before boarding my ship to Canada. My visits with them had always helped me unwind in the past. I wanted to see them one last time and to retrieve my personal belongings, which had been sent to them after I'd gone missing.

Their neighbourhood in North London was barely recognizable as I made my way towards their house. Dozens of buildings were flattened. I started to panic and began running up their street. Then I stopped and stared. The roof of their house was almost completely missing. God, were my sister and her family dead too?

Just then I saw Viola, Mac and young Wayne walking towards me from down the street. My sister and I hugged as they told me what had happened. The damage had been done by the next-to-last V-2 rocket, the latest of Hitler's miracle weapons, to fall on England during the war. They'd been asleep when the rocket exploded. Miraculously, all three came through with barely a scratch.

In the rubble they'd found one of the officer's uniforms I'd taken such pride in having made when I was on leave in

Toronto. Viola showed it to me. It was a rag now, with holes all through it. I told her not to worry. I didn't need it anyway.

Irene was waiting as my train pulled into Union Station. She was as excited to see me as I'd hoped, although she was startled by my appearance. Two large carbuncles that had appeared during the march still clung stubbornly to my neck.

Just as I'd feared in the letter I wrote to Irene from Luft III, it was obvious my readjustment back to civilian life was going to take time. Every little sound made me jump when we went walking on downtown Yonge Street. There were too many people, too much confusion. What seemed strangest of all was that things looked exactly the way I remembered them, as if the war had never happened.

After two days with Irene I went north to see my family in Penetang. Not more than two weeks later telegrams began arriving from Connie Mack, urging me to rejoin the team as soon as possible.

I ignored them at first. No way did I feel up to playing ball. All I wanted was peace, a long rest and time to forget. Every night I was jolted awake by nightmares, the sweat pouring off me. During the day I walked the town visiting old friends. It felt good being home. Secure. At that point I wasn't sure I ever wanted to leave.

Finally, Mack reached me by telephone. "Maybe you won't be able to pitch this season," the familiar high-pitched voice came over the line, "but it will do you good to be back with your team-mates. You have to think of your future. The sooner you get back into training the sooner you can get on with your career."

I have to admit I felt flattered the Old Man was so anxious to have me back. I'd been his ace in 1942 and no one had arrived in the meantime to take my place. Those seventeen wins were still the highest mark reached by any Athletics pitcher since 1935.

As he talked I started to think that maybe Mack was right.

Baseball was my livelihood, after all. He did say he didn't necessarily expect me to play. Just to work out at my own pace and get used to being back in the big leagues. It couldn't hurt to find out what kind of shape my arm was in.

I found myself agreeing to join the team several days later in Chicago. Irene tried to get me to change my mind, but in the end I felt I really had no choice. Who was I to say no to Connie Mack?

The team was having breakfast in the dining-room of their hotel when I walked in on July 6. Al Simmons and Earle Brucker rushed over to shake my hand and welcome me back. Mack rose from his table. "It's good to see you, Phil," he said. "I'm glad you're here."

Now eighty-two, the Old Man had hardly changed at all. He stood ramrod straight and his voice and hands were as as steady as before the war. Mack was still managing the team as well as running the front office on a daily basis. All the important decisions were his, just as they always had been. It seemed like he would go on forever.

Many of the faces around the tables were unfamiliar to me. Only Dick Siebert and Russ Christopher remained from the old gang. A few of the others I recognized from spring training tryouts or as September call-ups. Most of my old team-mates were still in the military.

One thing that hadn't changed was the team's position in the standings. Heading into that afternoon's game with the White Sox, the A's stood in last place with a record of 21–45, nineteen-and-a-half back of first-place Detroit. Towards the end of June the team had suffered through a twelve-game losing skid.

At Comiskey Park that afternoon I ran on the sidelines and did some light tossing with Earle Brucker. It was clear I had a long way to come back. My legs and arm felt weak, and I was winded after working out for just a few minutes.

"Nice and easy," Brucker kept saying. "The worst thing you can do is to try to rush back." He figured that if we slowly built up my strength and I worked hard through the winter, I might be ready by the following spring.

Every day I did my running and tossing, then sat back on the bench and watched as the team usually lost another one. The 1942 Athletics of Indian Bob Johnson, Sam Chapman and the rest had been a power-house compared to this squad. If this was what the war had done to baseball then I was almost glad I'd been away.

The new star of the team was the one and only Bobo Newsom, who joined the A's in 1944 after playing for the Dodgers, Browns and Senators the year before. Bobo was having his troubles. After notching his first victory April 21, he suffered through twelve consecutive defeats. At the end of the season his record was 8–20, yet his ERA was a more than respectable 3.29. That should tell you something about how bad the team behind him was.

Bobo was still being Bobo, never failing to touch both sides of the third-base line for luck, kicking dirt on the mound, arguing aloud to himself, quarrelling with umpires and challenging opposing batters to fights he had no intention of finishing. He was without a doubt the greatest showman in the game, a man who lived to be in the spotlight.

Bobo was also the only player I ever saw who could get away with talking back to the Old Man. Mack would just laugh it off, as if Newsom was some big, incorrigible kid who needed special attention and consideration. Only Bobo was allowed to take his wife on road trips. The soft-spoken, beautifully dressed Mrs Newsom seemed an unlikely match for the boisterous Bobo, but the two were inseparable. Mack probably figured that having her along was the only sure way to keep Bobo out of trouble.

My team-mates were gradually getting me caught up on what I'd missed while I was away. They all agreed the strangest aspect of wartime baseball was spring training, which was held in the north from 1943 on after federal authorities cut non-essential rail travel. The first camp I'd missed was held in Wilmington, Delaware, where the guys had a snowball fight on opening day. I heard how a total of six fans had turned out for a game between the A's and the University of Delaware.

Mack shifted the camp to the town of Frederick, Maryland,

for the next two springs. There, in the Blue Mountains, the weather was so bad the Old Man ordered horse-drawn sleighs to transport the players to indoor workouts at the local YMCA. When the weather improved, Mack made them walk the mile to the local ballpark, leading the way himself.

It wasn't always easy finding a game among the locals. The A's beat a semipro aircraft plant team 20–0. Less impressive was their 7–1 victory over the Frederick Hustlers, a squad the *Philadelphia Inquirer* said was made up of "a grocery clerk, a baggage man, a salesman, two schoolboys, a serviceman on furlough and four young, married men."

Newsom managed to convince Mack he'd be better off training at his home in South Carolina than in the north and missed the first few weeks of camp the two years he'd been with the team. Towards the end of the 1945 pre-season, Bobo called Mack and is supposed to have told him, "I read in the papers that your men haven't been doing so good so far. I guess I'd better come up and help you out. I'll be in Baltimore to pitch Sunday and I'll win twenty games for you this year. I've been running over the hills and pitching to the high-school kids."

Just as promised, that Sunday Bobo, accompanied by his wife and three dogs, wheeled his luxury automobile—equipped with neon lights that spelled "Bobo"—into the parking lot outside the ballpark. In three innings of work against the International League Orioles, he surrendered two runs.

By the time I rejoined the club in July, Bobo was well on his way to twenty *losses*, not wins like he'd promised the Old Man. To be fair, though, I don't think Cy Young himself could have won twenty pitching for that team.

My nerves continued to bother me my first few weeks back with the A's. My hands shook as if I had palsy and I was constantly on edge. My biggest struggle was overcoming the leftover fear that something terrible was about to happen. On every mission I'd spent hours scanning the sky for night fighters, always fearing the worst. During the march I never knew what to expect. One of our own planes could swoop down at any moment and strafe our column. Or a guard might shoot me because he was in a bad mood that day.

People kept commenting on how much I'd changed. A reporter who interviewed me wrote: "Yesterday as I sat beside him on the A's bench he brushed his hands over his forehead, pulled at his fingernails, scratched his chin, rubbed his eyes, constantly shifted his legs from one side to the other, squirmed in his seat and stopped and started conversations."

"I was on my way to the ballpark and suddenly something seemed to grab at my nerves," I told the interviewer. "I wanted to pick up a brick and toss it through a window."

No one around me seemed to understand the emotions I was experiencing. It was strange to see my team-mates indulging in the usual horseplay while there was still a war going on. When they did ask me about my experiences, someone would usually interrupt with a wisecrack.

"What date did you say you went down?" Bobo Newsom spoke up after I'd been asked to tell the story of our final mission.

"August 17," I answered.

"That was Connie Mack Night in Philadelphia," Bobo said. "That night the Yankees shot me down."

Newsom was constantly making cracks that got under my skin, belittling me in front of my team-mates. Maybe he was jealous because of the attention my return had been given in the Philadelphia papers. Or he could have been worried that once I got in shape I would take his place as the team's top pitcher.

Finally I told him to keep quiet or I'd be happy to shut his mouth for him. After that we got along fine. That was Bobo, all bluster. He really wasn't a bad guy. His problem was he just didn't know when to shut up.

Bobo had stepped over the line. But I had no right to blame my other team-mates for acting exactly the way ballplayers always had. Most of the fellows I'd played with before the war were still in the service. For the players who stayed behind—the 4-Fs rejected by the military, the aging veterans—life had gone on pretty much as it always had. I was the one who had changed.

Over the next few weeks I slowly began to unwind and enjoy life again. "I realize that if Greenberg hits me for a homer,

I'll still be able to go back to the hotel, eat a good meal, see a movie and laugh about the whole thing the next morning," I was quoted on one of my good days.

Even some of my team-mates' jokes were beginning to seem funny. Earle Brucker often asked me what the war had been like.

"Those Germans were taking a hell of a shellacking," I was saying about the raid on Bremen I'd seen while a prisoner. "When those Lancasters dropped their loads the ground rocked under us like a canoe."

"Bombings, huh!" Brucker laughed. "It couldn't have been any worse than our ninth innings."

It helped to have a sense of humour when you were with the A's. At one point in August our pitching staff was so threadbare from injuries and a general lack of talent that Newsom, always looking for the spotlight, went to Mack and offered to start both ends of a doubleheader in Detroit. There hadn't been a doubleheader victor since Cleveland's Dutch Levsen accomplished the feat in 1926. The rest of us thought he was crazy to put such a strain on his arm, but the big guy came through. Bobo pitched almost fifteen innings in the two games as we split with the Tigers.

There was one player on our ball club destined for the Hall of Fame, although none of us would have guessed it at the time. When third baseman George Kell came up with the A's towards the end of the 1943 season, both Mack and Al Simmons concluded he'd never be a major-league hitter. What they did like was his glove and arm. Kell was like a cat on his feet, jumping on bunts, making incredible grabs behind the bag.

A friendly, round-faced kid, Kell stuck with the A's on the strength of his defence and because there was no one else around during the war years to challenge him for the job. Mack finally traded him to Detroit for outfielder Barney McCosky in May of 1946.

With Detroit, Kell immediately blossomed into one of the game's best hitters, batting over .300 in eight consecutive seasons. I thought he was one of the toughest outs in the league.

Most batters like to get into a comfortable groove in the box. Not Kell. He'd change positions as many as four times in one at-bat. He was also a master of using the entire field, driving the ball to open spaces with one of the lightest bats in the game.

In 1949, Kell denied Ted Williams his third triple crown by edging him for the batting title on the last day of the season. A double and a single in three at-bats put Kell's average at .3429, while Williams, who went hitless that day, finished at .3428.

Like Williams in 1941, Kell refused to sit out even one at-bat. In the ninth he took his place in the on-deck circle, knowing an out would give Williams the title. But the game ended before he could bat when the Tiger at the plate hit into a double play. The next season Kell became one of the few modern hitters to drive in over a hundred runs while hitting fewer than ten homers.

Mack was big enough to admit he'd made a mistake in trading Kell. Hank Majeski, who took over third base for us in 1946, was a .279 career hitter who couldn't cover nearly as much ground.

I've sometimes wondered how much of a difference Kell would have made if he'd still been in our lineup a couple seasons later when the Old Man finally put together a winning ball club. It's just possible that trade cost Mack his chance at the final pennant he told everyone he desperately wanted to win.

With the Japanese surrender on August 14 the war that had lasted almost six years and cost millions of lives came to an end. On a personal level the war had forced me into most of the worst experiences of my life and cut three prime years out of my baseball career. Yet I've never regretted joining the RCAF or refusing the chance to stay safely behind in Canada. Like most vets, I'm proud of having done my duty when called.

It was early August when Mack dropped his bombshell. "We're having a day for you when we get back to Philadelphia," he told me. "I want you to start."

I'd honestly expected to stay on the sidelines for the remainder of the season. I knew I wasn't ready to pitch. So did Brucker. Everyone on the team thought it was too soon.

I wish I could say that Mack was just trying to do something nice for me to mark my return from the war. But the A's were on their way to a 52–98 record and attendance was down. I'm sure he figured that by heavily advertising my return he'd get one of the biggest crowds of the year at Shibe. With Mack money always talked.

I know for a fact that Al Simmons tried to talk him out of bringing me back so soon. Simmons told me he even suggested to Mack that I be sent to Florida on an extended vacation to regain my strength. I can just imagine the Old Man's reaction to that.

At the time I didn't see that I had much choice in the matter. Once again it came down to the simple fact that Mack was the boss. In those days players had to do what they were told. It wasn't possible to play out my option and sign with another team. Mack was such an influential figure in the game that it was entirely within his power to banish me from baseball altogether if I displeased him.

Now I wish I'd been a little less agreeable. Maybe if I'd stood my ground and refused to play the Old Man would have gotten fed up and traded me. Every other team in the majors would have been happy to take a chance on a pitcher who had won seventeen games in his last complete season.

I stepped up the tempo of my workouts. The plan was for me to get in at least one relief appearance before my start on Phil Marchildon Night, scheduled for Wednesday, August 29.

My return came August 17 in Cleveland, exactly one year from the day our plane was shot down. Newsom started for us, pitching well until the fourth when he was tagged for the tying run. On the bench between innings Bobo complained of a stomach-ache and Mack called me in from the bullpen.

"Nice and easy," Brucker said for about the thousandth time since I'd come back. "Don't worry about anything. It's not like we're in a pennant race." I laughed, took a deep breath and trotted in to the mound.

In two innings of work I allowed four runs on two hits, four walks and a wild pitch. I even made a fielding error on a routine ground ball. I took the loss as the Indians went on to win 6–4.

What was encouraging was the fact that the next day my arm felt fine—a little tired, maybe, but there was no soreness. My legs hadn't responded nearly so well. They felt wobbly for days afterward. That worried me. It's just about impossible for a pitcher, or any athlete, to be effective once the legs go. A pitcher needs strong legs to be able to push off the mound and get momentum on his pitches.

My thirty-second birthday was fast approaching and I couldn't help wondering how complete my physical recovery was likely to be. I sure didn't feel like a kid anymore.

Throughout the summer, ballplayers who'd been in the military were rejoining their old teams. On August 24, in his first game after returning from the Navy, Bob Feller threw a four-hit victory over the Tigers in Cleveland. Feller fanned the first Tiger he faced and eleven more. Briggs Stadium in Detroit had been packed for Hank Greenberg's homecoming from the Army July 1. Greenberg responded with a home run and then led the Tigers down the stretch as they fought Washington for the pennant.

With Detroit needing a win against the Browns on the final day of the season to prevent a play-off with the Senators, Greenberg iced the pennant with a grand-slam homer in the ninth. Detroit went on to take the World Series from the Cubs in seven games.

On our own club, Dick Fowler showed up in late August when his service as an infantryman in the 48th Highlanders was over. Sam Chapman was released from the Navy Air Force in early September. The two had probably been my closest friends on the team and now that they were back I realized how much I'd missed them.

I tried to keep my nerves under control as the big night at Shibe drew closer. The Philadelphia fans had been so supportive since my return that I was afraid of disappointing them. They were always calling out encouragement from the stands when they saw me throwing in the bullpen or doing my running before a game. My autograph seemed to be more in demand than ever among the kids.

Everyone was feeling such an immense sense of pride in the Allied victory and relief that the war was finally over that I think a lot of my popularity was simply the result of being in the right place at the right time. There was also the fact that unlike many American big-leaguers, who were kept safely behind the lines playing baseball exhibitions for the troops, I'd been on active service. The fans appreciated the difference.

When the night of the tribute finally arrived and I was standing at home plate listening to the A's announcer Byrum Saam recount the details of my career and war service, I found myself thinking again of my lost crewmates. There I was receiving the applause of over 19,000 fans when I could just have easily died that night with them. None of it made a lot of sense.

Saam brought me abruptly back to reality by calling me to the microphone and handing me a $1,000 Victory Bond on behalf of the team. Now that was a shocker. Mack had actually reached into his pocket to show me proof of his appreciation.

At that moment I was ready to rethink my opinion of Mack as a tightwad and look upon him as the benevolent old gentleman the public thought him to be. But it wasn't long before I reminded myself that Mack hadn't thought to pay me a bonus for winning seventeen games in 1942 and that now, with no concern for my physical condition, he was using me as a gate attraction. How many extra thousands of dollars was he pulling in that night because of me? Mack owed me every penny of that $1,000 and more.

Don't ask me what I said when it came time to make my speech. I was so nervous I'm amazed I was able to get any words out. It was basically just a short thank you.

Considering everything, I pitched pretty well against Washington that night. The next day one Philadelphia paper called it "five magnificent innings" of work. I'd allowed two hits and one run into the fifth when exactly what I'd feared happened. Reaching down to field a ground ball, I pivoted to make the throw and felt a stabbing pain that stretched from my right knee to my groin.

There was no question of my continuing in the game. I could barely walk. The next day the area around the injury was blood red. Our trainer taped me from just above my knee to the waist.

Despite the injury, I was enthusiastic after the game. Everything had been working for me. My fastball was jumping and the curve had all its old snap. For the first time I was convinced that I'd be able to make a successful comeback. I could hardly wait for the next spring.

I was so encouraged I foolishly decided to ignore my injury and start another game four days later against Boston. After two innings it was obvious I couldn't continue and Mack pulled me for a pinch-hitter. That ended my season.

The depression that followed me home from the war had almost disappeared by now. As the team played out the final weeks of the season, I was content to sit back and plan my future. There was a certain question I intended to ask Irene as soon as I got back to Toronto.

On September 9 I watched Dick Fowler make history as he became the first—and still only—Canadian to throw a no-hitter in the big leagues. He shut down the Browns at Shibe in his first start in nearly three seasons. One of the most modest men I've ever known, Dick always said his no-hitter was mostly a matter of luck.

"I came out of the Canadian Army and I was hog fat, at least thirty-five pounds overweight," he told a reporter a couple of years later. "For eight full innings it was a scoreless ball game. I retired them at the top of the ninth to sew up a no-hitter, but I was so dead tired from lugging all the weight around that I knew I'd never be able to pitch the tenth inning if we didn't get a run in our half of the ninth.

"Well, I was sitting under the stands behind the dugout, smoking a cigarette and trying to catch my breath, when Hal Peck led off our ninth with a triple. Irv Hall was next and when he rapped a single into centre field the ball game was over and I'd pitched a no-hitter. I can honestly say I was never in worse shape in my life. I have no explanation for it. It just happened."

As we mobbed him after the game, Dick had a dazed look on his face and a big goofy grin. A group of us went out and celebrated with a few beers at a local tavern.

It took me a while to work up my courage, but I finally proposed to Irene while we were watching a movie at Shea's Theatre in downtown Toronto. When I blurted out the question Irene laughed and said yes right away. Now neither of us can remember what movie was playing.

We were married November 16 in St John's chapel of St Michael's Cathedral. After a short honeymoon in Ottawa, we split the rest of the winter between Irene's mother's house in Toronto and my brother Pivot's place in Penetang. Almost every day when we were up north I went cross-country skiing to build up the strength in my legs. When Irene told me she was pregnant I added an extra mile to my route.

Now that I had a growing family to support I was more determined than ever to regain my place as the ace of the Athletics' staff. I'd win so many games Mack would have no choice but to finally pay me what I was worth.

CHAPTER
11

COMEBACK YEAR

"But I won seventeen games in 1942," I remember stammering to Connie Mack when we finally sat down to discuss my contract for the 1946 season.

"That was a long time ago," the Old Man answered. "I can't tell how you'll pitch. You're older now and you've been away three years."

He was offering me a raise to $7,500 from my last pre-war salary of $4,500. I had a pretty good idea that I was still the best pitcher Mack had and figured he was at least a couple thousand short. I told him I was willing to settle for $8,500.

"I can't pay you that," Mack said. "You have a bad leg. You're also going to get a late start on the season because you're so late reporting to camp."

At that moment I felt like reaching across the desk and

strangling the cheap old bastard. The reason I had a bad leg was that he had forced me to pitch before I was ready. And I was late reporting to the A's camp because I'd been holding out until he offered me something close to a fair salary.

After several more minutes of telling me how unreasonable I was, Mack finally agreed to review my salary in June. If I was pitching well, he'd give me the extra thousand I was asking for.

My hold-out was big news in the Philadelphia papers. After our session the reporters cornered Mack for a quote.

"I want Marchildon to show me he can pitch somewhere near as well as he did before he went to war," he said. "He doesn't have to win so often, because with our club that wouldn't be easy, but I want to be satisfied that he can still do good work and then I'll pay him plenty."

Needless to say, Mack's idea of "plenty" never matched the expectations I and the rest of his players had. There's the story I heard of a wartime Athletic who went in to discuss his new contract. The figure written in was so low the player thought there must have been a mistake.

"The Old Man started crying about how attendance was down and how poor he was, and I actually started to feel sorry for him," the ballplayer remembered. "I took a half-dollar out of my pocket and said, 'Here, Mr Mack, go and buy yourself a nice breakfast.'"

The knowledge that we were one of the lowest-paid teams in baseball grated on all of us. I remember how angry several of us were a season or so later when we compared salaries with Tiger pitchers during a game at Briggs Stadium in Detroit. In those days the bullpens at Briggs were side by side and the players would banter back and forth.

A Tiger pitcher who was only the third or fourth starter on the staff told me he was making several thousand dollars more than me. On down the line it went. To a man our pitchers were paid far less than players of comparable talents and experience on the Tigers.

Not that any of the teams back then were throwing their money around. Thanks to the "reserve clause" that was in every contract until the courts ruled it illegal in the 1970s, players had no option but to take what the owners were offering. Either that or quit the game.

The Yankees even tried to get Joe DiMaggio to agree to a $5,000 cut in pay after his magnificent 1941 season. Imagine the nerve of that. The Clipper had just hit in fifty-six straight games and led the Yanks to a World Series title. General manager Ed Barrow's reasoning was that there was a war on now and everyone had to make sacrifices. But somehow I doubt Barrow thought it necessary to cut his own salary.

Several well-known big-leaguers found it impossible to say no when Mexican millionaire Jorge Pasquel offered them contracts that seemed huge in comparison to what they'd been making to play in the newly formed Mexican League. Mickey Owen and outfielder Luis Olmo of the Dodgers signed on; so did second baseman Lou Klein of the Cardinals and pitcher Sal Maglie of the Giants. Attempting to establish instant credibility for his league, Pasquel offered Stan Musial a $65,000 advance and a multi-year deal worth in excess of $100,000 per year. Somehow Musial found the strength to turn Pasquel down.

No one came knocking on my door with a bag full of pesos, so I didn't have to face the temptation of making the jump. It was just as well. Most of the players who went to Mexico complained about the heat, the food and the primitive playing conditions. Mickey Owen tried to rejoin the Dodgers later that summer but, along with everyone else who had gone south, was barred from organized ball for five years by Commissioner Happy Chandler, who had taken over in 1945 after the death of Landis. Chandler later relented slightly, letting some of the jumpers come back in 1949.

Using the threat of the Mexican League as leverage, the players took the first steps towards forming the union that evolved into the powerful Major League Players Association of today. Though it doesn't seem like a very impressive list of concessions now, I can remember how excited we all were when, after season-long negotiations, the owners agreed to a minimum major-league salary of $5,000; a guarantee that a player could receive no more than a 25 percent cut in pay from one season to the next; incidental expenses in spring training of $25 per week; up to $500 in moving expenses for a player traded during the season; and a promise that injured players would receive their full salary for that year plus medical expenses.

From such humble beginnings came the multi-million-dollar contracts and all the other perks enjoyed by today's players. I wonder how many of them have even the slightest idea of how their fortunes got started.

Because of my contract squabble with Mack, I was almost three weeks late reporting to camp in West Palm Beach, where the Athletics had set up base now that the war was over. I'd been cross-country skiing all winter so I was in reasonably good shape. Even so, it took me most of that first full season to get back my leg strength. Many of the players who had been away in the military had the same complaint.

"I'm not so concerned about making a comeback, not if I can get my legs in shape," said Joe DiMaggio, who struggled to a .290 average in an injury-plagued season. "If your legs are right, your timing is right and everything else falls into line." After a great first half, Charlie Keller said his legs ran out of gas down the stretch.

It was wonderful having Irene along with me in Florida. We'd only been married a few months and we wanted to spend every moment we could together. Being a firm believer in the benefits of family life, Mack encouraged the players to bring their wives along. Irene hit the beach while I was at the ballpark. In the evenings back at the motel, we'd get together with the Chapmans, the Fowlers and several other team-mates and their wives for a barbecue and a game of shuffleboard.

The A's were a tightly knit group. Our kids got together for birthday parties and many of the wives were close friends. Few of my team-mates put down roots in Philadelphia, staying only for the duration of the baseball season. So it was only natural for us to socialize within our own little community.

When we were playing a series in New York, Irene, Joyce Fowler and sometimes Jodi Chapman would make the short train ride to meet us for dinner and a show. Most often we started out at Toots Shor's restaurant in mid-town Manhattan, a favourite hangout for celebrities.

Gossip columnist Walter Winchell had a table in the centre of the room near the entrance. Joe DiMaggio was a regular. So were film stars, Broadway actors and gorgeous show girls. Toots was a huge, gregarious man who always had a cigar in his hand and welcomed everyone like royalty. But he was known to be especially fond of ballplayers. Whenever he saw us he'd reach into his pocket and come out with complimentary front-row tickets to the hottest show on Broadway.

Tommy Henrich tells the story of how Toots was at the door one time greeting Sir Alexander Fleming, the discoverer of penicillin. Suddenly New York Giant great Mel Ott walked through the door. "Excuse me," Toots said to Sir Alex. "Somebody important just walked in."

Even with our late arrival in Florida, my comeback was pretty much on schedule. My arm was feeling good and my leg, while still a little tender from the injury the season before, was coming along. I expected to be able to take my regular turn in the rotation by the start of the season.

Right then just about the stupidest prank I've ever seen set me back several weeks and could have cost me my career. We had an outfielder in camp from South Carolina who liked to carry a knife and demonstrate to everyone who would watch how skilful he was with it. A group of us were sitting at a table having lunch when he pulled out his blade and started flashing it around. The next thing I knew blood was flowing out of a deep gash on the index finger of my pitching hand.

Mack was furious when he heard about the accident. He threatened to banish the ballplayer from baseball for cutting his star pitcher. In fact, the southerner played only nine more games for us and then was gone from the big leagues for good. I can't say for certain that Mack got rid of him because of what he did to me, but that was the feeling around the ball club.

The cut was slow in healing and I didn't make my first start of the season until May 17 in Detroit, when I lost a tough one to Virgil Trucks 3–1. Mack expressed relief about my performance to the press. "Yes, Phil looked mighty good out there. He's ready to take his regular turn now. He and Bobo should be a tough combination to beat. Now if the others perk up, our club won't be too bad."

Mack didn't know it yet but by this point old Bobo had taken just about all he could of playing for the hapless Athletics. On June 3 he asked the Old Man for his unconditional release.

"I'm no longer a frying-sized chicken," said the thirty-seven-year-old Bobo, who signed with Washington for the third time in his career a few days later. "I'm getting along in years and I want to make the best of the seasons I have left. I think a change will do me good. I really haven't been getting the breaks. I figure I'm still a good pitcher and Mr Mack didn't want me to go but said he would give me my release if I insisted."

I wondered if Mr Mack would be kind enough to give me my release if I asked. But something told me Bobo hadn't had to argue too hard to get the Old Man to release him from his $20,000 annual salary. I, on the other hand, was still working for bargain wages.

After I lost my next four games—two by 2–0 scores and two by one run—it was nice to know that I wasn't alone in my frustration. The *Philadelphia Inquirer* ran the following item:

"From far-off Sudbury, Ontario, Joseph MacDonald, Sandlot Baseball Commissioner for Northern Ontario, wired the sports editor of the *Philadelphia Inquirer* yesterday, asking the latter to advise Connie Mack that Phil Marchildon, a graduate of the Northern Ontario League, needs more hitting from his A's team-mates....Mr MacDonald concluded by stating Marchildon had to win games in Ontario without substantial swatting help, but he should get help now that he's in the majors."

My first win in more than three years finally came Friday, June 7 at Shibe in relief of Luman Harris, when I threw hitless ball in the eighth and ninth against the Browns to nail down a

5–4 win. From that point on things got a little easier. Going into the All-Star break my record was four and seven.

While the American League was pounding the National League 12–0 at Fenway Park July 9, Irene was in hospital in Philadelphia giving birth to our daughter Carol. The timing couldn't possibly have been better. Because of the break I was able to take Irene to the hospital and be right there when they wheeled her and our beautiful new baby girl out of the delivery room.

Irene, who had been listening to the game on the radio while she was in the early stages of labour, always called Carol our "All-Star Baby."

Just before the break I'd beat the pennant-bound Red Sox on a seven-hitter, and then in my next start I threw a two-hit win over Chicago. Funny thing, though. Connie Mack hadn't yet called me in to discuss the raise he'd promised if I proved I could still pitch. How much convincing did he need?

The writers kept asking me if the Old Man had come across with the cash. At first I told them to wait on the story, not wanting to make Mack angry by seeming to pressure him. Finally I got fed up and told the writers to go ahead and ask him themselves.

The next day Mack called me into his office and gave me the extra thousand. "I'm satisfied with your work," he said simply. "You've earned this raise."

Although they didn't always get their stories quite straight and I could have done without them referring to me as Froggy Phil in print, the Philadelphia writers treated me fairly. There was a different relationship between players and reporters in those days. They didn't try very hard to be objective. Most were unapologetic home-town boosters who bent over backwards to keep both the players and management happy.

Notable exceptions were the writers in New York and Boston, two cities where so many newspapers competed for the same audience that writers felt they had to be muckrakers in order to get their stories read. Ted Williams had a career-long feud with certain members of the Boston press who got on him for being a so-called draft dodger and complained that he never seemed to hit when it really counted—like in the 1946 World Series.

I always found that as long as I was honest and open with the Philadelphia writers I could trust them completely. They generally tried to make players, even the nasty ones they might have enjoyed cutting down to size, look like heroes. Some reporters almost seemed like employees of the club. They travelled and ate with us, usually at the team's expense, and they knew that if they consistently wrote items that displeased Mr Mack or the players their access could very quickly be cut off.

A lot of us old-timers have fond memories of sitting for long hours in the club cars of trains swapping stories with other players and the writers. The writers were part of the natural scenery and sometimes became close friends. When you were slumping, they agonized right along with you and even tried to keep the fans off your back by putting the best possible slant on your troubles.

I feel sorry for modern big-leaguers who travel everywhere by airplane. Air travel doesn't always allow players to get enough sleep or enable them to develop the closeness with the writers and each other that we had back in the days of train travel. After a night game a team today might not make it out to the airport until midnight or later, and then not arrive in the next city until four in the morning. It's impossible to be at your best on the field when you've only had four or five hours of sleep.

We never had that problem on the trains. Once you learned how to sleep in those tight berths and got used to the clickety-clack of the wheels, you could count on getting your eight hours. If the train arrived at our destination in the night or early morning, it was side-tracked so that we could sleep undisturbed until breakfast.

It was a plush way to travel. You could sit back and relax and watch the scenery go by, or get into one of the games of hearts, poker and gin rummy that were almost always in progress. But mostly there was time to discuss the one subject that interested us all more than anything else in the world—baseball. Al Simmons and the other coaches would tell tales about Babe

Ruth, Ty Cobb and other famous stars they had known. We discussed strategy, debated the strengths and weaknesses of the team we were about to play, and gave each other suggestions about improving our games.

Modern players miss out on so much of that travelling by airplane. There's not as much time to think and talk about the game, and maybe to get as much sheer enjoyment from being major-league ballplayers.

For a fact, we ate a lot better on the train than today's players do on any airline. It was like sitting around your mother's table for Sunday dinner. Porters in white suits served thick steaks, stews and chops in huge portions. Real silverware, linen tablecloths and vases filled with freshly cut flowers were set on every table. A lot of players said they ate better on the road than they did at home with their wives.

Train travel also provided the opportunity for players with nothing better to do to organize practical jokes. The most elaborate one I ever saw took place before the war when we were making the long trip from St Louis back to the east coast. In those days the Mississippi was the western limit of the major leagues.

There was a fellow on the team who rarely said a word to the rest of us, a country boy who was just about the last person anyone could imagine getting into trouble. The train was going to be passing through his home state. One of the organizers of the gag knew a local sheriff who agreed to come on board with his deputy and pretend to arrest the player on a charge of making moonshine at a still back at his home and then transporting it across the state line.

A bottle of white lightning was placed in his travel bag and, as arranged, the sheriff and his deputy got on at one of our stops. The sheriff loudly announced he had a warrant for the country boy's arrest. The kid could hardly believe what was happening. "But I didn't do anything!" he kept protesting. "You've got the wrong man!"

His luggage was brought out and searched. When the sheriff came up with the bottle of moonshine he ordered his deputy to clap the handcuffs on our team-mate, who was almost crying by now. "Get Mr Mack!" he was yelling. "Get Mr Mack! Don't let them take me away!"

Everyone managed to keep a straight face while all this was going on. Finally, someone cracked and then we all broke out laughing. The sheriff and his deputy bowed as we applauded their acting performance. After taking a few minutes to calm down, the poor kid, much to his credit, finally managed a smile and joined in the laughter.

While the team continued to struggle along in last place, where we'd been since early in the season, my own game was improving steadily. I was still more tired between starts than I remembered being before the war, but my arm felt fine and my legs were slowly getting back their strength.

My tenth win of the year came against the Tigers at Shibe August 21, a 4–1 seven-hitter. I literally threw away my chance at the shutout with two out in the third inning when, with a man on third base, I fielded a swinging bunt off the bat of George Kell and then fired the ball over our first baseman's head.

It was that kind of year. I was the lone Athletics hurler to make it into the double figures in wins. Dick Fowler had trouble getting back into shape and struggled to a 9–16 record. Luman Harris finished at 3–14. Altogether there were five pitchers who each lost fourteen or more games, which wasn't too surprising since the A's finished with a 49-105 mark, a whopping fifty-five games back of the Red Sox.

As I've said before, when you play for a club that finishes in last place year after year you take your fun where you can find it. You never want to put personal goals ahead of the team, but if your team is obviously going nowhere then there's not much else to keep you going.

One of my small ambitions as the season moved into September was to record a win over every club in the league. A 4–3 decision over the Yankees under the lights at Shibe September 4 left only Cleveland to go, an omission that was not to be corrected. I had already failed in three tries against the Indians and didn't get another start against them.

I would have felt less satisfied with my comeback year if I'd failed to beat the hated Yankees at least once. I was still smarting from my previous start against them back on June 28 at Yankee Stadium. With one on and the score tied 1–1 in the bottom of the eighth, none other than Charlie Keller strode confidently to the plate and whacked a homer to knock me out of the game. The man was really starting to get on my nerves.

New York was the one team everyone wanted to slice down to size. They always appeared so confident when they took the field, so businesslike. They even looked better than ballplayers had a right to in those tidy pinstriped suits of theirs. And they almost always kicked the hell out of us. My win at Shibe was only our fifth victory in fifteen games against the Yanks to that point in the season.

Although you wouldn't have known it to see them play us, there was a lot of loose talk around the league in 1946 that the Yankee dynasty was finally coming to an end. The Yanks finished in third place, fourteen games back of Boston, and they were without a .300 hitter for the first time since the dark days before Babe Ruth joined the franchise in 1920. Joe Gordon's average plunged to .210, and Rizzuto managed only .257. Even Tommy Henrich, the man the fans called "Old Reliable," hit just .251.

The Yanks were obviously a team in transition. There was new ownership and in May the players had been shaken by the resignation of manager Joe McCarthy after fifteen years at the helm. Bill Dickey took over, but by September he was fighting with the owners and resigned. Coach Johnny Neun ran the club on an interim basis for the remainder of the season.

As it turned out, New York was just regrouping for even better days ahead. DiMag and most of the other veterans regained their pre-war form the next year and new stars were coming up through the farm system. The two most impressive were Vic Raschi, a big, strong right-hander who would anchor the starting staff on into the 1950s, and a homely young catcher named Yogi Berra, who arrived for seven games at the end of the season and batted .364 with two home runs.

Looking back over the box score for my win against the Yankees recently I noticed something that made me nostalgic for the old days. It took us just one hour and fifty-six minutes to play that game. And it wasn't as if there were just a handful of hits. I only allowed four, but New York starter Floyd Bevens was touched for thirteen safeties by our side. Most nine-inning games were played in two hours or less back then.

I can understand people who say baseball is a boring sport. I get bored watching games that routinely last three hours and more. Fans who aren't old enough to remember the faster-paced ball games of years past don't know what they're missing.

Nowadays it seems almost every player is a hot dog. Hitters are constantly stepping out of the box to adjust their helmet and batting gloves, making certain they look just right. Every time they slide into a base they immediately call time and carefully dust themselves off. Don't they realize ballplayers are supposed to get dirty?

Maybe I sound like just another old-timer spouting off about how baseball was better in his day. But I don't think anyone can seriously question that a faster game is more entertaining.

We used to get right down to business. The umpire would give us hell if we stepped out for no apparent reason. Managers also didn't make as many pointless trips to the mound to talk to their pitchers. When one did come out it was almost certain the pitcher was going to get the hook. Players—and fans too—had to stay alert and involved in the game because things happened much more quickly.

I realize that a big reason games last longer now is to accommodate television commercials between innings. But a lot of time could be saved on the field by giving umpires the authority to force hitters to stay in the box and by limiting the amount of time pitchers can take between tosses.

To my mind, speeding up the tempo of the game is the single most important thing baseball can do to guarantee its popularity in the future. If an old hand like me gets bored watching a ball game, then something has to be wrong.

Remember how Charlie Keller complained about running out of gas in the second half? Well, he still had enough left in the tank to take me deep for his 30th homer during my last start of the season, a 7–4 loss September 22 in New York. That gave me a final record of 13–16, with 95 strikeouts, 114 walks, 16 complete games and an ERA of 3.49.

I felt I'd come almost all the way back to my pre-war form. For a better team, I might have won close to twenty. As it was, I accounted for over a quarter of the games won by the squad with the worst record in baseball.

Wilbur Wood, the sports editor of the *New York Sun*, published the results of a survey that placed me as the fifth most effective starter in the American League. Wood's rankings were based on the number of points a pitcher's personal won-and-lost percentage was above or below that of his team. Ahead of me were Bob Feller of the Indians, Spud Chandler of the Yanks, Hal Newhouser of the Tigers, and Dave "Boo" Ferris of the Red Sox.

I'd impressed the Red Sox enough that they asked me to join an All-Star squad of American League players they were organizing to play them in three tune-up games while they waited for the National League to decide a winner. Tied at the end of the regular season, the Cardinals and Dodgers were involved in the first play-off in the seventy-one-year history of the senior circuit.

There was no doubt that Boston could use the work. After being way out in front all season, they went flat in September. They had seemed listless when I threw a five-hitter to beat them at Shibe September 8. For two weeks they hauled around a supply of champagne before they finally clinched the pennant.

It was like a dream playing alongside such stars as Joe DiMaggio, Tommy Henrich, Hank Greenberg, Hal Newhouser, Dizzy Trout and Birdie Tebbetts. When I walked into the visitors' clubhouse at Fenway and saw all those famous faces I felt like a rookie again. Having played in that series helps make up for the fact that I was never chosen for a mid-season All-Star game.

The Red Sox must have regretted ever coming up with the idea of a tune-up series after Ted Williams, who was voted league MVP that year, was hit on the elbow in the opener by a pitch from Mickey Haefner of the Senators. "I tried to throw a curve to Ted, but my hands were so cold I just couldn't break it off," Haefner told us. The temperature was around the freezing mark in Boston. Williams's elbow blew up like a balloon and he went on to have a terrible post-season as the Red Sox lost to the Cardinals in seven games.

I mentioned how hard the Boston writers used to ride Williams. According to Ted's wife, Doris, the night following the injury "he was in agony." When he became restless the next day from sitting around his hotel suite, the two of them went shopping. Reporters then accused him of goofing off when he should have been getting ready to play. One even wrote that he'd gone fishing.

All proceeds from the games were supposed to be divided among the All-Stars, but the weather was so bad that only about 2,000 fans turned out for each match. I don't remember cashing a very big cheque.

I pitched three innings in the final game, allowing three hits. Maybe because there were so few people in the stands, none of us took the games very seriously. Mostly it was an opportunity to joke around and have a few laughs. Some of the Boston players told me I'd probably be playing with them next season. Joe DiMaggio said he wouldn't be surprised if I joined him in pin-stripes.

Just like before the war, rumours were flying that I was about to be traded to New York or Boston. "Either move would be fine with me," I told a Toronto reporter who caught up with me in Penetang after the season. As he interviewed me I was proudly shining the new grey Hudson sedan Irene and I had just bought. It had been quite a year: new wife, new baby, new car.

Well, on second thought, I figured maybe I would prefer Boston. New York was too big and dirty. "It sure would be a lot easier pitching behind guys like Doerr, Williams, Pesky and

DiMaggio," I said. According to the reporter, at this point I "sighed hopefully."

Over the next few months I went from sighing hopefully to actually being glad that Mack had once again resisted trading me away. In 1947, playing for the Athletics suddenly became a lot more fun.

CHAPTER
12

MAGIC SUMMER

If there is any one game I look back on as the absolute peak of my career, the point when I was pitching my best and the future seemed brightest, it would have to be Opening Day at Yankee Stadium in 1947.

In front of 39,344 New Yorkers I threw six–hit ball as we beat the Yanks 6–1. There wasn't a moment in the game when I didn't feel I was in complete control. My fastball and curve hummed and snapped, and the Yankee hitters were baffled by a new fork-ball I'd developed and unveiled for the first time. Even the New York fans appreciated the game I'd pitched, giving me an enthusi-astic cheer when I came to bat towards the end of the game.

It doesn't get a whole lot better. Just being at Yankee Stadium for an opener was a thrill, let alone getting the start and then such a convincing win. A Marine colour guard and the

Seventh Regiment Band opened the pre-game ceremonies. Ex-president Herbert Hoover was in the crowd as well as a variety of other dignitaries, including a delegation from the United Nations Security Council.

Beating New York starter Spud Chandler was especially sweet. Chandler had won twenty games the year before, including four of the five he started against us. In his nine years with the Yanks he'd beat the A's seventeen times.

Connie Mack, who loved seeing us stick it to the thirty-nine-year-old veteran, delivered his best line of the season. "What if he did win twenty last year?" Mack snorted. "That man's getting old and in this business you can't go on forever."

The forkball was something I'd experimented with on the sidelines before the war and finally gotten serious about that spring, working on it with the help of our catcher Buddy Rosar and Earle Brucker. I still felt I needed something extra besides the curve and hard one to keep the hitters guessing after my attempts at mastering a straight change had been a disaster. The forkball seemed like the perfect solution. It's a slower pitch delivered with the fastball motion. Released between the index and middle fingers, my forker was especially tough on left-handed hitters, breaking sharply down and away as much as a foot as it crossed the plate.

Bucky Harris, whose debut as the new Yank manager had been spoiled, told reporters he'd had trouble identifying my new pitch. He just knew it was nasty.

"We still don't know for sure," he said after the game. "I'll tell you one thing, when this fellow is out there pitching, the A's are going to be a tough club to beat this year. He looks like one of the better pitchers in the league."

I was full of juice and confidence. "With a few breaks I might be able to hit that twenty-win mark," I crowed to a swarm of reporters gathered around my locker. "And don't be surprised if we land in the first division. This is a different team than you've seen in the past. Now we know we can win."

The big difference in the A's was that the Old Man had dramatically improved our infield defence in the off-season by drafting veteran shortstop Eddie Joost and Ferris Fain, a young first baseman. Both had great range and were as good with the glove as anyone in the league at their positions. They gave every pitcher on the staff a huge boost in confidence. Pitching was so much easier when you could count on the guys behind you to catch the ball.

Joost was only a career .239 hitter, but he made up for it by getting to first on walks, leading the league with 114 free passes. Joost also had occasional home run power, hitting thirteen on the season. Fain was just getting started on a nine-year career that would see him win consecutive batting titles in 1951 and 1952. His on-base percentage was above .400 every one of those nine seasons, and only once did he strike out more than thirty-seven times.

Fain was one of the most hard-nosed competitors I've ever seen. One day that season he was tripped by Ed Pellagrini of the Red Sox while rounding third base. After he touched home, Fain ran back to third and hauled off and punched Pellagrini for "dirty play." It did a pitcher's heart good to watch Fain come fearlessly charging in toward the plate when he thought the bunt was on.

Mack also added hurlers Bill McCahan, Joe Coleman and Carl Scheib, who contributed twenty wins between them. McCahan, who had been a test pilot in the war, was especially effective that year, going 10–5.

That was all it took to transform us from the laughing-stock of baseball to a squad that hung in the first division for most of the season. We already had a solid outfield in Sam Chapman, Elmer Valo and Barney McCosky, who would finish second to Ted Williams with a .328 batting average. Pete Suder and Hank Majeski were steady if not spectacular at second and third, and our catcher, Buddy Rosar, who had played in Bill Dickey's shadow while he was with the Yankees, was one of the best backstops in the league.

Every time it looked like we were getting ready to fall back that season, we'd rally and win three or four in a row. Our pitching was outstanding right from the start. Fowler, McCahan and Russ Christopher all won ten games or more.

Mack went from predicting another last-place finish in spring training to answering "I think we can" a couple months later when asked if his A's could stay near the top. "But whether we do or don't," he said, "I'll tell you one thing: These boys won't quit."

I was feeling a little more kindly towards the Old Man. Without too much discussion he'd agreed to raise my salary to $12,000. That didn't exactly put me in the same income bracket as Bob Feller and Hal Newhouser, or even Bobo Newsom, but I considered it a reasonably fair hike. Now with Joost and Fain backing me up, I figured I'd be making as much as the big boys in no time.

The talk of baseball that spring was Jackie Robinson of the Brooklyn Dodgers, the first black to play in the major leagues. Many people seriously argued that integration would destroy the game. The owners themselves were firmly opposed to letting blacks in. Commissioner Chandler was forced to step in and overrule them after they voted 15 to 1 against allowing blacks to play in the big leagues.

Some of Robinson's own team-mates circulated a petition to get him off the team. Brooklyn boss Branch Rickey said he'd trade anyone who refused to play alongside Robinson. When reports circulated that the St Louis Cardinals planned to strike when the Dodgers arrived in town for a series, National League president Ford Frick threatened the Cardinal players with life-time banishment.

Having played in games against blacks as an amateur back home in Ontario, I had trouble understanding what all the fuss was about. Those players who objected to Robinson's presence were mostly Southerners who had grown up with segregation. I heard a couple of team-mates say they wanted no part of play-ing with "niggers." But the majority of us felt everyone deserved a fair chance. Many players had just finished fighting in a war that was supposed to be about preserving democracy. Well, didn't blacks, or negroes as they were most often called in those days, deserve their rights too?

The fact that the owners fought integration right to the end is probably the biggest disgrace in the history of the game. Judy Johnson, who, they say, was one of the greatest of all the black ballplayers born too soon to play in the big leagues, once asked Connie Mack why breaking down the colour line had taken so long. This was after Johnson had become an A's scout and a good friend of the Old Man.

"I asked him one day," Johnson remembered. "I said, 'Mr Mack, why didn't you ever take any of the coloured boys in the big leagues?' He said, 'Well, Judy, if you want to know the truth, there were just too many of you to go in.' As much as to say, it would take too many jobs away from the other boys."

On July 5, Cleveland Indians owner Bill Veeck broke ranks with his fellow American League owners and introduced a twenty-three-year-old black slugger named Larry Doby. But it would be years before baseball completely opened the doors. Including Robinson and Doby, by the end of 1949 there were only seven other blacks in the big leagues. I never had a black man for a team-mate.

After beating the Browns in St Louis for my second win of the season, I faced Bobo Newsom in a night game in Washington. Bobo and I matched each other pitch for pitch until he was lifted for a pinch-hitter in the eighth. With the score tied 1–1 in the eleventh, I came to the plate with two on and one out against reliever Ray Scarborough. Then I coolly crushed a juicy curve into centre field for a two-run single to put the game away.

Nothing to it. Not when you know exactly what pitch is on the way. Al Simmons, coaching at third, had decoded the signals passing between the catcher and Scarborough. Out of the corner of my eye I saw him gesturing with his arms two or three times, our signal to expect a curve.

If there's anything I knew how to do, it was kill a curve when somebody told me it was coming. I watched a couple go by. They were curves all right. Then I leaned into the third pitch.

Successfully stealing another team's signs gives the batter a tremendous advantage. But it can drive a pitcher batty when he suspects it's being done to him. After going through that stretch before the war when I telegraphed every pitch I threw, I probably worried more than most pitchers about giving anything away.

An alarm goes off in your head when someone who has never been able to buy a hit off you before suddenly digs right in and bangs a ball off the outfield fence. You pass the word to your coaches and everyone on the bench, telling them to look out for possible leaks. Then you huddle with your catcher and change the order of your signs.

Shielding his free hand with his mitt, a catcher flashes you a sequence of three or four signals. By pre-arrangement, you know that, say, the second sign is the pitch he wants you to throw. So now you change to the first or third signal and see what happens.

In a game against Boston that year I was absolutely convinced our signs were being picked up. I called Buddy Rosar out to the mound. "They can't be," he said. "Neither of those coaches can possibly see my hand."

Between innings I talked to Brucker. "Am I tipping my pitch? I've got great stuff today, but I'll be going along fine and then suddenly they eat me up." I'd also noticed that the Red Sox third-base coach seemed to be making a lot of unusual arm gestures. Brucker said he'd keep a close watch.

A couple of innings later Brucker had the answer. "They're getting it from second base," he said. "They've figured out our signs. The coaches can't see Rosar signalling, but every time they get a runner on second he can see the signs."

The gestures being made by their third-base coach were an attempt to throw us off the scent by making us think that he might be the one tipping the batter. What had actually happened was that early in the game a Boston runner on second had managed to decode our signs. Afterwards, any runner they moved up to second base was signalling the hitter.

It's the inside game, the things most fans never pick up on, that makes baseball such a great sport to play. You always have to stay alert, to think about everything that has happened and everything that might happen next.

There's a great story about the young Yogi Berra. When Yogi first came into the league he was a non-stop talker. He'd chat away when he worked behind the plate, he'd yap while he was at bat, and he'd talk with the fielders when he got on base. The only time he didn't talk was when he was on first and he'd been flashed the sign that the hit-and-run was on. Then he'd shut right up to concentrate. Naturally, it wasn't long before opposing teams noticed Yogi's pattern and regularly started throwing him out on pitchouts. The Yankees finally ordered him to keep talking all the time.

Berra later developed into possibly the best defensive catcher in the American League, but Ted Williams remembered a day when he was on first base and Yogi wasn't being careful enough in shielding his signals. He was dropping his knee, allowing Williams and Boston first-base coach Del Baker to decipher the Yankee signs easily. By the next time Williams came to the plate, Berra was fuming. "Boy, what dumb-ass pitchers we've got. Baker knows what they're going to throw every time."

Catching when I was pitching was certainly no joyride. I sometimes feel a little sorry for Buddy Rosar and the other catchers I worked with during my career. One night after I'd beaten the Yankees in a close one, Rosar told a reporter I'd put fifty balls into the dirt. "A pitcher has to have a tremendous amount of stuff to make fifty bad pitches in a game and win," he added.

That was my trouble, I often had too much stuff. My pitches would be hopping all over the place and many of them ended up in the dirt, although I think Rosar was exaggerating his count more than a little. Most of my team-mates refused to take batting practice against me because I was never able to just groove pitches over the plate. The ball seemed to have a life of its own.

The problems I had in the early innings of ball games can be explained by the fact that I was strongest then and my pitches had even more movement than they did later on. It seems strange for a pitcher to complain about having too much stuff, but that really was a problem for me.

So just imagine how great Rosar must have been defensively to be able to set the record for errorless games by a catcher while we were team-mates in 1946, fielding 1.000 in 117 games and then extending his perfect record to 147 games on into 1947. Only Berra, who put together a 148-game streak, ever bettered Rosar's mark.

As good as Buddy was, he was forced to sit on the Yankee bench for four years early in his career watching future Hall-of-Famer Bill Dickey do almost all the catching. It was easy to get lost in the Yankee chain in those days, which is why I've never really regretted that the Leafs didn't trade me to New York when I was still young and green. Even Charlie Keller thought about giving up and going back to college after he saw the great players he'd have to beat out for a job. When Rosar finally did escape New York, he became a five-time All-Star, twice for the Indians and then three times while he was playing with us.

Rosar likely had to scoop at least two or three out of the dirt in the first inning of my start against the Senators at Shibe May 23, when I surrendered a lead-off run before settling down and breezing to an 8–1 win. The victory put us at the .500 mark for the first time that season.

There's no question that Bob Feller was the outstanding pitcher of his generation. He was the standard by which the rest of us were judged. If the war hadn't taken almost four seasons out of his career, Feller would probably have retired with around 350 wins instead of the 266 beside his name in the record books.

Since I was the top pitcher for the A's, you might have thought that over the years Feller and I would have pitched against one another a dozen or more times. Yet we always seemed to just miss each other in the rotation. It's also possible that on other occasions Mack decided to hold me back when it was my turn to pitch against Feller, preferring to sacrifice another starter in a game in which the weak-hitting A's weren't likely to offer much run support.

Feller and I exchanged shutouts during a Sunday afternoon doubleheader in Cleveland June 8, with me blanking the Indians on four hits for a 4–0 decision in the opener, and Bullet

Bob throwing a three-hitter to whitewash us 2–0 in the second game. The split decision left us in fourth place, five games back of leading Detroit.

I could be wrong here, but I believe the only time Feller and I faced each other as starters was in my next outing, back home at Shibe on Friday, June 13. People have often told me that I had a lot of bad luck in my career. So what were my chances of winning against the great Bob Feller on Friday the 13th?

It was close, though. Feller fanned twelve and just narrowly came out on top, 5–4, as we both went eight innings. The difference was the successive homers I served up to Joe Gordon and Kenny Keltner in the fifth.

What sticks in my memory about that game was the experience of going to bat against one of the hardest throwers in history. When Feller was in his prime—and he was still at his best or close to it when I batted against him in 1947—he was said to throw about a hundred miles per hour. The ball looked like a pea coming in at you. Feller's motion was a tumble of arms and legs as he released the ball, making it almost impossible to pick up his release point. The ball was by you before you could move a muscle.

Was I scared? You can bet on it. Anyone who ever went to bat against Bob Feller was afraid for his life. We didn't wear batting helmets in those days, and getting hit in the head by one of his pitches would probably kill you. As far as I know, Feller never hit anyone intentionally. But like all successful pitchers he wanted the inside part of the plate and would brush back hitters who took liberties. The most frightening thing of all was that Feller had a tendency to be wild at times. Or maybe he just preferred to let batters believe that even he wasn't sure where the ball was going to go.

Although players may try to deny it, even to themselves, there's no question that fear is a factor when they step up to the plate. I know that some, including Mickey Mantle, have said they have recurring nightmares about getting beaned.

Later that season I saw Elmer Valo knocked cold by a fastball from Sid Hudson of the Senators. Valo toppled over like he'd been hit by a sledge-hammer. We watched as our trainer, Jim Tadley, put ice compresses on Valo's head, but he still didn't come to. Finally he was carried to the dressing room on a stretcher, where he regained consciousness and was taken to the hospital.

Valo was the third Athletic to be hit by an opposing pitcher in two weeks. Hank Majeski had suffered a concussion when he was beaned by Earl Harris of the White Sox, and Barney McCosky had taken a pitch in the elbow from Floyd Bevens of the Yankees.

Like a lot of former players, I'm convinced the game was rougher in the old days. Some pitchers lived by the rule that when someone hit a home run off them, the next two batters were going down into the dirt. Now players charge out to the mound ready to fight whenever they suspect the pitcher is trying to brush them back off the plate. Back then batters expected to be challenged.

A few managers openly encouraged their pitchers to throw at batters. Leo Durocher was famous for yelling "Stick it in his ear!" from the dugout. Connie Mack wasn't like that. Maybe he'd seen too many beanings in his day. I never once heard of him ordering a pitcher to deliberately hit a batter.

What's really amazing to me is that only one player has died in a big-league ball game—Ray Chapman of the Indians, who took a pitch in the temple from Yankee submariner Carl Mays in 1920. It's worth mentioning that the pitch Mays threw was said to have barely missed the strike zone. As usual, Chapman was crowding the plate.

Rarely are brush backs actually intended to hit the batter. They're thrown to send a message for him to move back off the plate. The next pitch is then usually thrown on the outside corner, out where the batter can no longer reach it. Brush backs are a basic part of pitching strategy. I can't understand why modern players expect to be able to get up close and comfortable without occasionally having to go down into the dirt.

I wonder how they would have handled batting against Dizzy Dean. "You all done? You comfortable?" he would yell at a batter who started to dig a hole in the box with his back foot. "Well, get a shovel because that's where they're going to bury you."

Although I didn't hesitate to pitch inside, I only deliberately threw at a player once in my entire career. It happened the next year in Cleveland when I was matched against Bob Lemon in the second game of a doubleheader. The Indians were pounding me all over the field and I couldn't understand why. My stuff wasn't that bad. After a few innings of this I knew they must be stealing our signs.

Finally I became so frustrated that when outfielder Hal Peck came to the plate I decided to knock him on his rear. Funny as it sounds, I chose Peck, who had played with the A's for a couple of seasons, because he was a friend. I figured the Indians would get the message I was on to them if I knocked Peck down.

"Why the hell are you throwing at me?" Peck yelled as he picked himself up out of the dirt after just managing to get out of the way of my brush back. "I had nothing to do with it." Peck's reaction confirmed my suspicions.

I don't have any proof that would stand up in court, but I later heard that Bob Feller, who had won the opener of the doubleheader, was hidden out in the scoreboard with binoculars stealing our signs, and was then somehow relaying them back to the Cleveland bench. Lemon and the Indians were tough enough to beat on any occasion. With an advantage like that I had no chance at all.

We hung right in there near the top of the standings on into July. My eighth victory of the season, an 8-4 decision in Boston July 3, put us into third place, six-and-a-half back of New York and a half-game behind Detroit. It was our fifth consecutive win over the reigning American League champs, a pretty good indication of how far we'd come as a team.

Another example of how much tougher we were was our ability to come from behind to win ball games. When we rallied for two late runs in Cleveland July 11 to nail down my ninth victory, it was our twentieth successful comeback of the season. Mack was right when he said we refused to quit.

Around this time I decided to abandon my experiment with the forkball. Not because it wasn't usually effective, but because throwing it was wrecking my arm.

I had developed a searing pain in my right forearm. Even before the pain started I noticed that I'd lost something off my fastball and my curve wasn't snapping like it used to. As usual I went to Earle Brucker for advice.

"You're using the forkball too much," he said immediately. "Take a week off, rest your arm, and when you get back into action, don't use the fork so often."

Another lesson learned. The time to start fooling around with trick deliveries is when you've already lost your fastball, not before. My heater and curve were still plenty good enough to keep me on top. A few more weeks of throwing the fork and I might have damaged my arm for good.

My arm bounced back fairly quickly and by the end of July I had twelve wins. My thirteenth, a shutout over the Browns at Shibe August 3, tied me with the Yankees' Allie Reynolds for the league lead.

I was enjoying myself more than I had at any other time in my career. When I was right, I felt I could beat anybody in the world. Best of all, the team was winning. We knew we were good and likely to get a lot better. Mack started telling reporters that the club might only be a season or two away from a pennant.

One great outing seemed to follow another. In early August I put together a stretch of twenty-five scoreless innings until I finally surrendered a run to the Senators in Philadelphia August 9. After that I coasted to an 8–1 win. I also hit my first and only big-league home run that afternoon.

I was basically a line-drive hitter, which explains why the round-tripper was so long in coming. In the third inning Sid Hudson hung a curve that I got all of and drove into the upper left-field stands. I felt like Babe Ruth rounding the bases. I waved at the boys in the bullpen, who laughed and waved back. We were always kidding each other about our hitting prowess and this would give me bragging rights for weeks to come.

"Ontario pitchers had their biggest day in the majors this year when Dick Fowler of Toronto, and Phil Marchildon of Penetanguishene, hurled the Philadelphia Athletics to twin triumphs over the Washington Senators, 2–1 and 5–2," read the lead of the American Press report on our game in Washington August 17. I had a perfect game going until Mickey Vernon tripled with one out in the seventh. Washington got to me for three more hits after that. The win was my fifteenth of the season.

Dick and I always got a kick out of being able to join forces the way we did against Washington. We both took a lot of pride in the fact that until we came along there had never been two Canadians in the same starting rotation. Now there were two good ones. Fowler's twelve wins were second best on our staff that year.

Less than two weeks later, on Tuesday, August 26, under the lights in Cleveland, I came even closer to being the first big-leaguer to pitch a perfect game since Charley Robertson of the White Sox turned the trick in 1922.

I can still see almost every pitch I threw that night. To this day, I get steamed when I think about how I was robbed.

I'd been staked to a one-run lead in the fifth when we finally got to Cleveland's tough right-hander Don Black, who had himself thrown a no-hitter against us July 10. Our run came on a double by Buddy Rosar, Sam Chapman's bunt and a single by Pete Suder.

I still hadn't allowed a hit or a walk into the eighth. With two out, Ken Keltner came to the plate, the twenty-fourth man to face me. You always had to pitch carefully to Keltner, who was one of the toughest outs in the league. He fouled a couple off and worked me to a full count. Then I threw a fastball that caught the outside corner of the plate. I was already a couple of steps towards our dugout when I realized that umpire Bill McKinley had called it a ball and Keltner was trotting down to first.

The next day a local newspaper said I went "ballistic," which is as good a description as any. I fired my glove from the pitching mound and ran in to confront McKinley. Rosar was already jaw-to-jaw with him by the time I got there. We ranted, kicked up dirt and called him every name in the book. Naturally, none of our arguments had any effect. Keltner stayed on first.

"What Bill McKinley apparently forgot last night," wrote Cleveland reporter Ed McAuley the next day, "was that when there's a doubt and a perfect game at stake, the pitcher should be allowed to keep the change."

My sentiments exactly. Besides, I know that ball was a strike. "It was right there, Phil," Rosar told me later. "It caught the corner. There's no doubt about it."

The only thing good I can think to say about McKinley is that at least he had the good sense not to toss me out of the game for throwing my glove and arguing the call. Under normal circumstances that would have earned me an automatic ejection. But even though my perfect game was ruined, I still had a shot at a no-hitter. McKinley allowed me to blow off steam and keep going. Punishment was delayed a couple of days until American League president William Harridge issued both Rosar and me twenty-five-dollar fines.

I tried to collect myself on the mound. Don't mess up now, I kept thinking. Stay calm. Joe Gordon, the next batter, hit a drive to centre field that Sam Chapman hauled in after a long run. Just three more outs to go.

Probably my greatest weakness as a pitcher was my inability to rein in my emotions. I'd fume inwardly when a team-mate made a bonehead mistake behind me or I surrendered a critical walk or home run. Sitting in the dugout that day I got angrier and angrier at the injustice of McKinley's call. I kept telling myself to focus on the next three outs. But I couldn't. By the time I walked back to the mound I had just about lost control.

I got a break when pinch-hitter Larry Doby swung at a couple of bad pitches and struck out to start the inning. Up next was George Metkovich, who wasted no time in pumping a single into the outfield to end the no-hitter. I went numb with disappointment. Dale Mitchell stepped in and slapped a single to left centre. Metkovich sprinted to third.

Not only had I lost the perfect game and no-hitter, but the Indians then tied the score when right fielder Hank Edwards hit a sacrifice fly that brought home Metkovich. I got the next two batters out and we headed into extra innings.

By this point I'd replaced my anger with a determination to win the game no matter what it took. I'd be damned if I was going to come out of this without something to show for all my aggravation.

I was tiring but managed to keep getting out of jams. A runner the Indians put on third in the tenth was thrown out at home on a failed suicide squeeze. When they got another runner to second with two away in the eleventh, Bob Lemon, one of the best-hitting pitchers in the game, was called in to pinch-hit for reliever Ed Klieman. Lemon went down swinging.

Cleveland's top reliever, Al Gettel, came in to pitch the twelfth. Gettel retired the first two batters before Pete Suder singled, bringing me to the plate.

What followed was one of the most satisfying moments of my career. Here's how Ed McAuley described it the next day: "But, ladies and gentlemen, there was only one story in last night's ball game and Marchildon, the slim and fiery Canadian who came back from a German prison camp to become the most effective pitcher in the American League, was easily its hero....

"Where he really proved himself a fighting man was in the twelfth. Marchildon was angry—he was sick with disppointment—and many of the customers were booing. So Phil smashed a double to left centre, and, for all practical purposes, the game was over. Suder streaked home with what proved to be the winning run."

The Indians' half of the twelfth wasn't quite as perfunctory as McAuley would have had his readers believe. Ken Keltner was trouble again, singling with one out. Joe Gordon hit a fly to make it two away. Then Pat Seerey, batting for Al Lopez, banged a loud foul off the left field wall. That scared me and I knew I had to end it right there. I reached back and threw one of my best pitches of the long night—a beautiful curve that caught Seerey looking. This time McKinley thrust his arm in the air and gave me the call.

By early September we started to fall back into the pack—but not with our customary thud. We continued to win more than we lost, ending the season just out of the first division in fifth spot with a 78–76 record. It was the first time since 1933 the A's had played better than .500 baseball.

The revitalized Yankees shook off the rust from the war and the turmoil of the previous season to take the pennant by twelve games over runner-up Detroit. What we found most encouraging was the fact that the spread between us and the Tigers was only seven games. Wedged in the second and third spots were Boston and Cleveland.

A happy, loose, confident bunch of Athletics played out the last month of the season. Word had spread throughout the league that we weren't push-overs anymore. At times in the past I'd been almost embarrassed to wear the uniform. We had always been the bums who attracted the smallest crowds on the road and who finished in the cellar year after year. Now we had respect.

My almost-perfect win over the Indians had been my sixteenth of the year. The way I was pitching, reaching twenty seemed a lock. Then one morning a blister appeared on the middle finger of my pitching hand and I was forced to miss a turn in the rotation. In my next start I lost a 1–0 cliff-hanger to the Browns. Suddenly time was running out.

Victories over Detroit and Boston improved my record to 18–9 as we travelled to New York for the last weekend of the season. The Yankees were preparing to play the Brooklyn Dodgers in a subway series which they ended up winning in seven games. After watching the Red Sox go flat the year before, the Bombers planned to stay fresh by playing most of their regulars over the weekend. There never was any such thing as an easy touch against New York.

I got the start that Saturday—September 28—against right-hander Floyd Bevens, who was only 7–13 that season but looked plenty sharp in the seven innings he worked that afternoon before giving way to star reliever Joe Page, who had saved a league-leading seventeen games. With the score tied at one run apiece, Page and I battled into the tenth. We finally won it 2–1 in our half of the inning when rookie shortstop Mickey Rutner, a late-season call-up, singled with the bases loaded.

After the game I went to Earle Brucker and asked if I could be on call in the bullpen the next day. If the game was close, maybe I'd be able to pick up my twentieth win in a late-inning relief appearance. "Don't worry about my arm," I told him. "I've got all winter to rest." Brucker said he'd talk to Mack.

Sunday was Old-Timers' Day at Yankee Stadium. I saw Ty Cobb lay down a bunt and Tris Speaker chase a fly in centre field. I also shook hands with eighty-year-old Cy Young, as well as Chief Bender, Frank "Home Run" Baker, Duffy Lewis and Harry Hooper. And for the only time in my life, I saw Babe Ruth.

I walked around the field like an awestruck kid asking the game's immortals to autograph a baseball that became one of my proudest possessions. More than two dozen former Yankees and other American League stars were there as guests of the New York club for the upcoming World Series.

After master of ceremonies Mel Allen completed the introductions, the old-timers squared off for a two-inning exhibition before the start of our game. The old Yanks were coached by Joe McCarthy; the American League stars by Connie Mack. The sixty-one-year-old Cobb came to the plate first, holding the bat almost vertically, with his hands far apart in his familiar stance. Playing first base for the pin-stripers was Wally Pipp, the man whose famous headache had given Lou Gehrig his chance to break into the Yankee lineup. Among the pitchers in the game was former Athletics star Chief Bender, who had broken into the big leagues in 1903.

The festivities ended with an appearance on the field by Babe Ruth, looking frail from his losing battle with cancer. When he spoke into the microphone, Ruth's voice was so raspy you could hardly understand a word he said.

Mack told Brucker he'd try to get me into that afternoon's game if the situation seemed right. Pitching for us was a

talented kid named Lou Brissie, another September call-up.
With the score tied 1–1 in the sixth, the Yankees got two on
and I started getting loose in the bullpen. But I guess the Old
Man wanted to see what Brissie could do under pressure and he
left him in. The Yanks got four runs and that was that. We lost
the game 5–3.

I was disappointed at not getting that one last win, but the
future seemed so bright that I didn't dwell on it. I felt certain I'd
win my twenty the next season. Just shy of my thirty-fourth
birthday, I figured I still had three or four good seasons left.
Now that the A's were an improving team, there was no telling
how many games I might win before I was through.

I have to admit I get a charge out of opening baseball
encyclopaedias to the pages covering 1947 and seeing my name
listed among the leaders in so many American League pitching
categories. I tied with Allie Reynolds for the second-most wins
(Feller was first with 20). My total of 21 complete games was
fourth best. I held batters to the third lowest batting average
(.224), was third in innings pitched with 277, and third again
in fewest hits allowed per game (7.41). I also recorded
the fifth-highest number of strikeouts (128). My ERA was a
solid 3.22.

One stat I was much less happy about was my league-leading
141 walks, but that was nothing new. I'd also led in that catego-
ry back in 1942, my other big year.

A few weeks before the end of the season Bob Feller called
with an invitation to join his team of travelling all-stars on a
post-season barnstorming tour through the southern states and
into Mexico. One of the canniest businessmen in the game,
Feller organized similar jaunts every year to supplement his
already sizeable income. Among the stars joining him this year
were the National League's home run champ Ralph Kiner,
Ken Keltner, Jeff Heath, Gerry Priddy and Eddie Lopat.
When I heard who was going, I told Feller to count me in.

Everything was fine until we got to Mexico, where Feller
had us playing in some of the dustiest, hottest, most God-
forsaken towns in creation. A few of the boys came down with

bad cases of Montezuma's revenge. Then we got into an argument with Feller about money we thought he owed us. I began counting down the days until the tour would end in Monterey.

I do have a funny story I like to tell about the trip. We were playing a game in yet another miserable Mexican town when we noticed a commotion in the outfield stands. Time was called, and we watched as a couple of hundred fans climbed down out of their seats and proceeded to pick up and move an entire section of the bleachers. Seconds later an old-fashioned steam train slowly chugged through the gap and across the outfield. We had noticed the tracks out there when we were warming up, but they were level to the ground and we'd figured they hadn't been used in years. Play resumed once the train was gone and the fans had finished putting the stands back in place.

To me the best thing about being from a small town is the feeling that people genuinely care about one another and are proud when someone from the community goes out into the world and makes good. The dinner given in my honour that November 13 in Penetang was even more special to me than the night organized by Mack after my return from the war. The difference was that I didn't have to question the motives of my townspeople. They had always been my biggest fans.

Arranged by the local Chamber of Commerce, the dinner brought together two hundred friends and members of my family at Laboureau Hall. Joining Irene and me at the head table were my seventy-two-year-old father, my brothers and two of my sisters, Elizabeth and Jeanne. Looking back, I'm especially thankful that my father was able to be there. Just a few months later he died of stomach cancer, the same disease that took my mother.

On behalf of the town, Mayor W. M. Thompson presented Irene and me with a sterling-silver dinner set for twelve. "We are terrifically proud of you, Babe," the Mayor said. "Phil is a credit to this town and country in sport. We in Penetang and district wish him every possible success in 1948. I personally would like to see him win at least twenty-five games."

Judging by the cheers of the crowd, that made two hundred of us.

CHAPTER
13

THE LONGEST SEASON

O ver the winter I tried to psych myself up for what I figured would be an exhausting, drawn-out battle with Mack over my new contract. After the season I'd had, I wanted a big raise and was ready to hold out until I got it. I wasn't going to listen to any of the Old Man's excuses about how poor he was. He was either going to pay me what I was worth or I was going to demand to be traded.

When the contract arrived in Penetang, I could hardly believe my eyes when I saw that Mack had written in $17,500. That was exactly the figure Irene and I had in mind. Maybe the Old Man was going soft in his dotage. Or maybe he decided it was just good business to keep his top pitcher happy. He'd been telling reporters that his dream was to win one last pennant, and he may have figured he needed my enthusiastic help to do it.

After Irene and I finished dancing around the living room of our rented house, I quickly signed on the dotted line and mailed the contract back in the next post—just in case there had been some kind of mistake.

I'd never seen Mack as chipper as he was that season. Winning was a tonic for him. His step seemed to be quicker and he said he woke up in the morning with a new purpose in life. By mid-season he was telling everyone that this was his favourite team of all, because it was "the fightingest."

Mack was content to open the schedule with the same everyday lineup as the year before. "Why change?" he asked. "I know what I've got now. We've got solid men at every position. Pete Suder plays a substantial second. Majeski has arrived as a clever third baseman, and so has Elmer Valo in left. Sam Chapman should come back this year—he hasn't got over the slump that started when he was let out of the Navy. Barney McCosky was the second-best batter in the league last summer—and that's good. And show me a catcher who equals Buddy Rosar!"

The only significant new addition was aging slugger Rudy York. Mack had hoped he would provide occasional power as a pinch-hitter. But by that point York's best friend was a bottle, and he hit just .157 with six RBIs for us in what would be his last season.

The press was calling our young pitching staff one of the best in baseball. I was the only greybeard in a core group that included Fowler, Coleman, Scheib and newcomer Lou Brissie, all still in their early to mid-twenties. "Maybe they're one year away from greatness," Mack said, "but I'll bet my hat they'll come through before long and make their mark as stars."

Mack had every right to be pleased, especially considering the fact that the team's entire payroll was just $75,000. That was an incredible bargain, even back then. You had to hand it to the Old Man. He'd managed to construct a legitimate pennant contender for what the Red Sox were paying Ted Williams alone. No wonder the spring was back in his step.

Now eighty-five, Mack seemed to be better loved by the public with each passing year. In spring training as he called out instructions and encouragement while sitting in a folding chair placed along the sidelines or behind the batting cage, crowds gathered behind the fence to stare at him, not at the players on the field. For many people, Mr Mack was baseball.

Now that our disagreements over money appeared to be behind us, I found myself becoming as susceptible to the the Old Man's charm as everyone else. I didn't forget how he'd rushed me back into action after the war or underpaid me early in my career. But I did start to appreciate Mack's many good points.

I never once heard him use profanity. "Gracious" and "my goodness" were two of his strongest expressions. Mack's way of speaking and his courtly manners were from an earlier age.

Some of his better qualities rubbed off on the rest of us. In an era remembered for its fierce bench-jockeying, when players and managers would scream vicious obscenities across the infield at one another, the Athletics bench was probably the quietest and most polite in baseball. We weren't exactly choirboys, but it just didn't seem right to us to sink to the level of the other teams when the Old Man was sitting there looking so proper in his high-starched collar and dignified summer suit.

His trade-mark collars, by the way, were made specially for him. When they had gone out of style around the turn of the century, he had convinced the manufacturer to keep him personally supplied.

The older Mack got, the more his players and coaches felt protective of him and insisted that others treat him with the proper respect. "Hello, Connie!" Bobo Newsom loudly greeted Mack when he joined the A's during the war. The next day a group of his new team-mates surrounded Newsom. "We call him Mr Mack, understand?" the leader said. Bobo got the message and was careful to address his employer properly from that day on.

Mack always arrived in the dugout fifteen minutes before game time and had one particular place he would sit. He was handed a scorecard and then wrote down the lineup and scored the game himself. If it was a warm day, he would take off his jacket and hang it up. "Would you please stop babying me," the Old Man sometimes snapped when a coach reached over to place a fresh bath towel behind his back.

Maybe the most endearing thing of all about him was the way he showed his appreciation to a player who had just done something special on the field to help the team. Most managers in those days were too hard-bitten to do more than grunt their approval.

Mack would be standing up when you got back to the dugout, reaching out to shake your hand. "Thank you," he'd say with a sincerity that was impossible to doubt. Sometimes it looked like there was the beginning of a tear in his eye.

Mack only rarely visited the clubhouse after a game, making it all the more memorable when later that season he opened the door after we'd won a big one, looked around the room to catch our attention, and then brought his hands together in applause. "This is for you," he told us quietly.

"People ask me if I'm tired of baseball," Mack said that year. "I can only give one answer. There is nothing in baseball I dislike. I'll stay in the game as long as my mind is clear. When I reach a stage where I don't know my business or trade a .300 hitter for a .200 hitter, then you'll know I'm unfit.

"If I did quit," he concluded, "I'd die in two weeks."

Mack gave me the ball for the opener in Boston April 19, my third and last opening-day start in the big leagues. Boston's management had decided to do things differently that year, with a game in the morning and then another in the afternoon, with two separate attendances. Rookie Lou Brissie worked the second game for us.

Pitching against eighteen-game-winner Joe Dobson, I got the win, but it sure wasn't easy. In the second inning I served up successive home-run balls to Stan Spence, Vern Stephens and Bobby Doerr—the first into the right-field bullpen, the second into the left-field screen, and the third over the left-centre wall. That just about covered the whole ballpark. The consecutive round-trippers tied a big-league record—not exactly how I'd hoped to get my name in the record book.

Things could only get better after that. We scored one run in the fifth and then tied the score in the eighth. Growing stronger as the game went on, I pitched into the eleventh and was able to hold the lead for a 5–4 win after Joost singled home Rosar and utility outfielder Don White added an insurance run with a sacrifice fly.

Mack was predicting greatness for Brissie, a twenty-three-year-old, 6' 4 1/2" rookie left-hander whom no one could ever accuse of lacking character. During the war his left leg had been all but ripped off by an enemy shell in Italy that had wiped out the rest of his unit. Brissie begged the doctors not to amputate and, twenty-three operations and forty blood transfusions later, he was in the big leagues, wearing a plastic shinguard to protect the scar tissue and exposed nerves of his ankle and lower leg.

In the sixth inning of the afternoon game, a rocket shot off the bat of Ted Williams struck Brissie just below the knee and just above his shin-guard.

"Damn it, Williams, pull the ball!" Brissie yelled as he lay on the mound.

He got back on his feet and refused to come out of the game, hanging in all the way for a 4–2 win. After the game, when our trainer got a look at the ugly black-and-blue bruise on Brissie's bad leg, he ordered him to the hospital for X-rays and an overnight packing of ice bags.

The next morning the kid awoke to find himself a national hero. Hundreds of congratulatory telegrams had arrived along with offers to appear on popular radio programs and in advertisements. None of the attention seemed to faze Brissie. He was already the cockiest rookie I'd ever met.

I had trouble believing someone pitching just his second game in the majors would have the nerve to challenge Ted Williams. But I suppose without that type of self-confidence Brissie would never have been able to come back from his injuries.

I seemed to have picked up right where I had left off the year before, pitching strongly almost every time out. My second start was a 3–2 loss to Early Wynn in Washington, but then I beat the Senators and Browns in tight games at Shibe. By May 6 we were in the middle of a ten-game winning streak and stood in first place, a half-game up on New York and one ahead of Cleveland.

Usually when fans start getting on an umpire's case, nobody takes it seriously. Cries of "Kill the umpire!" are a part of base-ball tradition. But there were times during my start in Washington May 27 when I thought I might actually see a crowd carry through on the threat. The reaction of the 13,012 fans at Griffith Stadium after a mistake by umpire Red Jones cost the Senators a run was one of the strangest and most fright-ening things I've ever seen on a ball field.

In the eighth inning, Jones got in the way of Mickey Vernon's peg to the plate, allowing Sam Chapman to score our seventh run. The ump was out of position and Vernon's throw bounced off his chest protector.

The play meant only the difference between a 6–3 and 7–3 score, but the way the crowd erupted you would have thought the World Series was at stake. Before we were through, the game had to be interrupted three times while bat boys cleared the field of empty beer cans that had been hurled at Jones. The ump finally warned Washington manager Joe Kuhel that if the abuse didn't stop he would forfeit the game to us.

After I'd set down the Senators in order in the bottom half of the ninth to seal the win, Jones held his mask over the top of his head and ran for the tunnel leading from the Senators dugout to the dressing rooms. Several hundred fans tried to fol-low him, pressing in against a police cordon formed around the dugout. We could still hear them out there howling like wolves as we took off our uniforms. The police finally ordered the park lights turned off and hauled the worst offenders away in paddy wagons.

The victory was our fifth in a row and my record now stood at 5–2, a pretty fair start to what looked likely to be my best season yet.

A few days later I was working out with Buddy Rosar on the sidelines, just getting loose and building up a sweat. I remember how pleased I was with the way I was throwing. My fastball and curve seemed as good as they ever had—maybe better.

I was in the middle of my wind-up when suddenly I felt dizzy and kind of numb. The feeling is hard to describe. Looking around the ballpark everything seemed strange. It was like I didn't belong there.

I tried to shake the feeling off and concentrate on throwing my next pitch. Now the ball felt like a lead weight in my hand. My arm and the rest of my body seemed drained of all strength. When I released the ball it barely went twenty feet, bouncing the rest of the way to Rosar.

"What's wrong?" he asked walking up to me. "You look funny, Phil. Are you all right?"

I didn't know how to answer. I'd never felt this way before. "I think I'd better go home," I said. "Tell Mr Mack."

Once I was with Irene and Carol, I began to feel a little better. But I was still weak and my nerves were on edge. Over the next days and weeks I found myself chain-smoking and becoming increasingly irritable. I fell into funks that became more and more difficult to snap out of.

The team doctor said the weakness was probably caused by a virus. He thought it was possible that the dysentery I'd had during the war had returned. As for my nervousness, well, I had always been known as the high-strung type, especially since my return from the war. Just try to relax, he said. Once the virus worked itself out of my system I'd probably feel fine again.

Although I slowly regained most of my strength, I continued to be bothered by little aches and pains and never felt quite right. I got creamed 8–1 by the Red Sox at Shibe June 1 as Vern Stephens and Bobby Doerr each slammed two homers off me. Fortunately, while I slumped the team continued to win. Starting the month we still led the Indians by a game.

Speaking at a baseball writers' dinner, Mack predicted that we'd finish the season in third spot. When the writers wanted to know why the Old Man didn't give his players more credit, he replied, "I'd rather surprise than disappoint."

But we could tell he thought we had a legitimate shot. For one thing, he'd started waving his scorecard around to position his fielders with more enthusiasm than he'd shown in years. When we were in the cellar he'd rarely bothered.

The problem was that Mack's eyesight was starting to fail, and now when he waved his scorecard he often had players bumping into one another. Our fielders learned to take a step or two towards where Mack was pointing and then drift back to where they thought they should play.

Life with the Old Man was never dull. Though the dugouts in Detroit, Boston and a couple of other American League clubs were connected to the bullpens by telephone, Mack still preferred to use old-fashioned sign language when summoning a pitcher.

For instance, Mack might have one of his coaches or players step out of the dugout, wave to attract the attention of Brucker in the bullpen, and then pound the nearest stadium wall to indicate that the man wanted was Carl Scheib—as in Shibe Park.

When the services of Bob Savage were required, someone would hold his hand over his nose in exaggeration of Savage's oversized honker. As the staff's only lefty, Lou Brissie was easy. The signaller simply went through the motions of pitching with his left hand.

The actions of a man shovelling coal brought Joe Coleman running. And for Dick Fowler, the messenger would stoop as though he were picking flowers. Mack, who had a habit of mispronouncing names, often referred to Dick as "Flowers." He sometimes shortened my name to "Marsh."

While Boston had Ted Williams and the Yankees were led by Joe DiMaggio, the Athletics didn't enjoy the benefit of a superstar who could carry the rest of the team along on his shoulders. Most of our wins were by committee. Fain, Valo and Joost were all having solid years. Sam Chapman continued to struggle, but the runs he did drive in were usually important ones. Our top pitcher at that point was smooth right-hander Joe Coleman,

with six wins against only one loss. Mack had been tipped about
Coleman by his old friend Brother Gilbert, the Xaverian who
more than thirty years earlier had put Baltimore Orioles' owner
Jack Dunn onto a young pitcher named Babe Ruth.

One Athletic enjoying a career year was third baseman Hank
Majeski, on his way to a .310 batting average with 120 RBIs.
Later that season Majeski set a record by hitting six doubles in a
doubleheader.

The Canadian connection sputtered on June 6 when Dick
Fowler and I dropped both ends of a doubleheader and surrendered first place to the Indians. My troubles continued in my
next outing as I was shelled for five runs in the opening frame of
a two-inning stint against the Browns.

The entire team went flat, losing five in a row and dropping
to four games behind the Indians. Then we showed the old-
time fight that made Mack so proud and slowly began to narrow the gap.

Mack did something then that was uncharacteristic for him,
and perhaps demonstrated just how badly he wanted to win that
last championship. After veteran reliever Nelson Potter came in
and blew a game against the Browns, Mack loudly dressed him
down and gave him his release in front of the entire team after
the game.

"If that's the best you can do get your cheque," he told
Potter, who had been purchased on waivers from the Browns a
month before. "I paid $20,000 cash for you and that was my
mistake. I don't care how good any player ever was, has been or
could be. All I care is how good he is now."

The Old Man's treatment of Potter put a chill on the feelings
of affection I'd started to develop for him. Like all owners, when
it came right down to it he was first and foremost a hard-nosed
businessman. Mack was ready to discard in a second anyone
who had stopped being of use to him.

He hadn't even been right about Potter. Signed shortly
afterward by the National League Boston Braves, he went 5–2
down the stretch and helped put the Braves into the World
Series. When Mack released Potter there were grumblings

among the A's that he'd just cost us our shot at the pennant.

Baseball was more popular than ever in the years immediately after the war. The economy was booming and people wanted to get out and enjoy life again. Attendance had never been better. Our double-header loss in Cleveland June 20, when I was convinced Bob Feller was stealing our signs from a perch in the scoreboard, drew a record 83,434 fans. In the American League, New York, Detroit, Boston and the Athletics all set new team attendance records, and Cleveland's total of 2,620,627 was an all-time high.

Every seat at Shibe was filled and thousands more were turned away when Cleveland visited July 15. Crowds started gathering outside the stadium in the early morning even though the gates didn't open until after five o'clock. There was such a crush that the police stopped all automobile traffic heading towards the park.

The dogfight for the top spot included the Indians, the Yankees, the Red Sox and us. Although no one seriously considered the Athletics to be the best team, they had to admit we were hanging tough. By July 4th, the turning point of the season, we were just a half-game out of first. We'd won seventeen of our games by one-run margins.

"The A's are not the best team in the world, but they just don't know when they're licked," one opposing manager told a Philadelphia reporter. "They never quit trying."

Hank Greenberg, who after his retirement as a player at the end of 1947 joined Cleveland as the Indians vice-president, had this to say: "Are we afraid of the A's? The answer is no. We aren't afraid of the A's. Neither is anyone else in the American League. No one is afraid of the A's—and the team that plays the A's in the World Series won't be afraid of them, either."

I'd waited so long to play for a club with a legitimate shot at a pennant, and now when my chance finally came I wasn't doing anything to help. My next win didn't arrive until July 5, and even then the Senators knocked me from the box in the fifth. Bob Savage bailed me out with four innings of masterful relief.

I was still feeling on edge. Before a game I would pace around impatiently, sweat soaking my uniform. During road trips I hardly spoke to my room-mate, Dick Fowler, who was such a great guy that he never took offense. I walked the streets of whatever city we were in for hours. When I got tired, I'd go into a movie house. Sometimes I watched three movies a day.

The team doctors continued to blame my troubles on what they called chronic influenza. Mack said he thought the problem might be that I smoked too much, which didn't make sense to me at all. It's true that I was lighting one cigarette on the butt of another, but that was the result of my problems, not the cause of them.

The good news was that my arm felt fine and I was still capable of throwing effectively—at least for a few innings. I'd be mowing down the hitters like I always had until, at some crucial point in the game, my stomach would turn to knots and I'd start to get wild. Before I knew it several runs would have scored and I'd have to come out, more frustrated than ever.

Mack kept trotting me out there every four days hoping for the best. My start against the Tigers in Detroit August 1 is a good example of what I was going through. A win would give us sole possession of first place, a game up on Cleveland. Pitching against Dizzy Trout, I only allowed five hits but I was constantly in and out of trouble all afternoon.

Leading 4–1 in the bottom of the ninth, my nerves started jumping and I almost threw the game away. I walked Johnny Lipton to start the inning. Then Eddie Mayo forced him at second and Freddie Hutchinson fouled out.

Okay, two outs, no problem. But do you think I could get that last man? I hit the next batter on the back of the leg with a wild pitch to load the bases. I looked into the dugout and could tell the Old Man was getting agitated. When I walked George Kell to force in a run, he'd seen enough. Charley Harris came in from the bullpen and tossed one pitch to Vic Wertz, who hit a grounder to Pete Suder, and first place was ours.

That game is also memorable because I let go with one of the great wild pitches of all time. In the fourth inning, while I was pitching to Wertz, the ball broke off my little finger and sailed well up the first base line and deep into the stands. The ball struck a spectator who was in the process of lighting a cigar, getting him squarely on the head. When he came to, the fan told a reporter that he had only himself to blame for the accident because he'd taken his eyes off the ball.

I knew the team was counting on me, and that put even more pressure on me to come through. Mack said openly we couldn't take the pennant unless I started winning. But it seemed the harder I tried the worse things got. Even though I often pitched well enough to win, the breaks just weren't going my way. Of course, that made me brood even more.

My best performance in weeks was wasted in a 2–1 loss to the Browns August 6. An error brought in the first St Louis run and a double that was fair by inches cashed in the other. I felt like cutting my throat afterwards.

But by far my most disappointing outing of the season came in a packed Yankee Stadium on August 15. Pitching the second game of a Sunday doubleheader, I had a 2–0 lead going into the bottom of the ninth and was absolutely determined not to let this one get away.

When I walked Bobby Brown to start the inning, I stayed cool. Tommy Henrich popped out. That brought Joe DiMaggio to the plate. I still wasn't worried. I'd been getting him out on curves all day and that was all I intended to show him now. My curve was so sharp that afternoon it was almost unhittable.

Strike one, strike two. Yankee Stadium was hushed. New York stood only one-and-a-half games behind us in the pennant race.

I called time and motioned for Rosar to come to the mound for a conference.

"What do you think about wasting a fastball, then coming back with the curve?" I asked. "That should throw him off."

"Okay," Rosar nodded, "but make sure you waste the fastball."

And that's exactly what I did. I swear that pitch was up around his eyes, a mile out of the strike zone—but DiMaggio took a wild tomahawk chop at it and knocked the ball out of the park. I guess by that point the Clipper was so glad to see a fastball he was ready to swing at anything.

That sent me to the showers and the game into extra innings. We finally won, but once again, I hadn't gotten the job done.

The next day, New York and the rest of the baseball world went into mourning when Babe Ruth died in the city at the age of fifty-three. Connie Mack was taken to see him just before he passed away. "Hello, Mr Mack," Ruth said. "The termites have got me."

An estimated 100,000 fans passed by Ruth's coffin as he lay in state in the lobby of Yankee Stadium. Thousands more lined the streets around St Patrick's Cathedral to catch a glimpse of the funeral cortège in which Mack was one of five honourary pallbearers. "It rained that day," wrote Arthur Daley in the *New York Times*. "Even the skies wept for the Babe."

By the end of August we stood in fourth place. A season-long run of injuries was finally beginning to take its toll and, though we hung onto fourth, we steadily lost ground throughout September and finished twelve-and-a-half games back, with a record of 84–70. Every one of our position players and our starting pitchers had missed at least part of the season.

It had been fifteen years since the A's last finished in the first division. The Old Man said he was proud of us and that he expected to do even better next season. He was still counting on winning that one last championship.

I thought Mack was going to have to make some changes if he expected his dream to come true. It wasn't just the injuries that had held us back. The truth was we couldn't score runs with the big boys. As a team, we had at least 117 fewer runs batted in than each of the three clubs ahead of us. We needed a DiMaggio, a Musial or a Williams to put us over the hump. There just weren't enough of them to go around.

Overall our pitching staff performed well, which helped take some of the heat off me. Fowler's fifteen wins led the club, with Scheib, Brissie and Coleman kicking in fourteen victories apiece. I finished at nine and fifteen, with an ERA of 4.54.

As my problems continued late into the season, I heard whispers that some reporters and possibly even one or two of my team-mates thought I was malingering. When the doctors weren't able to say for certain what was wrong with me, people began to question my desire to win. There didn't seem to be anything wrong with my arm. So what was the problem?

Finally, a reporter asked me if I'd heard the rumours. "I'm over thirty," I said. "I haven't got so many years left that I can afford not to do my best. When I pitch, I pitch with everything I've got."

In my heart I knew I'd done the best I could, and I think most of my team-mates appreciated that I was just as puzzled by my bad season as they were. But the insinuations hurt. I couldn't believe anyone could seriously question my commitment to the team.

We watched as Cleveland, Boston and New York fought down the stretch in one of the greatest pennant races ever. The Indians and Red Sox finally tied for first, the Yankees falling back only on the second-last day of the season. It was the first dead-heat finish in American League history. Cleveland won the one-game play-off on the strength of two home runs by Lou Boudreau and then beat the Braves in a seven-game World Series.

I hoped that once I got back to Penetang, far away from the pressures of a pennant race, I'd begin to unwind and enjoy life again. But my dark mood followed me home. When I still wasn't feeling any better by early December, I decided to check myself into Sunnybrook Hospital, a veterans' institution in Toronto, for a thorough going over. I had to get some answers.

"They discovered I have controlled tension, only I can't control it," I was quoted in *Sport* magazine a few months later. "Controlled tension is good for a fellow, particularly an athlete. It makes him do his best. The only trouble is that when it becomes uncontrolled it plays tricks on his body. It affects the nerves in the head, the stomach, the eyes—all over." The headline of the *Sport* profile of me was "The Heebie-Jeebies."

After putting me through a battery of tests and long sessions with psychiatrists, Sunnybrook's doctors concluded that my problems were a hold-over effect of the stress of the war. There was nothing wrong with me physically. They could find no traces of dysentery. The weakness and little aches and pains I'd felt during the season were probably all psychosomatic. They were seeing hundreds of former servicemen who had seemed fine for a year or two after they got back, but were now finding it difficult to cope with everyday life.

I had to try to lighten up, they said. Stop thinking about my troubles. Try to concentrate on all the positive things in my life. If I could stop my brooding and control my moodiness, all my physical problems would disappear.

The doctors thought it might help if I had something to occupy my spare time, so they suggested I try leatherwork. While I was in hospital, I sewed a big bunny for Carol, who was two years old now. I made it from pale yellow and green leatherette and stuffed it with cotton. It wasn't the best-looking rabbit in the world, but Carol loved it and carried it with her everywhere.

Just finally knowing what the problem was made me feel a lot better. I could snap myself out of this. The doctors were right. There were all kinds of reasons for me to be happy—a wonderful wife, a beautiful daughter and a career in the big leagues that had gone only temporarily off track. My arm was still sound and I would come back and win my twenty in 1949 for sure.

Then I took a call from a local reporter. "Connie Mack said he expects you to take a full 25 percent pay cut next season. Says you have to prove that you can still pitch. What's your reaction, Phil?"

I told the reporter I couldn't talk now. Suddenly I wasn't feeling so good.

CHAPTER
14

FINAL INNINGS

B y the time I arrived at the A's training camp in the spring of 1949 I had more or less resigned myself to Mack's demand that I accept a full 25 percent cut in pay, the maximum allowed. Not that I thought it was fair. During the winter I read in the newspapers that he had turned down an offer for me from the White Sox for $100,000 and some players. So the Old Man must have thought I could still pitch.

I just didn't feel like fighting him anymore. The last thing I needed was the stress of a long hold-out. After my stay in Sunnybrook I felt calmer than I had the previous summer, but it was still a struggle to keep my nerves under control. All I wanted was to concentrate on regaining my old pitching form and help the A's chase a pennant. I knew the surest way to start feeling better was to win a few games.

Mack and I met in his office at the training complex in West Palm Beach. "Let me see the contract," he said straight away. "I think maybe we were a little too severe." He took his pen and wrote in $15,000, a cut of only about 14 percent. "Get back to where you were two years ago and you may do better. Meanwhile this will have to do."

At age eighty-six the Old Man was still full of surprises. I appreciated his change of heart. What I couldn't understand was why, when he knew I was going through a bad time, he had caused me all that unnecessary worry in the first place.

Following two winning seasons there was a real feeling of optimism in that Athletics camp. The guys now felt they could play with the best teams in the league. With our fine young pitching staff, anything seemed possible.

Earle Brucker confided to reporters that his hurlers were looking so good it almost made him uneasy. "Lou Brissie has the ability to make Connie Mack forget Rube Waddell," he raved. Carl Scheib was "physically equipped for greatness." Joe Coleman looked "ready to take his place with the best in the American League." Brucker also felt certain Dick Fowler would improve on his staff-topping fifteen victories of the previous season.

There was almost an embarrassment of riches. Among the rookies in camp was 5'7", 143-pound Bobby Shantz. "Shantz is too small... but beats everyone," a scout reported to Mack. Quickly given the nickname Jumbo, Shantz had a sneaky fastball, a curve that Ted Williams was soon calling the best he'd ever seen, and a deceptive change of pace. Once Shantz matured, he became the toast of Philadelphia. In 1952 he won twenty-four games and was named the league MVP.

Two new but familiar faces in camp belonged to Wally Moses, who returned to the team as a bench player only to end up replacing the injured Barney McCosky in the outfield, and Jimmy Dykes, the former Athletics great who had signed on as a coach.

"Jimmy, I'm afraid we can't pay you enough money," Mack told Dykes when he offered him the job.

"Do we have to start in where we left off sixteen years ago?" Dykes answered back.

I was pitching well in the early going. My arm felt great and my thirty-five-year-old legs were holding up. I began to let myself feel optimistic about my chances of coming back. Everyone in camp seemed to be pulling for me. The Philadelphia writers gathered daily to watch me pitch on the sidelines, checking anxiously with Brucker about my progress. Despite the success of the younger fellows on the staff, my recovery was considered essential if the team was to move up in the standings.

"It's all up to Phil Marchildon," Mack said. "He's the balance wheel of our pitching staff. If he can come back, I think we've got a great chance at the pennant. If he can't, it will be just a chance."

My first start of the season was an afternoon game against Boston April 21 at Shibe. For eight innings I threw as well as I ever had. The only problem was that Mel Parnell, pitching for the Red Sox, was just as good. Neither side had scored as we headed into the ninth.

Ted Williams singled to open the top half of the inning—but he was forced at second on Vern Stephen's attempted sacrifice. Then I got Stan Spence on an outfield fly. I could feel the butterflies start to churn in my stomach. Stay calm, I kept telling myself.

Suddenly I couldn't find the plate. Successive walks to pinch-hitter Bill Goodman and catcher Birdie Tebbetts forced in a run. When I walked the next batter, Mack gave me the hook.

As I made my way toward the dugout the crowd started booing. At first it was only a few fans, then more and more joined in until it was an angry roar. "You stink, Marchildon!" a foghorn voice cut through the din. "Choker! Bum!"

I was stunned by the crowd's reaction. It had never occurred to me that I might be booed at Shibe. Not after the way they'd welcomed me home after the war. Not after I'd been their winningest pitcher since Lefty Grove.

I felt so disgusted with myself and angry at the fans that I waved in derision and then squeezed my nose to let them know I thought they stunk. The booing grew even louder and followed me as I walked down the tunnel from our dugout to the clubhouse.

Although I refused to admit it for a long time afterward, that game finished me. When I got out of bed the next morning following a sleepless night there was a shooting pain in my arm. I couldn't raise it above my shoulder. Something must have snapped during the ninth inning but I'd been too pumped with adrenalin to notice.

The team doctors weren't certain what the problem was. Even if they had known they wouldn't have been able to do much for me. In those days medical science didn't cover the repair of a damaged pitching arm. You played through the pain and hoped your arm would miraculously heal itself.

It was pretty obvious the doctors suspected this might be just another of my psychosomatic complaints. After a while I even began to wonder that myself.

I foolishly tried to start again five days later in New York. After throwing only two pitches, both wide of the plate, I had to pull myself out of the game. My arm was killing me.

I went out again in Detroit on Memorial Day, May 21, and was bombed for seven runs in three innings. Then the doctors decided to try giving my arm a complete rest for a couple of months. That didn't work either. In late August I allowed two hits in two-thirds of an inning of relief work against the Browns, and was battered for six runs in just over three innings of work in a start against Detroit a couple of days later.

The uncertainty I felt that season was pure hell. Until then I had always been able to convince myself that I'd be able to come back. As long as my arm felt strong there was no real reason to believe otherwise. Now I was just another sore-armed pitcher trying to hang on.

The Philadelphia fans continued our war. When I sat in the bullpen during home games they never failed to get on me.

"When ya going to start earning your big salary, ya bum!" "What's the matter, Marchildon? Can't stand the heat?"

When the team wasn't able to make that final jump to the top, the fans took their frustration out on me. They couldn't forgive me for going sour just when their expectations were so high. By the end of the season the A's had dropped one spot in the standings from the year before—into fifth place and out of the first division, sixteen games back of the pennant-winning Yankees.

While I felt badly about letting down the team, I knew I hadn't cost the A's the pennant. Our biggest problem continued to be an inability to score runs. The man the fans should have blamed was Mack, who still hadn't gotten us the big bat we desperately needed.

By September I'd hit bottom. After I was clobbered for five runs in the first inning of a loss to Boston September 2, the Yankees screamed bloody murder, charging that by using "Nothing Ball" Marchildon, Mack had as much as forfeited the game to Boston. The two teams were scratching for every win in a pennant race that went down to the last day of the season. Yankee manager Casey Stengel demanded I be given a start against his team to even things out.

So I'd come full circle in the nine years since I'd first joined the Athletics as a September call-up from the Maple Leafs. In 1940 there had been an outcry when Mack announced he was starting me in a game against one of the pennant contenders. The complaint had been that I was too inexperienced. Now everyone figured I just plain wasn't good enough. This was worse.

At first the Old Man assured the Yankees he would even things up. "I want to play it fair and square with both the Yankees and the Red Sox," he said. "I promised I would use Marchildon against the Yankees after I used him against the Red Sox, and I will keep my promise."

I was still trying to convince myself that my arm would heal and I'd get back to my old form. There were days when I looked pretty good on the sidelines. I could still throw effectively for short bursts.

"Maybe I'll surprise them," I said bravely when we arrived in

New York for my scheduled start the last week of September. "I'm throwing the ball hard and I'm liable to beat them."

I never got the chance. By now the newspapers were on their high horse, saying that Mack was jeopardizing the integrity of the game by starting me. The outcry was so great he had no choice but to pitch Dick Fowler in my place. "They aren't going to point any fingers at us," said Earle Mack, speaking for his father.

I don't think I could have gotten through all this without Irene. She was always giving me encouragement, trying to ease my mind about the future. When it got to the point where I hated to leave home for the ballpark, it made all the difference to know that when I got back she'd be there with a smile and that Carol would come running to jump into her daddy's arms. There were still two fans in Philadelphia I could count on.

For a fellow who never expected to play professional baseball, I fought long and hard to hold on to the career I'd built. It was such a wonderful life when things were going right. While other men worked in factories and on construction sites, I played a little boy's game on a beautiful green field in front of thousands of fans. People were excited to meet me. They asked for my autograph and wanted to be my friend. Ballplayers weren't just men—they were heroes.

Now it seems obvious that I should have retired at the end of the 1949 season and gotten on with the rest of my life. My stats for the season were brutal. In seven games I was 0–3, pitching just sixteen innings and surrendering twenty-four hits for an ERA of 11.81.

But I didn't quit because I was still hoping my arm would come back. I let myself be encouraged by those brief moments on the sidelines when my stuff seemed as good as ever. I also had no idea what I might do to make a living after baseball. The thought of going out into the real world frightened me.

I was only back in Penetang a few days after the end of the season when I read in the newspapers that the Athletics had fired both Al Simmons and Earle Brucker. The news shocked me and everyone else in baseball. For the first time, the club's directors had made a decision that went against the wishes of Connie Mack.

In other words, the Old Man was no longer in complete control of the ball team. The directors included Mack's three sons, Earle, Roy and Connie Jr., and Benjamin Macfarland, a grandson of the late Ben Shibe, Mack's original partner. Connie Mack Jr. said the directors' decision was "for the best interests of the club. We decided a change in our coaching set-up would prove beneficial to the team."

Connie Mack issued his own statement: "They [Simmons and Brucker] both are wonderful fellows and I thought they did a fine job for us. But the board of directors decided we could do without them and they have the final say in running the ball club."

I couldn't imagine what the directors were thinking when they let them go. I've talked about how much Simmons meant to the team. He was always there whenever a player needed a few words of encouragement or advice. His intensity helped keep each one of us focused on winning. Mack was right when he said Simmons was the heart and soul of the Athletics.

Earle Brucker had merely been the single most important influence in my career. There was a good chance he had kept me in the big leagues by changing my pitching motion when I was a rookie. Over the years he had spent countless hours working with me on the sidelines and talking strategy, reminding me over and over again to do all the little things that make a pitcher successful. He gave me the knowledge and the confidence I needed to be a winner.

Mack, who had a reputation as one of the most astute judges of pitching talent in the history of the game, said Brucker deserved most of the credit for developing the Athletics' excellent young staff. It's true that overall our pitching hadn't been quite as good in 1949, but how could anyone imagine that Brucker was to blame?

Just a few days after the firings, the Athletics sent me to Johns Hopkins Hospital in Baltimore so that Dr George E. Bennett, the famed surgeon who had removed the bone spur from Joe DiMaggio's heel the previous spring, could examine my sore arm.

There were rumours circulating that the Yankees were interested in trading for me, but insisted on seeing the medical report before completing any deal. New York was supposed to be offering outfielder Johnny Lindell. One newspaper report said Mack was holding out for more.

I don't know how much more Mack could possibly have hoped to get after the season I'd just had. I'm certain that before I visited Johns Hopkins the feeling was that most of my problems were psychosomatic. The Yanks may have been counting on the magical healing powers of pinstripes to cure whatever ailed me. There was a long history of players' careers reviving the moment they put on the famous uniform.

Once Yankee general manager George Weiss got a look at the doctor's report the deal was off. I never saw it myself or was told what was in it. But I didn't need an expert to tell me I was seriously damaged goods. Although I've never had my arm re-examined in all the years since, my own guess is that I had a torn rotator cuff, the injury that has probably killed more pitching careers than any other. In those days it was untreatable.

I reported to spring training at West Palm Beach, still hoping for the miracle that would save my career. That camp was Connie Mack's fiftieth as manager of the Athletics. It was also his last. At age eighty-seven, the Old Man was finally starting to look and act his age. At the end of the 1950 season, after guiding the club to a miserable 52-102 last-place finish, Mack stepped aside and was replaced by Jimmy Dykes.

"I am not quitting because I'm too old," he said stubbornly. "I am quitting because I think the people want me to quit."

My miracle refused to happen. I could still throw hard for an inning or two, then my arm would begin to throb with pain and I lost sight of the plate. Yet despite being ineffective almost every outing that spring, I was fool enough to be surprised when on the last day of camp word came that I'd been sold to the Buffalo Bisons, the A's International League farm club.

"We went along with him as far as we could," Mack told the reporters. "I wish him all the luck in the world."

That was more than he told me. In fact, no Athletics official sat me down to tell me the news. Somehow my release became public knowledge and I heard about it from another player who had heard it from someone else. Not exactly the greatest way to find out you're being sent down.

Irene was given the news by Jodi Chapman, Sam's wife. "Stick by him," Jodi said. "He's really going to need you now." Seeing the way the A's callously dumped me, Irene said that if we ever had a son she wouldn't let him grow up to be a ballplayer.

After all my years with the Athletics I deserved better treatment than that. Mack could have at least come over to shake my hand and say goodbye. For the previous two or three seasons he'd been more than fair with me about money and I'd actually started to grow fond of him. I thought my feelings of resentment were all in the past. But I was wrong. I've never been able to forgive the Old Man for the way he handled my release.

I didn't know what else to do except report to Buffalo as ordered. Maybe a stint against easier competition was exactly what I needed to get back on the beam. It had worked for me eleven years before when the Maple Leafs sent me down to Cornwall of the Can-Am League.

No such luck this time. In my first outing for the Bisons, I issued eleven walks. After five losses without a win, Buffalo manager Frank Skaff had seen enough and released me.

Now when I look back I think it would have been better if my arm had been so badly damaged I hadn't been able to throw at all. But because I still seemed to have my stuff during brief warm-ups on the sidelines, I hoped for a recovery. Along with a lot of other people, I also began to wonder if my trouble wasn't all in my head.

"I've thought of that, and I honestly believe there may be something to it," I told a reporter. "It could be that my difficulty is psychological rather than physical. Every time I go to pitch, this arm ailment is in the back of my mind. I can't seem to relax. That's why I think that, with a little warm weather,

I might loosen up. Once I get started, I'll be more at ease."

I hung around Buffalo, pitching batting practice for the next few weeks, still hoping. Then it began to look like my arm might actually be getting better. I was throwing so hard in batting practice the Bisons offered to re-sign me.

I turned them down for a better offer. My old battery mate, Buffalo native Buddy Rosar, who was then catching for the Red Sox, heard of my seemingly miraculous recovery and suggested to Boston general manager Joe Cronin that I be given a try-out.

Early in July I travelled to Boston and threw to Rosar at Fenway for about half an hour. "You look as good as you ever did," Cronin said. "How'd you like to join the Red Sox?"

What a shame that my opportunity to play alongside Ted Williams, Bobby Doerr and Dom DiMaggio arrived too late. Cronin didn't realize that half an hour of hard throwing was just about my limit. My one appearance in a Boston uniform came at Fenway in the high-scoring opener of a doubleheader against the Indians July 16. I'd been up and down two or three times in the bullpen before I finally got in, and by then my arm had stiffened. I surrendered one hit and two walks in an unimpressive one-and-a-third innings of work.

Cronin, who'd been my boss for all of two weeks, handled my release with the type of class and consideration I'd hoped for but hadn't received from Connie Mack.

"How do you feel, Phil?" he asked when we sat down in his office. "My arm's shot," I admitted. "I know I can't pitch anymore." Cronin then wrote out a generous severance cheque and very politely wished me the best of luck.

Still I didn't quit. I should have, I knew that even at the time. But that winter the Toronto Maple Leafs invited me to their camp the following spring and I found myself agreeing to try one last time.

Leaf general manager Joe Ziegler was an awfully persuasive guy. "Maybe all you need is to be close to your home and family," he said. "This is where it all started for you, Phil. The fans love you here. A season in Toronto might be just the thing to get you straightened away."

Ziegler knew that if I could come back I'd be a big gate attraction with the Toronto fans. After my signing was announced, one loyal supporter wrote to a Toronto newspaper to suggest it would be a nice gesture if the Leafs were to reserve the opening day start for me. "Even should Marchildon fail," he wrote, "the fans would not care a hoot, and the ovation he would receive would be something he could remember forever."

"I'm convinced Phil has his stuff left," Ziegler said. "He has been working out at Broadview 'Y' all winter and is in good shape. He's much more settled than a year ago and we may have something."

What I showed in spring training at Avon Park was exactly nothing. Although I was on the roster when the team broke camp, I sat on the bench once the season started and was released on April 30 without getting into a game.

There would be no more comebacks. I played that season and the next in the Intercounty League, a semi-pro circuit in southern Ontario that paid me just enough to get by. I didn't even try to pitch anymore. Now I was a hard-hitting outfielder who one year batted .367.

Those were tough years for me and even tougher ones for Irene. She went back to work full-time and bought a house in Toronto with the money we had left, hoping that might force me to find a real job. By that point I'd lost all confidence in myself. Friends arranged job interviews and I wouldn't show up. Most days I sat around the house brooding and drinking beer.

I'm not the only former athlete to have trouble adjusting to real life at the end of a career. As a player you love the game so much that somehow you fool yourself into believing it will always be there. What's really hard is accepting that it doesn't want or need you anymore.

Finally, a friend brought over an application for a job at A. V. Roe Canada, the aviation firm that produced the Avro Arrow fighter. This time I forced myself out the door to apply and was surprised when I landed a job as an expeditor, the person who makes certain all the necessary materials are on hand.

It wasn't easy going from being a famous baseball star to just another guy with a lunch bucket, but I made the adjustment and came to enjoy the job and my new friends. When the government cancelled the Avro project and the plant closed down, Bob Knight, an old neighbour from Penetang, offered me work at Dominion Metal Wear Industries, a manufacturer of hospital furniture located just outside Toronto. I stayed there until I retired at age sixty-five.

I owe a lasting debt of gratitude to all the friends I made at those two jobs after my playing career was over. They helped me learn one of the most important lessons of my life—there is happiness after baseball.

CHAPTER
15

THE WIND-UP

I n sight of the Ferris wheel and with all the familiar hubbub of
the annual Canadian National Exhibition swirling around us,
I was inducted into Canada's Sports Hall of Fame during a
ceremony on the front lawn of the museum on August 28, 1976.

The rain that had been threatening all day held off until the
end of the proceedings, prompting veteran Toronto sportswriter
Milt Dunnell, whom I've known since the 1940s, to write: "You
can discount those superstitions that once the old whammy
overtakes an athlete it never lets go. Phil Marchildon, the one-
time forkball thrower, entered the Canadian Sports Hall of Fame
at the CNE carnival lot without a slip, a hitch or a mishap."

Dunnell was right. The cloud of bad luck that had seemed
to follow me during my career had vanished. On the day of my
induction I was feeling like the luckiest old ballplayer alive.

The news that I'd been voted into the hall came entirely out of the blue. Without telling me, our friend Jack Reinhardt, who had been Irene's boss at the Singer Sewing Machine office during the war, put my name forward for nomination. My election was something I never expected or even allowed myself to hope for.

Sharing the day with me were the three people who mean the most to me in the world: Irene and our daughters Carol and Dawna, who was born in 1955. I've said before that it's a wonderful thing for a man to have a taste of fame in his life. It's even better when you can share its rewards with the people you love.

Among the other inductees were skier Kathy Kreiner, swimmer Cliff Lumsden and fitness coach Lloyd Percival. When it came to my turn at the microphone I was brief, as I always am when making a speech. "Being elected to Canada's Sports Hall of Fame," I said with absolute sincerity, "is the greatest honour of my life."

The years since then have been good to retired ballplayers like me. Fans have become nostalgic for the days when baseball was played outdoors and on real grass, the way it was meant to be. For many years after I left the game it seemed that I was almost forgotten, even here in my own country. Now every week in the mail I receive letters and requests for autographs from fans throughout North America.

It's nice to be remembered. Although many fans in this country are still unaware of the Canadians who made it to the big leagues before the arrival of Fergie Jenkins, the situation is slowly improving. In part this is due to the efforts of The Canadian Baseball Hall of Fame, founded in 1982. Along with George Selkirk and James "Tip" O'Neill, a native of Woodstock, Ontario, who hit .435 for the St Louis Browns way back in 1887, I was one of the hall's inaugural inductees.

It's easy to understand why many fans look back so fondly on the era when I played. Sometimes I think baseball continues to prosper in spite of itself, not because of the product on the field.

I don't pretend to be unbiased, but in important ways today's game just isn't as good as it used to be. Now you routinely see free-swinging lead-off men who don't know how to work the pitcher for walks, young hitters whose inability to adjust at the plate enables pitchers to strike them out on the same pitch time and again, and outfielders who miss the cutoff man. Those things didn't happen in the old days. By the time they got to the majors, ballplayers knew how to play the game.

There aren't enough quality players to go around now. With almost twice as many teams as when I played, the talent pool has been diluted and youngsters are being promoted before they've had time to learn the fundamentals.

I'm not forgetting that it wasn't until I went up to the Athletics and met Earle Brucker that I learned the proper mechanics of pitching. But I was the exception to the rule. Most players only made it after a long internship in the minors. I was actually older than the average when I was called up, and no one ever doubted that I had a major-league arm.

Another reason I think we're seeing so many mistakes on the field is the complacency that naturally sets in with players who have signed long-term, multi-million-dollar contracts. Al Simmons was right when he said it's almost impossible for a player to keep his edge once he starts to make the big money.

In the old days almost everyone signed one-year deals. Slump even slightly and your salary was certain to be cut. Have two bad years in a row and face banishment to the minors. You were forced to go out and hustle day after day just to hold on to your job. Now players are set for life after signing one big contract. That has to effect the performance of at least some of them.

I certainly don't begrudge today's players the money they're making. For too long the owners had it all their own way, nickel-and-diming us while most of them were making fortunes. Though I'm not certain any ballplayer is worth five or six million dollars a year, you can't blame the players for cashing the cheques the owners are handing out. I just wish I could have gotten in on a little of the action.

Despite my criticisms of today's game, I'm also happy to admit that most modern players are better athletes than we were. They're bigger and faster and stronger. They also work on their conditioning all year long, something most old-timers didn't do.

You see plays now that never would have been made in the old days. Outfielders climb walls and make impossible leaps to haul in fly balls. Every team has a shortstop with the moves of an acrobat. The oversized modern gloves help, but I think most of the sensational plays are the result of the players' greater athleticism.

There's more speed in the game now, which I like. Most teams have two or three players who steal twenty-five or more bases a season. On the Athletics, the team leader usually had around fifteen and most players swiped no more than three or four.

A strong argument can also be made that pitching in the big leagues is better than ever. Teams now employ pitching coaches at every level of the minor leagues, which means kids arrive in the majors with more poise. Starting staffs are thinner in talent because there are more teams, but relief pitching is much improved. Once regarded as simply not good enough to start, relievers are now specialists. The bullpen closer is often the hardest thrower on the staff.

I don't even mind the designated-hitter rule. And, remember, this comes from a pitcher who could hit. I like the extra offence it brings into a game. It also gives the fans the opportunity to see popular old sluggers play every day. I think the game has to keep as many big stars playing as possible.

The lack of superstars, or at least ones who have captured the public's imagination, might be the modern game's greatest weakness of all. None of the young millionaires have replaced Joe DiMaggio, Ted Williams and Mickey Mantle, who after all these years are still the game's most popular stars.

I met DiMag again in the spring of 1991 at a dinner in Toronto sponsored by The Canadian Baseball Hall of Fame to commemorate the fiftieth anniversary of the season of his streak. Also in attendance that night were Bob Feller, Ken Keltner, Bobby Doerr and Johnny Vander Meer, the National League pitcher who once threw back-to-back no-hitters.

At a press conference before dinner, Joe was kind enough to single me out in front of my hometown reporters and talk about how tough a pitcher I'd been. Then the conversation got around to the ways the game has changed.

DiMag thought artificial turf was one of the biggest differences.

"I think specialized relief pitching…and more running," said Bobby Doerr.

"Dollars and cents, I guess," answered Johnny Vander Meer, who said his highest salary had been $21,000.

"It's show business, entertainment—merchandising, shall we say," Bob Feller said. "One difference is the lack of pitchers who go nine innings. I did it more times in a month than they do in a whole season now."

I found myself thinking about Connie Mack as I listened to their answers and wondering how the Old Man would have felt about all the changes the game has seen since the days when he was pinching pennies as the owner of the Athletics. I imagined what it would be like to go into his office as a player today and dicker over a multi-million-dollar deal.

"Gracious, I can't pay you that," he'd say.

"Well, Mr Mack," I'd answer. "That's my final offer. We can always go to arbitration, but that could end up costing you even more.…"

You know, maybe the modern game isn't so bad after all.

MAJOR LEAGUE PITCHING RECORD OF PHIL MARCHILDON

Year	TM/L	W	L	PCT	G	CG	SHO	SV	IP	H	H/G	HR	BB	BB/G	SO	SO/G	ERA
1940	Phi-A	0	2	.000	2	1	0	0	10	12	10.8	1	8	7.2	4	3.6	7.20
1941	Phi-A	10	15	.400	30	14	1	0	204	188	8.3	15	118	5.2	74	3.3	3.57
1942	Phi-A	17	14	.548	38	18	1	1	244	215	7.9	14	140	5.2	110	4.1	4.20
1945	Phi-A	0	1	.000	3	0	0	0	9	5	5.0	0	11	11.0	2	2.0	4.00
1946	Phi-A	13	16	.448	36	16	1	1	227	197	7.8	14	114	4.5	95	3.8	3.49
1947	Phi-A	19	9	.679	35	21	2	0	277	228	7.4	15	141	4.6	128	4.2	3.22
1948	Phi-A	9	15	.375	33	12	1	0	226	214	8.5	19	131	5.2	66	2.6	4.54
1949	Phi-A	0	3	.000	7	0	0	0	16	24	13.5	3	19	10.7	2	1.1	11.81
1950	Bos-A	0	0	—	1	0	0	0	1	1	9.0	0	2	18.0	0	0.0	9.00
Total	9	68	75	.476	185	82	6	2	1214	1084	8.0	81	684	5.1	481	3.6	3.93

PCT = winning percentage
CG = complete games
SV = games saved

H/G = hits allowed per 9 inning game
BB/G = bases on balls allowed per 9 inning game
SO/G = strikeouts per 9 inning game